W9-AFE-414

# Ten Africans

# TEN AFRICANS

*edited by*

Margery Perham

NORTHWESTERN UNIVERSITY PRESS

*First published 1936*
*by Faber and Faber Ltd., London*
*Second Edition 1963*
*Published in U.S.A. 1963*
*by Northwestern University Press*

*Printed in Great Britain*

# Contents

[*Note:* All these Africans, except the two from Nigeria, belong to the Bantu-speaking peoples. In their languages the prefix *a*, *wa*, or *ba* added to the stem of the tribal name denotes the plural, *m* the singular.]

# Illustrations

*after page 16*

*Illustrations*

# Introduction

*by Margery Perham*

We have grown accustomed to the peculiar condition of empire under which we control the destinies of people we do not understand. In Africa, especially, our agents regulate in considerable detail the lives of some tens of millions of human beings of whose languages and ways of life they still know little, and with whom they have none of those ordinary social relations through which people come to know and to like each other.

The main reason for this is the 'backwardness' of Africans. It is an obvious and fundamental fact, but one upon which we are apt to lean a little too hard in order to make ourselves comfortable in a difficult situation. In default of true knowledge we too often make do with assumptions: the primary one, that Africans are backward; next, that they are all almost equally backward; even that they are inherently, and so permanently, backward. Cut off, as most of us are, from any contact with Africans as individuals, we think of them or deal with them in the mass, according to our various standpoints, as 'natives', or the 'native problem'; as 'the heathen'; as 'hut and poll tax-payers', or as 'native labour'. We see the strange, stupid or cruel things they do and, ignorant of their motives, forgetting what we ourselves did yesterday, what, alas! Christian nations are doing today, think them relatively more stupid and cruel than they are. We allow black skin and negro features to shut Africans off from those perceptions which we turn upon members of our own race.

When, here and there, an African differentiates himself from the mass in a way which we cannot ignore, he often rouses in us a kind of resentment. Is this, perhaps, because it is troublesome to adjust towards an individual an attitude which for our convenience or our prestige we habitually turn towards a race?

The very poverty of the Africans is a barrier between them and peoples who have enriched—some would say, complicated—their lives with the innumerable products of modern industry. We see semi-naked peasants living in mud huts, satisfying their elementary wants apparently in the most primitive ways. Surely, we think, people living like that cannot have personality as we reckon it! Forgetting a moment the most obvious facts of anthropology, and the long ages of evolution during which we shared, until yesterday, their primitive culture, we may even make the unscientific remark that they are near to the animals. And yet, perhaps, if at night some of the elders should come and sit round our camp fire, and its flames should suddenly paint their faces as they talk, we may be startled by a sudden doubt. For these faces are all different; each has taken the stamp of life in its own way. Naked torso, foul rags, outlandish tongue, greedy hands stretched for tobacco or coins, cannot hide the truth. There is the authentic sculpture, that of human experience working upon genuine and sometimes fine material. In the middle squats the elder statesman—or is he, perhaps, a bishop?—white beard, thoughtful eyes, grave lines, still posture. There is the man of action, the renowned hunter, straight-lipped, keen-eyed, restless, assertive. Next to him is the humorist with roving self-conscious glances, and puckish twist to mouth and eyes. These are people of full human stature, rich personalities some of them, and it is our loss as well as theirs that we do not know them.

This lack of mutual individual knowledge has its consequences. There are certain methods we find it quite natural to employ towards masses, which would seem inappropriate or embarrassing if we tried to use them towards groups of individuals some, at least, of whom were known to us. In India all the competence and integrity of our administration has not been able to compensate for this lack of individual, mutual understanding. In many parts of Africa we see a clumsy dictation in place of the experiments in partnership which are open to us and which in one or two places are actually being begun. The dictation may be inspired by the best intentions. It is possible to work in a spirit of high altruism *for* 'natives': it seems more natural, on the other hand, to work *with* 'individuals'. Their wishes and feelings begin to come into the picture as well as our standards of what is right and efficient.

This division of man from man means loss of a less measurable kind. People who are shut off from communion with human beings around them, whether it is within their own wealth, rank, nationality, or race that they are confined, begin in time to impoverish themselves. A purely negative attitude, a vacuum, cannot be maintained, and prejudice fills up the void. And in those made to feel themselves outcasts unfortunate qualities grow rank. Their injured self-respect makes for hypersensitiveness, and they seek compensation in self-assertion. Some of the most valuable human qualities are denied growth in them or distorted in growing. The defence or exaltation of their depreciated race becomes a will-o'-the-wisp in pursuit of which intellectual power is wasted, facts dodged and history perverted. Bitterness saps the power to appreciate or to co-operate. There is no exercise for the sense of responsibility. There is no room for that dual foundation of man's belief in his own value as an individual person and as a member of his community, upon which alone he has hitherto been able to build up his contribution to civilization.

I do not for a moment suggest that this situation is due entirely to human perversity or that a little right sentiment will open up a golden age of mutual understanding. The barriers between the civilized and the less civilized are there, and they are solid. Nothing of course need hinder us from achieving reasonable relations with fully 'educated' Africans, except certain fears which do little justice to our dignity and common sense. But the fully 'educated' (I am using the word in our own somewhat arrogant sense) are few. Only those who are exceptionally patient and disinterested will succeed in getting on friendly terms with Africans in all the awkward fractional degrees of education. As for the very primitive, perhaps only saints or scientists can learn to know them well. Are we, then, to sit down on our side of the barrier, or, recognizing the present waste and future danger it represents, shall we make some effort to cross it?

The younger anthropologists are doing much to sap that ignorance of Africans which is chiefly responsible for the disdain in which they are held. They have done much and will do much more in the next few years to reveal tribal society as an intelligible working whole, rather than as a field for the collection of strange customs or quaint handiwork. Yet it is not all anthropologists who can breathe upon the dead bones, nor is it everyone who will read works which are labelled anthropology. Other means of insight are needed.

My own work in Africa demanded much travelling. I could know few places or persons intimately. Yet from time to time, in Africa or in England, I have been able to make contact, and in one or two cases to make friends, with Africans. In the light of their opinions, old cherished assumptions began to look strange. To explain ourselves and our policies to them was instructive and sometimes uncomfortable. But it was an adventure, a new kind of African exploration coming as the old kind gives out, to discover for myself behind all the admitted differences of race and culture what in theory I knew to be there, our common nature, easy to know, and sometimes easy to like and respect. I almost blush as I write this, knowing that I may offend some of the initiated among my own people by committing to paper something at once so personal and so obvious, while some Africans will be offended that it should be necessary to speak of it at all.

These were the ideas that prompted this collection. I wanted to share my experience; to introduce English readers to a group of Africans, individuals and individualities, so that they might obtain a sense of that intimacy which few of our people can achieve in life. That, let me hasten to say, is the extent to which this book is propaganda. I maintain here no theory about Africans unless, in the eyes of some, what I have said already constitutes a theory. These Africans have not been carefully selected to represent any special virtues or qualities. Still less—and here I can only offer my word—have their stories been tampered with, and light, shade, and colour redistributed so as to build up the picture that my collaborators or myself might wish to present. There is, I think, sufficient internal evidence of the truth of this. That knowledge of Africans as persons makes it impossible to dismiss them all as savage or backward is a truth which has its reverse side: it is also impossible to regard them all as uniformly good, simple, unfortunate, or oppressed. These Africans, like any other ten persons, vary in character and also reveal contradictions in themselves. They were chosen at random, and these stories are, in fact, those that materialized from four or five times as many which, as the outcome of innumerable talks and letters, were promised or attempted. In the case of six of them I asked certain people, who were qualified by their knowledge of an African language and their sympathy with the project, to select an African and to record the story of his or her life. I did no more than offer a few tentative suggestions as to the lines upon which the narrator should be guided if guidance should prove possible without injury to the spontaneity of his subject. The African should be encouraged to sketch the main events of his life; should be coaxed to explain any customs which he might otherwise regard as requiring no explanation; should refer to the coming of the Europeans if that event seemed to interest him, and should be invited to philosophize a little at the end, if philosophy seemed to come naturally to him. (If only it had proved possible to reproduce on paper the wealth of gesture and expression with which these stories were told by people to whom talking is a joy and an art!) Chief Kumalo and those who have recorded their own lives in English were known to me in Africa or in England and I approached them directly. The exception to this is Mr. Coka, with whom I got into touch through the kind offices of Mr. W. Ballinger.

Although it would be against the principles expressed in this introduction to say that the subjects of these lives are typical, I must own that I have endeavoured to present people who have undergone widely different degrees of European influence. By that standard the stories have been arranged as far as possible in an ascending scale, with effects which will not escape the discerning reader. At a certain point across most of them runs a band rather like that igneous intrusion which forces itself among the old sedimentary rocks, altering their character and all the contours which form above them. Has this European intrusion been for the happiness of these individuals? Have its effects been deep or superficial? Perhaps the three stories that start above the line may in part provide an answer. But it is not for me to instruct the reader as to what he should find: each will discover different things according to his knowledge and perception.

A word as to my activities as editor. I have already said that there has been no tampering with this material. The stories are almost untouched except that, for reasons of space, one or two of them have lost a few of their less significant passages. The question of notes presented some difficulty. These stories contain much that is of anthropological and historical interest. Kumalo's story, for instance, deals with the occupation of Rhodesia, while Coka's reveals the inner history of the first Bantu attempt at Trade Union organization. But how is the reader to judge of the accuracy of the information offered him? It would have been possible, at the cost of a great deal of work, and very extensive annotation, to have given him some guidance. But this book is not offered as a contribution to anthropology or history. Its function, as I have tried to show, is something quite different. It is a book for the layman, and must stand or fall by the general impression it gives of the way Africans think and live. Those most interested in the anthropological, and other, aspects will be able to supply most of their own commentary; to the rest it will be a matter of no great moment. I can, however, offer them my partly substantiated opinion that not quite all, but by far the greater proportion, of the facts contained in this book are true. I know that three of the recorders, two distinguished anthropologists and a missionary of long experience, all deeply versed in the customs of the tribes from which their subjects are drawn, could not have sent to me without comment material they knew to be inaccurate. Notes having been renounced, short introductions were provided for some of the stories, and occasionally a translation or explanation by the recorder or the editor has been embodied in the text in square brackets. I have used my discretion in the matter of European names, and have omitted them in some places. As it has sometimes been difficult to refer doubtful points back to the recorders, any errors or omissions should be charged against myself, as editor. Finally, with regard to the stories written in English by Africans, I have, for the most part, left them as they stood, except that in each I have corrected anything from four to twelve verbal or grammatical errors which obscured the sense.

It only remains for me to thank the recorders who have worked with such skill and sympathy and the Africans who have so frankly revealed themselves to us. They have done what they have for its own sake and without asking for any material reward. By agreement the royalties will be devoted to a cause of interest to Africans.

## Note to 1963 Edition.

I am glad that the publishers are reprinting this book. As a historical document it is right that it should be reprinted just as it stands. These intimate human stories have today a new and enhanced value. In a rapidly changing Africa they are a social landmark. They show how Africans of various tribes, types and ages saw themselves and their lives before the second world war and especially how they had taken the impress of British power and influence. Since this book appeared many Africans have written books about themselves, but in the changed setting of our time most of these tend to be more political and more self-conscious in tone. The royalties will again be devoted to an African cause.

MARGERY PERHAM

'Individuals and Individualities'

*Photograph by Margery Perham*

'The Authentic Sculpture'
*Photograph by Margery Perham*

Babemba Elders round their Chief

*Photograph by Audrey I. Richards*

The Priest Chimba

*Photograph by Audrey I. Richards*

The Blind Singer at the Chitimukulu's Court

*Photograph by Audrey I. Richards*

Udo Akpabio and his Schoolmaster Son

*Photograph by the Rev. W. Groves*

A Scene in the Matabele War from the film *Rhodes of Africa*

*By Courtesy of Gaumont-British*

Chief Ndansi in the Part of Lobengula
*By Courtesy of Gaumont-British*

Angoni Warriors

*Photograph by Margaret Read*

Washing Day in Nosente's Country

*Photograph by Margery Perham*

Nosente

*Photograph by Monica Hunter*

African 'Boy' on the Road in Southern Tanganyika
*Photograph by Margery Perham*

Kikuyu Women

*Photograph by Margery Perham*

Martin Kayamba (*left*), the Kathi (judge) and other notables of Tanga

*Photograph by Margery Perham*

A Johannesburg slum-yard

*Photograph by Margery Perham*

Kofoworola Moore as a child, with her father

# I

# The Story of Bwembya of the Bemba Tribe, Northern Rhodesia

*recorded by Audrey I. Richards*

## Foreword by the recorder

The narrator is a member of the Bemba tribe (A-wemba), which occupies the Tanganyika plateau of North-Eastern Rhodesia. He appears to be between fifty and sixty years of age. Though actually only a head-man of a small village just outside Kasama, he yet carries himself with an air of authority and is usually attended by one or two followers who accord him the small courtesies and privileges reserved for a chief. This rank he can in fact claim, being a member of the royal family of the Babemba, and having inherited the name, and according to Bemba belief, the spirit of one of the former Paramount Chiefs. Here is, in fact, a man who has little real authority or position in the modern world, but yet commands a good deal of respect among his fellows by virtue of descent and personality. The poverty of this old man, measured in terms of material possessions—his tumble-down hut and the frayed cloth in which he is swathed—is in striking contrast to his commanding presence. His insistence on the small ceremonies due to his rank is, in fact, probably the result of his own realization that according to present-day values the young men of his village—

mostly wage-earners in Kasama—are wealthier than he is himself.

Brought up at the court of one of the most famous of the old Bemba chiefs, Mubanga Chipoya, he saw the coming of the white man as a youth, and thereafter travelled widely over Africa to countries as far distant as Somaliland and Zanzibar. But, in spite of these varied contacts with white civilization, it will be seen that his interest in the past and his deeply rooted belief in the power and importance of the Bemba chiefs remain unchanged. This is, I think, a very usual characteristic of older natives who have served the white man as Askari or police, rather than of those who have come in contact with the European industrial system, either in mining areas or in big towns. On the other hand, association with white men seems to have increased Bwembya's natural shrewdness and quickness in dealing with men and affairs, and he has an almost uncanny knowledge of what each particular European is likely to expect. 'He knows how to talk to white men,' as one of his fellows said to me. At a meeting for Bemba chiefs held by the late Governor of Northern Rhodesia neither the government officials nor the chiefs themselves were able to command the silence of this enormous crowd. Bwembya got up and told the crowd exactly what he thought of them, obtaining perfect silence at once.

It must not be supposed that this narrative is historically accurate. Old natives love to dwell on the splendour of their former rulers, and delight in bloodthirsty tales of their ferocity. Their descriptions of what were probably occasional border raids usually give the impression of incessant and violent warfare. The present narrative is typical in this respect. The English reader will probably find it hard to reconcile this glorification of war and conquest with instances of what would seem to us arrant cowardice. The Mubemba somehow manages to combine heroic endurance and loyalty on some occasions, with acts which often shock the Englishman by their apparent treachery or lack of spirit. This is a never-ending puzzle to the white man, which this narrative does not solve. It does, however, give an idea of that complex attitude of admiration and fear which the Mubemba has for his chief—an attitude which cuts across ties of personal loyalty or kinship sentiment. It may also throw light on another perpetual problem. Why did this warlike people immediately accept, with practically no fighting, British rule? Bwembya's account of the rule of the great chief Mubanga Chipoya gives us some idea why the sudden collapse of the whole institution of chieftainship in a society accustomed to such autocratic rulers led to the temporary disintegration of the whole social system of the tribe.

## The Story of Bwembya

I am Bwembya. I am a great chief. I am not just a headman as you white people think. I am a grandson of the Chitimukulu [the title of the paramount chief of the Babemba]—the son of his sister's daughter. Therefore I am a member of the Crocodile clan—the clan of our chiefs. Besides, I have inherited the spirit of Bwembya, and Bwembya was once the Chitimukulu himself. It is true that he was chased away by his nephew Chitapankwa because he was born dumb, and had not strength to hold the chieftainship. But nevertheless they honour his spirit still, and call on his name, and reverence the spot where he died, and I, who inherited his spirit, am therefore a great chief. That is why the people give me such respect.

# *The Story of Bwembya*

Bwembya died when I was just a boy. I was then at my grandmother's village, the great Chandamukulu, the mother of the Chitimukulu, whom they used to call 'the Sun of Lubemba'. All the elders assembled at this village and said, 'Let us find a grandson of the Chitimukulu to inherit the name of Bwembya, for it is the spirit of a great chief.' Then they clothed me in a new cloth and gave me the bow of Bwembya and the beads which he used to wear. These are his beads which I am wearing today. They are very old, these blue beads. You cannot buy them at the store, for the Arabs brought them here long before the Europeans came.

My mother, the chieftainess, died when I was very small. It was Sampa, who was then the Chitimukulu, who took me with my brother to his village and brought us up there. He said, 'Let me fetch my grandchildren who belong to me. They shall grow up at my court. How should I leave them at their father's village, they who are of the rank of chiefs?' [The Babemba follow matrilineal succession.]

But this Sampa died very soon, for he was an old man when he took us to his capital. And, of course, when he died we all fled, I and my brother and those who were with us, the sons of Sampa and his courtiers. We fled in the night because we were afraid we should be killed. For it was the custom of long ago that when a great chief died many of his followers were killed. Some of his favourites they slew because they said, 'You, you people who received food every day from the hands of the chief, and beer and meat and cloths and every good thing, now you can follow your chief where he goes!' Others whom they killed were just slaves. They hit them on the forehead with a pole, and those who carried the chief's body stepped over the dead slaves as they bore the corpse out of the royal enclosure. Others were his wives and body servants whom they killed so that they should hold the body of the chief in his grave. This is why those who stood near to the chief fled when he died. You know that even now we call the hour before dawn 'kupakwa kwa mfumu' [the time of the announcement of the death of the chief].

So we fled to the village of Mwamba, who was the son of Sampa's sister, and the next most powerful chief of the house. [Both Chitimukulu and Mwamba are permanent titles of chieftainship.]

Now the name of this Mwamba was Mubanga Chipoya, and he was a very great chief, so great that his power came to rival even that of the Chitimukulu himself, and everyone gave him respect and brought him their troubles from all over the land. It was at his court that I grew up with my brother, working for him, and learning all the legends and tales of the past. You white people, I know that you do not believe the splendour of our chiefs in the old days, how great they were. And this Mwamba was the greatest that I ever saw. Why, his village alone! It was bigger than this white town of Kasama. I suppose it had over fifty divisions in it, each with a man of rank at its head. The chief's private enclosure was as large as the entire village of the present Chitimukulu. And then the wives he had! My word! I should think he had as many as sixty wives living there in that enclosure!

The chief used to sit on top of a big ant-hill inside his courtyard with all his people gathered round him. We boys used to sit at the bottom of the slope, just staring all day long. All the councillors and notables of Mwamba used to like to sit with him. They sat on the ground at his feet, for this was how they showed him respect. Sometimes the ground would be black with people—I should say from here to that tree right over there. They would sit there sometimes until the sun set, talking of this and that, and listening to affairs of state. This is the way they honoured the chief and waited for him to give them things. For to feed the people is the splendour of chieftainship. So that all may say, 'See that chief, how many people he has!' Have you not noticed how I myself am always giving food and snuff to the people? Not only my own family, my daughters and their children, but others as well. Look at those three old women over there. Those women stamping their corn! I feed all those three women, and make their gardens for them. They came to me and said, 'We are in great misery. We are left alone with no man to look after us.' I said, 'My mothers, you are my people. I am your chief.' So now I care for them. And in the same way this Mwamba I am telling you about was always giving presents of one kind or another to his courtiers, for he was a king indeed! He was not like the chiefs of today, who have no wealth to give their councillors. This Mwamba was always dividing out beer and meat between them, and sometimes he would pass round his great snuff-box to those who sat nearest him, or reward his favourites with cloth, or with hoes, or any kind of valuable.

You could see he was a great chief as soon as you looked at him. At different times of the day he would come out of his hut wearing different cloths—sometimes bark-cloth very elegantly sewn, and sometimes white cloth, or blue, or red, all cloths which the Arabs had brought him. And his neck would be hung with beads. Sometimes he wore a feather headdress, as was the custom of men of rank in those days. Mwamba of today has the headdress of Mubanga Chipoya, but he only wears it now when you white people come to his village. That is how the Bwanas like to photograph him—dressed after the fashion of the past.

Well, I can tell you many things about this Mubanga

Chipoya. I remember the tales of the past because I am a grandson of the chief. When I was a boy I used to watch Mubanga Chipoya sitting like this all day long in the centre of his court. He had often a big hubble-bubble pipe in front of him, and one at each side, for he was a great smoker. He had one wife to swish the flies off his head, and another to kneel beside him holding his snuff-box in case he should need it, and another to hold the big umbrella above him. These carved umbrellas came from the country of the Kazembe to the west, from the Balunda, whom we call our elder brothers, since they came with us on our journey from Lubaland long ago. We ourselves do not know how to carve wood, nor do we understand iron-work, or any such arts as other tribes practise, but all the same they used to honour us more than the rest. Why? Because they were afraid of us. We Babemba took their lands and made them work for us. We are fiercer than other tribes! . . . You can see this umbrella at Mwamba's court today. I have heard all over the place how you yourself took a photograph of it.

Well, if there was no important case to be heard, Mubanga Chipoya used to call another wife, who would kneel in front of him holding a small gourd of beer. But if there were some serious matter before him the chief sent the beer away and called all the elders to listen to the affair. Everything was done silently and in order. All the children would be sent away. It was not like the courts of the present day, where sometimes you see a chief hearing a case with no one to listen except the Government clerk, just a young man. Why, even the Chitimukulu allows a crowd of children to tumble about all over the place. Nowadays, in fact, the elders often stay away because the chief no longer respects them, nor honours them with gifts. He has nothing to give them now, since he has no ivory or cloth or tribute from his people. Besides, he is always trying to do what the Government wants, and therefore he listens to his clerk instead of his councillors. He thinks, 'That young man understands the ways of the white men. He will teach me best.' It was quite different in the old days. The elders would sit silent then, perhaps twenty or thirty of them, for Mwamba had a very big village, as I told you. First the injured man would state his grievance, and, as he spoke, one of the councillors would clap the points, one by one. So everyone knew that the court had understood what was said. Besides, it was the way in which they honoured the chief, to clap like this. Then Mwamba would sign to the accused man to state his case, or perhaps the head of the family would speak for him. Then they would call those who had seen the affair with their own eyes. Then, after this speaking, the chief would turn to his councillors and say, 'My friends, you elders, what judgment shall we give?' Then each would speak what it came into his heart to speak, first one and then the other, the oldest speaking first, and the chief being silent all the time. Then suddenly he would stop all the talking and give his judgment, and everyone would shout to the litigants, 'Salute the chief! Salute to the ground, both of you! You have received justice! Salute the chief!' The men of both families would roll on the ground before him, and the women would kneel and clap, and cry their salutation in the way you know that women do. We older boys used to watch all these things happen, for we knew that we were the grandsons of the chiefs and so we listened to the judgments given. Sometimes, too, we would crawl up to the fire in the evening when the old men were talking of the things of the past. They told each other tales of this ancestor and that, so that a boy with a good heart would remember many such stories. But as you know some boys have hard ears and remember nothing, however much they hear.

Everyone came to see the Mwamba, and to give him respect. I remember how the priest, Chimba, once came to visit Mubanga Chipoya. [The Chimba is the chief hereditary priest of the Babemba. The recent holder of the title so presumed on his position that he defied the present Chitimukulu, and held up the work of tribal government by refusing to perform the necessary ceremonies for the Paramount Chief. After perpetual friction the Government reluctantly consented, in 1934, to his replacement.] It was that Chimba who has just been chased away by Chitimukulu. He was chased away for his pride and presumption. Even the Government official finally agreed that he should be chased away. For years we had been saying, 'That man, Chimba, is a sorcerer. It was he who bewitched Ponde so that he died.' But, of course, whenever we took the case to the Boma the Bwana said, 'Go away! You are foolish! There is no such thing as witchcraft!' So we had to hide this affair, and it is only now that the Government believe what we say, and have agreed that Chimba should be sent away. But he was proud even in the days of Mubanga Chipoya. When he arrived at the chief's court they brought him some beer as a sign of respect, but Chimba was so proud that he sent back the messenger, saying, 'Go and tell the chief to give me also a slave to hold the pot of beer while I drink.' Mubanga Chipoya was exceedingly angry. He said, 'Does this man speak like a chief? He is defying me!' First he sent Chimba two very fine pieces of bark-cloth to show his magnificence. Then he sent again and said, 'Tell the chief to return to the country from which he came. We are poor, miserable creatures here, and we evidently do not understand how to treat chiefs of another country. Let him return from whence he came.' So they chased him away in the dark. They did not even allow him to sleep a night. This Mwamba did to show he was a great chief. I tell you he was very proud in his dealings with all his fellow chiefs. They were afraid of him for he had more power than even Chitimukulu himself. For this Chitimukulu—Makumba—was very old indeed. When Sampa died, Mubanga Chipoya could have succeeded him, for he was strong enough, but he let Makumba succeed because he had really a stronger claim, being the brother of his mother. Besides, he was afraid that, if he did not let him succeed, Makumba might die with a grievance in his heart, and then his spirit would return and wreak vengeance. You see Mubanga Chipoya had killed one of Makumba's sons, by accident, in a raid. That was why he was afraid. Besides, he thought that Makumba was very old, and would die soon. But, as you know, Makumba did not die for many years!

He was so old that he was quite deaf when I saw him. He used to sit by himself before a tiny fire, all alone. He only ate sweet potatoes. He used to sit roasting them in the fire himself, pulling them out and eating them just as a child does. He ate fish too, and, when they brought in the fish in baskets as tribute, he would pull a fish out and roast it in the fire there and then. And he never drank beer at all. He just gave the beer away in a haphazard fashion to whoever made obeisance to him. He just smiled and gave the beer away. He never heard anything they were saying. It was his councillors who managed his affairs for him, and his eldest son, Seluka. His nephews? No, of course not his nephews! For the nephews of the chiefs are chiefs themselves. They are all heirs. Therefore there would be jealousy between them. That was why they called Makumba's son to manage his affairs, and not his nephew.

## *The Story of Bwembya*

You want me to tell you some more about the court of Mwamba? Well, I will tell you everything, for I, Bwembya, remember all the things of the past. You ask about the drums and dancing? No, no one would dance inside the chief's enclosure. They were too much afraid. But the young men and the girls danced outside in the village when the moon was full, and we boys of the royal court would slip through the palisade and dance with the rest. But inside the enclosure only the chief's praise-songs could be sung. Old men, usually blind, sung songs in praise of the chief. They sang all day long. Whenever it came into their hearts to sing, they would leave their huts, with some little boy to lead them across the village. They sang all the way with their young men behind them beating the drums. This was the way they honoured the chief. Dreams would come to them in the night, and in the morning they would wake and say, 'I have dreamed good things. I have dreamed a praise-song to Mwamba,' and they would walk round and round the village singing, so that the chief's heart would be lightened, and he would give them great rewards. I have heard them say that sometimes such a chief would be filled with pride at these songs and he would say, 'This singer shall never leave me to go to another court.' Then he would begin constantly to find fault with the man, until one day he would put out his eyes just for some little fault, not a grave charge at all. But I did not see such a thing done myself. It is only a story they tell. Of course the blind singer you saw at the Chitimukulu's court last month had his eyes put out because he stole one of the chief's wives. That was a long time ago. They call him *Chishale shale* ['a thing which is left behind'], because he is so old and his fellows are dead. But for weeks after he had been blinded such a singer would sit in silence, because his heart was heavy and bitterness had caught him at the throat. He would sit inside his hut in the dark all day long, and every day the chief would send him presents--pots of beer the people had brought him as tribute, or meat, or honey or the like. This he did to appease the blinded man. Then after a time his heart would grow still again, for his eyes had healed so that they no longer pained him. And then, all of a sudden, he would begin to dream new songs. Yes, and he would sing again in praise of that very chief! For you know what such men are. They sing because it is in their hearts to sing and they cannot keep silent long. Besides, such a man would be afraid to fly to another village, for what can a blind man do without his people, alone in a new country?

Now then, about another matter. This Mubanga Chipoya, whom I am telling you about, had many wives, for he was a very great chief. He would send out his men to bring him the girls whom he wanted. They were washed and shaved and rubbed with oil so that their skins shone, and then they were brought before the chief. He would give them new clothes and ivory bangles to wear, and houses to live in where they sat and laughed and played, and did not work like their fellows. So that they were glad and said, 'Indeed I have married a great chief.' Sometimes they were mere girls. These were his granddaughters whom he had a right to demand in marriage. They brought them to his court as children and they grew up to womanhood there. The whole court came to dance at their initiation rites. But then later on the trouble came. There were so many of these young girls, the wives of the chief. In time they began to say, 'I am young. Why should I have to sleep alone on my bed every night? I am not like these head-wives who have cast their womanhood behind them.' And phew! In a moment they had slipped through the wooden stockade on a dark night and found themselves lovers after their fancy outside. And so there was always trouble, for Mubanga Chipoya was a very jealous man, after the fashion of great chiefs. Once Kanyanta, the nephew of Mwamba, seduced one of his wives. Seeing she was pregnant, the chief asked her the name of her lover. First she sat silent for a long time. Then she said, 'Sir, it was your sister's son.' Without a word the chief sent and razed his village to the ground! Of course he could not kill the adulterer for it was his sister's son.

But sometimes his anger was worse than this. It was bhang that made Mubanga Chipoya so violent. He was a great chief, and he gave good judgments, but sometimes when he had sat smoking all the evening with his big pipe it was as though he was drunk—as though he were mad. We could see that his face was all swollen and his eyes bloodshot. Then we of the court would creep about and whisper to each other, 'Look out now! Do not make him angry! He is like a madman tonight.' We were all afraid. For we knew that if anyone offended him in such a mood he might order that their hands be struck off or their ears slit.

And so one day when this temper was on him, he became suddenly furious because he found out that one of his young wives had been unfaithful. So he cried out that the whole company of this girl's fellows should be burnt alive. They were all to be burnt, about twelve of them, on a great platform, with all the young men of the quarter of the village to which the adulterer belonged.

No! the girls never tried to beg for mercy, they were afraid. They just sat silent on the ground holding on to each other. Only when they had dragged them outside the enclosure, they began to shriek, 'Alai! Alai! It was not I who deceived the chief. Let me go! Let me go!' But who knows? Perhaps they were all guilty all the same. You know what women are!

Did the fathers and brothers of these girls try to help them? Why do you ask me that? Of course they had run away a long while ago. They had run as far as Kasama [about ten miles] in the night. They said, 'The chief is killing our children, do not let him kill us too.' They were afraid of such a powerful chief. After it was over, Mwamba made them come and do obeisance to him. He said, 'See how your daughters have wronged me!' And always after that these people took care to bring Mwamba presents. They brought beer or fish whenever they had it, for they were always afraid that he might remember how their daughters had done him wrong.

Did I try to help the young men, my fellows, who were about to be burnt? You ask if I pleaded for them. No indeed, I was running to fetch the firewood. I went with the others. The whole village was running to and fro bringing in great logs and piling up the fire. You never saw such a commotion, and such work going on. Men who never fetched firewood for their wives were staggering in with enormous logs on their heads. You see they were afraid they might be burnt too, if they seemed to hang back, because the chief was like a madman that day. And the fire they built! My word! The big fires they make when the Government officials go on tour, they are nothing to this fire. They built a high platform above it after the fashion of the granaries we build out in the fields. It had bars across to keep the people in.

When the fire was lit, we caught hold of the girls and the boys and hoisted them up, and thrust them on to the platform. They were all crying out, 'Let go! Let go! I never did wrong.' But, of course, it was too late to cry out then, for the chief had already given the order that they should be burnt. They did not scream for long, either, because the fire was so big. We boys were all standing watching. For a moment they all shouted like madmen, 'Ai! Ai! I am dying! Take me out!' But then they stopped crying quickly. It was the smoke in their nostrils that stopped them crying out.

After it was over we went to tell the chief. He sat silent then. He said nothing, for the ferocity in his heart had spent itself. There was quiet in the court for many months after that, for the madness had worn itself out. Nor did he ever burn the people again in this way. Yes, that is true, he might have been afraid the spirits of the victims would haunt him. You are right when you say that those who die unjustly accused return as vengeful spirits to kill their persecutors. But then I think to myself, why should a chief as great as that be afraid of the dead?

Yes truly, I am going to speak of my own life now, since that is what you ask me. But I tell you all this because I am Bwembya, and I know all these things that happened in the past. Besides, wasn't it at this Mwamba's court that we grew up, I and my brother? When we were young we played with the other boys who had been sent to be brought up at the chief's court. All day long Mwamba's wives cooked us food. We ran in and out of their huts, teasing them to give us little bits of meat from the joints they were stewing for the chief's labourers. We hid behind the doors of the huts and hooked out tasty morsels with pronged sticks! And the chief only laughed when they complained, and said, 'Let them be! They are grandsons of the chiefs. All the food in the courtyard is mine.'

But as we grew older we had work to do too. We did not have to cut the trees to clear the gardens, as the village boys did, but all other work we did, carrying the chief's messages everywhere, and showing great respect and good manners to his elders.

I learnt to hunt, too, and even now I hunt, as you know, and that is why the people give me great respect. I have shot elephants in this country and in distant countries far away. I shot four in Uganda when I went with a white man to teach him how to shoot, and now I am the hunter of Mwamba and Chitimukulu. But in those old days the chief's elephant hunts sometimes lasted a month long. We all went out together with the men who owned the strongest elephant magic. There was wonderful game to be had, too, before you white men came. Yes, I know you brought us good things, but we hunters long for the old days. The chiefs were very fierce, and killed the people, as I have told you. But then, not everyone was unlucky, and all could kill meat. Besides, nowadays everyone has to pay tax, and that we never had to do.

We followed Mwamba to war, too. He was a fierce chief. They called him the 'Bow of Lubemba'. You know how we were always fighting the Angoni, and they were a very ferocious tribe. We took all the country of the Babisa, too, right down as far as Lake Bangweolu. All the guardian spirits of that land are Bisa chiefs. We Babemba pray to them to this day. Mwamba chased out the Balungu, too, further north. They are people famous for their magic. Why did we take their land? Well, why did you white people take ours? Because you saw what a lot of elephants there were here, and how many people there were to work for you. But even the white people were afraid to come into our land for a long time. One of our chiefs put a row of heads on spikes across the road to dare the white men from Fife to come any nearer. I have heard old men say that the Europeans could never have taken our land but for a terrible misfortune. The sacred relics of one of our chiefs were burnt by accident in a forest fire. So everyone was afraid. They knew some calamity would come. I do not know if this is true, what they say, for I was only a young man then.

I myself went to fight three times. I went against the Wiwa in the Isoka District, but this fight was stopped because the white men came. I went with Makumba against the Banyika too, right over the border into Tanganyika Territory, north of the Government Station at Abercorn. And another time, too, I followed Chikwanda, who became the Chitimukulu, against the Balala, near Serenje.

Yes, indeed, the present Chitimukulu, Kanyanta, also fought as a young man, for this was the work of all great chiefs. He told me how he came to the shores of Lake Bangweolu and got together a lot of canoes. Then he sailed across the lake to try and capture some sheep. They were the sheep of the Baunga, who live on the islands in the swamps. He did not know how to get across the lake, but he made the shore natives paddle the canoes. When he drew near, he saw the sheep feeding on the bank. It was the village of Kasama, one of the chiefs of the Baunga, but it was not a fine village like our villages, for all the huts were built of reeds. They have no trees, the Baunga. They have to make even their fires of reeds. Yes, I will tell you what happened to Kanyanta after this. Our men got out of the canoes quickly and ran to hide in the Manioc gardens near the shore. The Baunga heard them and came rushing out shouting. They had arrows and spears, and our men had arrows and spears too. Kanyanta had some guns, too, but he had no shot to put in the guns because he had come very far from home. But he always had these guns carried with him. It was for pride that they carried them, to show that this was a great chief. Then Kanyanta stood up and shouted to the enemy that his men had come to take their sheep, and that they must submit to him because the Babemba were a very fierce people, as they all knew. But these Baunga are very treacherous. One of them quickly shot at our chief with his arrow. The arrow stuck in his arm. He fell back, crying, 'Ai! Ai! I have hurt my arm!' Several of our men were hurt, and their hearts were hot so that they began to shoot arrows. Our men were angry, because they had not thought the Baunga would wound our chief like that, and there were a great many of these villagers, whereas the Babemba were very few, for there were not enough canoes to cross the lake. The shore people had hidden their boats from our men. The chief was still groaning because of the pain from his arm. He said, 'Let us get back to the canoes, my people. My arm is hurting. Hold me up. Besides, these sheep are very small. They are not like the sheep on the shore. And how could we get them into the canoes?' So they shouted at the Baunga and shook their spears at them and they ran to get into the canoes. The Baunga just stood and let us go. They were frightened of us, you see, because they knew we were a very fierce people.

But this was a little fight. Often we went in great companies, and our fights lasted for two weeks long or even three. The chief sent to gather his men to the capital, and he took omens as to their success. The diviners threw bones, or perhaps a man possessed by a dead chief's spirit would prophesy success. We had wonderful war-magic in those days. The chiefs would pray to the ancestral spirits, too, before we set out. What did they pray? All sorts of words. They would probably say, 'You, my spirits, my grandfathers and my mother's brothers, protect us as we go. Bring us good luck on the way. Go in front and lead us. Make it that we find our enemy lying asleep so that we can quickly kill large numbers before they wake up. Let us bring home many heads to the chief to show our bravery. Let us dance the Malaila, the triumph dance, with our axes covered with blood.' So the spirits listened and gave us help. We grew up in this way in the service of the chief, following him wherever he went.

It was in these times that you white men first began to come into the country. The first white man had come before. We called him Cinyondo, and he came from the east, from Ikawa [Fife]. The people came running to tell the chief Makasa that they had seen men who were white. Makasa only laughed. He said, 'You foolish people. These are only Arabs that often come to our country with cloth.' But the messengers answered, 'No, these have different clothes. They do not wear white kansas at all. They have sandals of leather on their feet and cloth around their legs.' Then they started to tell Makasa about their guns. They told him of the way these white men killed elephants from far off with a new kind of gun. Everyone cried and shouted, 'Witchcraft! That must be magic!' But the chief himself sat silently all the while. He was thinking about these guns. He cried, 'Yangwe! Shall we escape?' But for a long time nothing happened.

Then another white man came [probably the assistant collector from Fife, who came to ask for permission to build a station]. He came to see Mwamba. He walked straight into Mwamba's presence with a little dog at his side. Everyone stared at this little dog, and they did not know what kind of man this was. He stood up in front of Mwamba and spoke his business. We were all staring at his face. He was not still, after the manner of a chief, but he stood there twirling his moustaches and looking quickly about him from right to left. But Mwamba was silent, and he looked straight in front with his eyes. Afterwards, people said, 'That white man is like his little dog the way he quickly turns from side to side. His eyes are always looking here and there, and are never still.' Then he struck a match to show us, and everyone cried out. They thought it was fire, for we were very foolish in those days. We still made fire with bits of wood out of the bush, whereas now we all buy matches at the store.

After these things I began to work for the white men. They gave us white cloth. Mwamba called me to him and said, 'Do you leave me now, your grandfather, who brought you up since you were a child?' I said, 'Sir, we will not leave you,' but we went all the same, because we wanted this cloth.

I became a mailman. I carried letters from Kasama to Mpika for six years.

During this time Mubanga Chipoya had been very ill indeed. People said he was ill because his brother Ponde had bewitched him. It happened like this. Ponde's sister had reached puberty, and they should have brought the news to Mwamba at once, but they delayed because of the enmity between the two chiefs, the brothers. Mwamba grew anxious, but in time the messengers of Ponde came carrying white chalk to announce the news. They saluted Mwamba and put a streak of white chalk on his forehead, as is our custom when such news is announced to the head of the family. That evening Mwamba cried out suddenly, 'The cold! The cold! Light me a fire!' And though it was the hot weather they lit him a fire, and he was never warm from that day. It began to hurt from the moment the chalk touched his forehead. People said it was Ponde who had bewitched him, but there were a lot of other stories too.

When Ponde heard of the illness he came near and waited. Mwamba heard the drums going in the distance, and he began to be frightened. They told him, 'Sir, it is your brother Ponde who is come because you are ill,' but he only said, 'My brother is killing me. He is waiting for me to die.' And all the people flocked to Ponde, because they liked him and because they thought, 'We will make Ponde chief when Mwamba dies.'

All the cleverest doctors were called to Mwamba's court, but they failed. Every diviner of note in the country was there. At last a man came and said, 'There is a white man in Makasa's country. Send for him. They say he is the greatest witch-doctor of all.' So Mwamba's chief captain went to fetch the white man with presents. This Bwana was the Bwana Shikofu [Bishop Dupont, the first missionary to enter the country]. He rose at once when he heard that the chief was ill. They carried him in a litter six days' journey to where Mubanga Chipoya lay. When he arrived at the chief's village, the people wanted to kill him. They crowded round his litter threatening him with axes. But the white man said, 'It was Mwamba who called me.' So they let him pass through to see the chief. Mwamba was very ill. They were holding him up in their arms. The Bwana felt his hand and his arm. Then he pricked the chief with a needle. He said some prayers, and he said, 'Perhaps he will live and perhaps he will die, for he is a very sick man.' Next morning the chief was dead. Of course, they accused the white man of witchcraft, but I do not know if this was true. Perhaps it was one of those stories the people tell in whispers whenever any great chief dies.

Then the people rushed to fetch Ponde, and he moved into Mwamba's country, but he was afraid of the Bwana Shikofu, for he had taken under his protection all the wives and the sons and the subjects of the dead man. The Bwana camped on the hill where they have built the mission now. He called it Chilubula, the place of salvation, because he saved those people from being killed by Ponde.

Then the Bwana McKinnon came down from Abercorn. He built the first station at Kasama. He destroyed the village of Ponde, and there was a big meeting of chiefs to discuss the succession to the mwambaship. You all know how the white men appointed Kanyanta, and not Ponde.

At this time we were all working for the white men, building houses and making bricks and every kind of work. And I myself have worked for the Bwanas in many countries. After I had been a mailman they put me in charge of carriers going with a white man to Fort Jamieson, Blantyre and Chindi. When I got back to Kasama I found a Bwana gathering men to fight as askaris. I thought, 'This is my work. I know how to fight. I will fight for the white man now.' They took me as far as Zomba, and then I was in Mombasa, and in Nairobi for three years. When I was at Nairobi I went with a Bwana on a hunting trip, and it was here that I bought a charm. I gave a cow for this charm to a very educated fellow, a native who had been to a Mission school. He could read and write, and he had learnt every kind of magic. He sold me this charm to kill elephants, and you see that now, even though I am old, I kill elephants even to this day. I killed two last month for the chief Nkolomfumu, and brought the ivory in to the Boma, and now Chitimukulu wants me to shoot elephants for him. Unless an enemy is using witchcraft against me I always kill.

I was still an askari then, and went to Tanganyika Territory to fight against some tribes there, and then to Somaliland, where there was no fighting. We just sat down in this place and stayed there. From there I went back to Nairobi and then they took me to Zanzibar. From Zanzibar we came back in a steamer across the water. My word!

You should have seen what a big steamer that was and how many men it held! I got back to Kasama in 1911 and I said to the Bwana, 'I must rest now.' So I rested in my village, and after that I became Government messenger and I worked in this way for ten years. I was one of their best men, because I always did right, and the Bwanas gave me great respect. Besides, they surely knew I was a chief, and not like an ordinary man. I worked for them so long that I became the head Government messenger, telling the Bwanas in everything what they should do. They gave me a village made of all the people who were working for them, messengers, mailmen, carpenters and bricklayers. It was not like an ordinary village for the people were not kinsmen, but they were all living together because they wanted to get money from the white men.

After that I retired and the Government gave me a very rich present. Yes, it was a pension—a lot of money. With it I bought another charm to kill elephants with, for such magic is sold at a high price, and usually from a native of another tribe.

This is the third village I have built. I have built my court right in the centre, with my subjects all around me. Here, can't you see? This is the court, where we are sitting. No, it is true there is no royal enclosure around my house. But is it not a court where the chief sits?

Yes, that is true, what you say. Those houses over there are bigger than mine. But then they are the houses of the young men who work for the Bwanas. It is their pride that makes them build houses as big as that. The white people come to look at them sometimes. They say, 'Look how big these huts are! This is the village of Bwembya!' Last week the head white doctor came up from Livingstone to see our village. He came and shouted to us here. He said, 'You people, you live like animals. Why don't you build a big hut with three rooms, so that a man may sit and eat with his wife?' But of course he did not know that it is already the fashion of many of the women of this village to eat with men. For many of the women have bad hearts nowadays. They care for nothing but clothes and beer. They want to wear shoes and stockings and blouses, and so they are always looking for men. That is why they are willing to sit and eat with men. Men and girls sit and eat together with no sense of respect or decency. But the Bwana doctor did not know all these things, so we were silent. We said, 'Yes Sir!' and clapped our hands. He told us to build windows in our houses. So, many of the young men made windows, for some of them are carpenters, you see. Yes, those are the windows, over there. Cannot you see? Those are windows like the white man has. Afterwards they put in wood and straw to keep out the cold which they found in their huts at night. They have tables and chairs to sit on too, some of these young men, and many other things. I have a lamp in my hut, too. My grandchildren and nephews bring me such presents because I am the headman of this village. But all the same, the men are very unruly here, and the women too. Their hearts are not good. They are always making trouble in my village so that it is constantly splitting up, and there is always noise, and no respect for the elders. The Bwana at the Boma calls me in and says, 'You must stop all this drinking in your village and these quarrels that go on.' But I say, 'The young people of today have no respect. They don't listen to the words of their chiefs.' I tell you it was better in the days before the white man came. But then sometimes I think in my heart, 'But where could we find the clothes and the salt and the matches that we buy at the stores?'

# II

# The Story of Udo Akpabio of the Anang Tribe, Southern Nigeria

*recorded by the Rev. W. Groves*

## Foreword by the recorder

The subject of this autobiography is a member of the district of the Calabar Province, Nigeria. This tribe Ukana clan of the Anang tribe in the Ikot Ekpene has an estimated population of 290,000. It stretches like a wedge through the heart of the province. Ethnologists have stated that the Ikot Ekpene district is the most thickly populated area in the whole of the African Continent apart from the Nile Valley.

The social structure of the tribe is patriarchal and communal. The Ete Ufok, Father of the House, is the head of the Ekpuk, or family. The family with its subdivisions dwells together in one large compound. Two or more families constitute a village. The democratic principle of government is the foundation of their constitution. From the heads of the families one is elected as the Obon ke Ison, the Lord of the Earth, or village chief. The powers of such a position are limited.

The Government forces first entered the Ikot Ekpene district after the Aro Expedition of 1901. The Aros were a dominant, slave-trading people to the north, whose 'Long Juju' was an oracle or court of appeal for all this part of Nigeria. After much fighting and burning of villages, the people were subdued. In 1904 Ikot Ekpene was made a seat of government. Direct rule was established; this was the only possible course to adopt when nothing was known of the indigenous organizations.

Udo Akpabio was elected by the people of Ukana Ikot Ntuen to be their representative and so became a 'chief' by Government warrant. He held this position until the introduction of indirect rule, or, in other words, the reorganization of administration on native lines, by which councils have replaced the warrant chiefs. This reform has lately been introduced together with direct taxation and native treasuries.

He is a big man in every respect. He is big in body and mind. Standing over six feet in height, with square, broad shoulders, he is one of the finest examples of African manhood I have seen. His mind is keen and alert. A great believer in the benefits of education, he gave of his land and substance to help the youth of his town and district. Two of his sons have received secondary-school training; one of them is the certificated headmaster of a Mission school, and the other is a clerk in one of the Clan Courts. He was held in high regard by all administrative officers who had dealings with him, for his frankness, sincerity and high sense of honour won their esteem. As president of the Native Court or as an assessor, the other warrant chiefs paid deference to his judgment. During all my years of residence in Ikot Ekpene I cannot recall any instance where his judgment was questioned. Neither have I ever heard any word that would suggest he was guilty of taking a bribe, and this is more than could be said of many other warrant chiefs. The strength of his influence in the district was revealed during the 'Women's Riots' in December, 1929. Peace reigned in every village under his jurisdiction, and he gave valuable assistance to the officer administering the district at that time.

One of the most wonderful things about the African is his capacity for friendship. As this bond strengthens, there develops a loyalty that death does not destroy. He gives himself whole-heartedly to a specific trust. Amid all the influences operating upon his life from youth to manhood—contacts with the impatient demands of our Western civilization, his veneration for the 'Old', and the appeal of the 'New' organization of life—Udo Akpabio was faithful to the trust placed in him as a warrant court chief. Doubtless under the new reorganized 'indirect' administration he will join in leading his people and helping them towards a fuller freedom of life.

Sir Donald Cameron, addressing the Legislative Council of Nigeria on March 3rd, 1935, in summing up the financial situation, said: 'We were saved from disaster by the indomitable spirit of the people.' Hope for the future was to be found in their 'unflagging industry and tenacity of purpose'. Udo Akpabio is one of these people.

# The Story of Udo Akpabio

My father, Udo Umo Ntuen, was the Obon [head] of all the Ukana clan. My mother's name was Akpabio Essien Ita of Akpa Uton. My father died when I was very young and I was left under the care of my elder brother. My father's possessions were wasted and his lands mortgaged as the result of the many death-feasts and sacrifices we had to make. My mother had then to work very hard to feed me and herself. She was given in marriage to another man. Unfortunately, she gave birth to twin children and had to leave the town. According to our custom twin children are unnatural and the mother of such children is considered unclean. She is banished to a lonely part of the forest called the Ikot Iban Ekpo [Bush of the Women Devils. It is believed that one of the twin children is the result of association with an evil spirit] and the children are killed. Sometimes they were put into water-pots and left in the bush; other times they were placed in white-ant hills. My mother was not allowed to walk the ordinary roads in the village or go to the same spring for water that was generally used by the people. Neither could she pass to the farmland that had been given to her. At this time she used to make many sacrifices and offer many prayers to the gods and devils who were believed to have brought the twin children. She did this in the hope of freeing her relatives and neighbours from a similar fate; that she might not bear twins in the next world; and that her two sons might not marry women who would become mothers of twins. No one was allowed to have any dealings of any kind with such women. In this despised condition my mother was sold to the Ibo people, who did not treat their women in this fashion.

There is a story we tell to our children that teaches the sacredness of the land and how punishment comes to those who neglect to obey the laws affecting it. For no mother of twins can walk across any farm owned by another person. If she does, the crops when planted will be cursed and the harvest a failure.

A certain man went to clear his farmlands by cutting down the bush and burning it. When he was tired he sat down under the shade of a tree to rest. Then he drew his big pot of palm wine towards himself and his servants sat around him. He took his bag that was hanging from the branch of a tree. Inside the bag were some calabash drinking cups. Taking the biggest, he filled it with wine. Pouring some of it on the ground, he prayed: 'O Earth, watch this farm for me and let all the crops I sow bring forth bountiful harvests. Do not show me any evil thing. Likewise I will not show thee any evil.' Then he drank the wine that was left in the cup. Taking some food from another large calabash, he sprinkled it on the ground in the same manner and repeated his prayer.

The Earth was glad to hear what the man said and agreed to keep the promise. The Earth said: 'Good, I will see who will break this promise.' When the day's work was done the man went home.

At the appointed time he went to sow his seeds. He walked with all kinds of people to help in the work. Some had bad sores and running ulcers on their feet and legs. Others had nose ulcers and were continually spitting on the ground. To make matters worse, some mothers of twins accompanied the workers. Then the Earth grew very angry for the farmer had broken his promise.

When the work of sowing was finished the man went home with a glad expectation of a good harvest. But the Earth laughed at him and did not yield anything that year. During the harvest the farmer was surprised and ashamed that he did not reap anything. He grew very angry and cried: 'O Earth, what have I done to thee? What a terrible mischief thou hast shown to me! Before I planted I made a vow with thee.'

'Vengeance,' the Earth replied. 'You had first broken the promise on the day you had sowed your crops by the filthy people you brought unto the land.' The farmer went home sorrowful, regretting what he had done.

The story is also told to teach this lesson. *If you want your friendships to last, try and avoid doing anything that will annoy your friends.*

I suffered many hard things in those days. My brother did not take a proper care of me. He was worried about his own business and I had to look after myself. This was a period of deep thinking for me. I had to consider how to feed myself, as my father's farms were taken by other people. I tell my children I do not want them to suffer as I suffered and that they should study me if they want their lives to be good in this world. I am glad that I was poor for my poverty has taught me to think deeply and work hard. My early struggles of boyhood and young manhood have taught me to understand life better than anything else.

I set myself to learn all the handwork my people could do. Having succeeded in this, I was able to get a piece of land, which I planted. I began to save food and from food I was able to save money. Then I bought some fowls and a cow. In the course of a few years I became a cloth-seller. There was no proper trade route at that time. Ten miles' travel was a long journey. Before a man could go on such a task he had to be well armed with knives and a gun. He also had to have friends in all villages through which he walked. If not, he would be caught and sold or killed. Abasi—God—saved me and helped me to success.

When I was a child I was strictly advised by my mother and relatives not to eat or drink carelessly with other people. I know this advice has saved my life on several occasions during my travels. That is why you never see us drink the last drop of water or wine from a cup. We always leave a little at the bottom and throw it on the ground. Should there be any poison in the drink it generally goes to the bottom of the calabash. But I was taught this in order to protect me from eating rats and snakes. These are thought to be injurious and poisonous to our people. There is a belief that whenever a Ukana person eats a rat or a snake his body will swell from his feet to his head and he will die a dreadful death. Thus it is considered a terrible curse to say to anyone: 'Iso nte ata ekpu' ['A face like one who eats a rat']. These words are always applied to people with a swollen face. This curse has been the cause of much fighting and many deaths and curse-borne prayers. This is also true respecting the Ibom, the puff adder. The souls of our ancestors are supposed to dwell in them. That is why we never cut down the thick bush at the foot of the big trees where these snakes live.

As in most other clans here, social life and intercourse with mothers of twins is strictly forbidden. Any persons found guilty of such conduct, both men and women, were either killed or sold as slaves to Inokon, the Aro people. Thus in my early life I was led to see the evil of indulgence with such women. From that time I have done my best to observe and obey the laws of the town. Indeed, I am quite clean so far as these women are concerned. But I shall never forget the life-taking trouble of my early manhood. Although I was careful and watchful of my doings, yet I was tempted to commit a crime for which I was ordered to be killed. I am sorry to confess it was the crime of adultery. It was not a matter as in this age of paying a five pounds' fine in the Native Court. It was something greater. It meant that a person who was guilty of such a crime had to hide himself for fear of being killed. Thus I had to hide myself and send some people to beg the offended husband to allow me to pay a fine as a ransom for my life. He would not consent to do this at first. As I was humble and courteous to many, giving them a helping hand when I was able to do so, they voluntarily made it their duty to plead for me. After much pleading the stony-hearted person consented to terms of peace. The case was tried and I had to pay a fine of fifteen hundred manillas.

Where was I to get this money? While I was fretting

over this, one kind old man pointed me to a village in which my father had married. He explained to me that the woman had been sent away from my father's compound and that the head-money had not been repaid. I went to the village and caught a man, as the custom was at that time. The owner of the man refunded the amount due to my father. This was how I managed to get out of my trouble. The purchase-money of this divorced woman is the only direct inheritance that I have obtained from my father's possessions.

It was because of this palaver of mine that I began to understand something of life. When I am talking to my sons and family I always begin my advice by saying: 'Study me if you want your lives to be good in this world. Do not make the mistakes that I have made. Learn to walk by night and learn how to lie down and throw a spear.' This teaches that if you practise evil, practise also how to receive the effect of evil when it comes. For if you throw away every fire that gives smoke you will sleep coldly. Meaning, that if you want to part with every bad man you know, you will have no one at last. I always tell them that people climb up an oil palm that ripens two bunches of fruit and observe the one that ripens three. This to show them that from small beginnings people come to greater prosperity. To teach them that they must work and not lose hope by thinking that their time is past and success will not come again, I tell them that a man's growth does not cease until he dies. To encourage them to work hard and not waste their time, and to save them from regrets and crying over lost opportunities when they get older, I point out to them: when the hawk takes the chicken and passes over the river, there is nothing more can catch that fowl.

In the early days fathers always selected husbands for

their daughters. If they refused they were severely dealt with or they were sold. But they were good sons and daughters at that time and they were ever ready to obey. The repayment of the purchase money nearly always resulted in a sort of war between the villages. If a woman ran away the husband could catch any person from the village to which she had gone. That person was sold as a slave. Supposing a wife died and the purchase money had been fully paid, another girl had to be given. Even if the second died another had to be given in her place. This might be continued as long as the man desired to claim the privilege of this custom.

On the marriage day, there is erected in the village playground a mound of clay about six feet high and three feet broad. Every inhabitant of the village is present, except those who are sick. The bride with her mother and friends arrives first. Then come the fathers of both families, each bringing a pig. They cut the throats of the pigs in turn, each assisting the other, and squirt the blood around the foot of the clay pedestal. The blood of the pigs mixed in this fashion carries the idea that the two families become one. The bridegroom climbs to the top of the pedestal and announces before all gathered, his name, his family name, the name of the girl he has bought, her family name and how many goats he has paid for her head.

I did not marry at once without consideration. I thought of what I should give to a wife before I entered marriage. When I found that I had enough foodstuffs and manillas for the maintenance of a wife I began to set about the business. From the grain I got by trading in cloths I was able to buy back my father's lands. The people then began to recognize me. They saw that I was not only growing in wealth but in wisdom as the result of my work and travels. My elder brother then came to me and sought to teach me about the government of our people. He took me to the village council and this brought me into the company of the other Ukana chiefs. They liked to hear me speak of other people I had seen and the things they did. Sometimes my brother used to send me to represent him on important matters in our clan. In hearing palavers I was always fearless in giving justice. From that time I became one of the chiefs of the town and gradually took my father's place. The people preferred me to my brother. I think it was for this reason and my love of justice that I was elected to represent my town as Warrant Chief.

I have now with me seventeen wives, and two are dead. I have also married for my sons twelve wives of which eleven are alive. As a blessing from the marriages I have now got thirty children of which eleven are females, not counting those which are dead. I have got at present twenty grandchildren. I do not record this to show my wealth, but to be a lesson to my people when comparing my beginning with the present standard. I believe that my life has been spared by the Aqua Abasi [Great God] for the purpose of teaching my children, myself and others an important lesson.

My reason for saying this is because I have taken an active part in much fighting. I have been wounded on many occasions. People with much smaller wounds than I received have died. I have now in my left thigh, near the groin, a big, deep scar which a bullet from the gun had made. Many people tried to work the bullet out but failed. It is there now. I think it has given an additional bone to the number of bones in my body. If such is the case, I have more bones in comparison with the rest of my fellow creatures.

When my father was about to be crowned as a chief he was told to go to Ikot Obio Osun and live there. This place was the head of government for our people in those days. As my father was a powerful and wealthy man he persuaded the other chiefs to allow him to stay in his own town and have the crowning there. They agreed. He then began to make improvements in many things. After he had considered for some time he sent for all the Ukana village chiefs and revealed to them his thoughts. One of the things he desired to possess was a big drum. This was for the purpose of bringing the people together on important occasions, to assist in keeping order in the clan, and to be a means of protection for fugitives from other clans. When any stranger beat the drum it meant that he had fallen under his feet and became a slave of my father. It was not to be beaten at all times like other drums. It was to be used on the anniversary of the day he was crowned, and for the purpose already stated.

It was agreed that he should go on with this work. He made a search of all our forests to find a big tree of hard wood. This was found, and labourers came from every village to assist in the work of cutting it down and removing it to the place where the drum now is. Each village sent a representative wood-carver. They carved on the drum figures of all the animals they could remember they had ever seen. They also carved my father's staff—Eto Ubon—and his crown—Ntinya—on the drum. The work was very hard and it took three years to finish.

My father then made a great feast in which all the villages joined. A sacrifice was made that the drum should be set apart for its special work. Two men were killed and their heads placed one at each end of the drum. I have never seen so many animals killed at one time before nor since that day. Neither have I ever seen so great a feast. While the people were feasting they were told that they must run to the drum at once when they heard the sound of her big voice. If any stranger should beat the drum they would have to defend him against any persons seeking to do him harm. [The drum is cut out of the tree in the form of a woman with head and legs.]

Every harvest, after the seed-yams have been selected and stored, the drum was beaten and there would be much feasting. There would be thousands of yams in one enclosure. They are put together in rows of twenty upright and fifty rows horizontal. Two men were always killed and their bodies were hung at each end of the enclosure. No one ever went near the place until the flesh was gone from their bones. This was done to warn thieves. When the next planting season came round three men were caught and killed and the drum was beaten. Two of these men were for Ikorok [the drum] and the other for the seed-yams. His body was cut to pieces and the blood sprinkled on the yams before they were planted.

At first we heard a rumour that a certain power had fought against the Inokon [Aro people] and destroyed many things. After this we were informed that this warlike people had come from Ibibio to Ifuho near Ikot Ekpene. They were seeking Ukpon Inokon who was a slave trader. He was one of the big chiefs and a leader of the people in the slave trade. During the fighting and the destruction of the 'Long Juju' the Aros were scattered throughout all this district. The white men had been informed that this man was hiding at Ifuho. They caught him, fastened ropes around his ankles and he was hung on a tree with his head downwards. They cut off his head and went away.

In a few years they returned to Ikot Ekpene. When we heard this we all ran away and hid in the bush. We used to go to the spring and to our farms for food at night. The soldiers came to Ikot Nwo and Ikot Akpabio, villages near to us. They fired at the people and burnt all the houses as they went. They came on to Ikot Ntuen where we fired at them in return. The same day they returned to Ikot Ekpene.

When the other Ukana villages heard of this they all came together. Adiasim joined with us. We armed ourselves to go and fight the white men and their soldiers. Everyone of us said: 'What a disgraceful thing it is for another people to come and fight us on our own land. We have no palaver with them. Let us find out where they are and fight with them. Are they not men like ourselves?'

We found that they were resting at Ikot Inyang on the other side of the Qua Iboe river in Chief Ibanga Umo Ekere's compound. When we reached Abiakpo Edem Idim the people advised us not to cross the river or none would ever return and we would fall a prey to them.

A few days passed and one morning we heard the sound of a bugle. We sent messengers to call all the other chiefs and people. We beat the big drum and our bugler blew his horn. When all were gathered together we went out to fight and met them at a place called Anwa Oko on the borders of Ikot Ntuen. There the battle took place. We were the first to fire and we killed their bugler. Then they grew very angry and fired at us. They did not shoot at first but waited until we had ceased firing. We were pressed back into the bush. They came on until they reached the centre of the town where the big drum is now. Here we had a big fight and many were killed. It was on this day that Udo Esi Idomo, a big chief, was killed while taking snuff.

At this time we could not find many of our people again, not even our bugler. Everyone had escaped into the bush. The British soldiers marched as far as Nsasak and slept by the riverside. Everyone of us slept in the bush.

The next day we wanted to go and make peace, but we did not know how to reach them. As soon as we came out of the bush at Ikot Akpabio they fired on us. It was on this day that our old chief, blind with age, and his old wife were killed. Their bodies were found in the bush that same evening. During that day they tried to burn my father's drum but failed. They burnt down my big compound, destroyed all my property and farms and returned to Ikot Ekpene.

We desired peace as so many people had been killed and so many towns burned. We sent messengers to meet the white men at Ikot Ekpene. They returned saying we had to supply a white goat, a cow and twenty thousand manillas before they would agree to any taik of peace. This we did at once.

[In 1930 there was a visitation of Nkpayo, or locusts. This was the first that I had known. On inquiry, I found that the previous visitation was just prior to the coming of the Government to Ikot Ekpene. In discussing the matter with the old folk, I found that locusts were a terrible omen of evil. Their crops and palms were badly destroyed and there was a serious outbreak of Mfat Ito, or smallpox. Then the white men came and fought strongly against them and conquered them. These old men said with bitterness: 'If we had known, we would have fought much harder aganst Nkpayo to destroy them and not let some of them get away. Then we would have had greater power to defeat the white men.']

The court was then established at Ikot Ekpene. Summonses and warrants were issued free of charge. Okodi Iya of Ikot Ekpene, Akpan Etok Akpan of Ikot Esetan, and Inyang Ata Udo of Ikot Obong Edong were the first Warrant Chiefs. [These three villages adjoin each other around the Government station.]

A year passed when a charge of eighty manillas was made for every summons and warrant. Then it was changed to sixty manillas and one fowl. The white men used to buy the fowls for food. Some were also sold to the clerks. It was during this time that I was elected as a Warrant Chief. The sitting fee was five shillings per member and ten shillings to the president of the court per month. From this time we began to be less afraid of the white men. They also began to be friendly with us. When money was first given to us we did not like it. The commissioner persuaded us to know the use of shillings and that it was not so heavy to carry as our own money. This brought about the issue of summonses and warrants for five shillings.

At Ikot Ekpene we used to build all the houses the Government required without payment. We also had to keep them in good repair. We were compelled to clear the bush, make roads through the towns and keep them clean. Everybody was employed in this work, men, women and children. The roads were portioned out to the different villages. If a road was bad, or anyone refused to go and work, the chief of the village and that person were arrested and fined or imprisoned. It was very funny sometimes in making the roads. One commissioner would tell us to make the road flat. Another would make us change it and make a hill [camber] in the centre. Another would tell us to make drains by the side of the road and then a new one would come and tell us to fill them up again. Some of these changing ways of the white men used to make us laugh, but we did not let them see us laughing.

All transport in those days was on the heads of our people. The carrying of loads was by compulsion. The carriers were paid according to the distance they travelled. If the chiefs failed to send carriers to the office when they were wanted, they were arrested and fined. But if the chief could prove that he had given the token [a zinc disc with a number on it] to any man who had not gone to do his work, the man was punished.

The cleaning of the court house, prison, offices and houses of the clerks was done every week by women from the villages. No payment was given for this work. After a while this method was changed when female prisoners were given to the chiefs of the court. They were held responsible for their protection and care. These women were all connected with marriage palavers. There was no accommodation for women in the prison in those days, neither were there any women warders. These prisoners were kept by the chiefs until the purchase-money had been repaid into court. Then the women and girls were handed over to their families to be remarried.

The work of the court and its power in the district were increasing every month. Our sitting fees were increased to three pounds per member and six pounds to the president. We had to work very hard. The court was in session from morning until evening five days every week.

We looked upon the first Commissioners as our fathers. As we grew to know and understand each other they trusted us as we did them and followed their guidance. Every elected chief was given a warrant and a cap with the number and name of their court and the King's Crown on the front of the cap. We were told it was our duty to help all we could to develop the district for the good of our people, their happiness and peace. Wherever we went we were respected by white and black. The chiefs were the only people who had power to decide cases in the courts without any interference by non-members. The District Commissioners always consulted us when there was anything of importance affecting our people. As regards the Government service I have always tried to give satisfaction in any work that has been given me to do.

Things have changed very much during the last few years. The beginning of Native ['indirect'] Administration and taxation has not all been good. The old men and chiefs are much poorer than the young men today. Children were more obedient to their parents than at present. Strong-headed sons and daughters were mercilessly punished. The young men lived in their fathers' compounds and worked for them. They might work for others and have some money but they could not make use of it without the knowledge and consent of the old men. The Father of the House had to protect them and provide food and clothing. He would marry wives for his sons and give them some yams to add with their own to maintain themselves with their wives. They had to continue helping the old men and the people of the compound. Now, they look after their own interests. Sometimes they will give assistance if there is any big trouble. But at present, it is very hard for some people to get a helping hand if they have no money, for every small piece of work needs payment.

Before taxation we were informed that the price of palm produce would be raised, but now, oil and palm kernels are very little valued by the Europeans. As palm produce is the chief means of living, I do not know what the life of the people will be in a few years' time as regards the payment of tax and the buying of food. It is a struggle to work out ways and means for maintenance and taxation.

Taxation has also increased the number of thieves. There are many whose names have been recorded as taxpayers, but they have no means of fulfilling this condition. They have no proper work and neither can they get any in these days. Many come to me for help, asking for work to save them from stealing. I do my best for them. When the time comes to pay the tax there seems to be a plague of thieving. Sometimes the young men run away to different parts of the country and do not return to their homes for a long time. Some will stay away for one and two years. During this long absence the Father of the Family has to find the money to pay the full assessment of the tax. He has to pay for the absent ones and can get no relief unless he can prove that they are dead.

The paying of tax has done another evil thing. Young men apply to the District Officer for work as clerks, messengers or labourers. The officers refer them to the chiefs. If the applicants are disappointed in their request they put the blame on the chiefs. They do not consider that we cannot find work for all who want it. The result of this is that they refuse to pay their share of the tax to the chiefs. The chiefs are then summoned by the Government and fined. Action is taken against such young men and they are punished by the chiefs. For this they find ways and means of killing their chiefs.

In the native courts there are many more disturbances than there used to be years ago. In judging cases many people stand up and give their own decision even though they are not the elected chiefs. The District Officers of this time differ very much from those we had formerly; whenever they go to some courts they tell the non-members that they all have right in everything just because they have paid the tax. I wonder what business the tax has in regard to deciding cases in court. For example, when some people are dissatisfied with the court judgment they would appeal to the District Officer. The chiefs are then asked to review the case. I think this method is not quite good, because when some untrained chiefs have hated a man, it would be very hard for them to give him justice.

A large number of the present court members are new and have not had much experience.

On the other hand there are many advantages derived from this new fashion of government. There are many new and better roads throughout the district. We are not now compelled to make and look after them. There are special labourers who work every day to keep them in good condition. They are paid from taxation funds. We have no trouble about carrying loads. This is all done by motors bought from the tax money. When we are called to build any house or do any kind of work we are now paid for it. Many bridges have been built. In some places where the people have to walk many miles for their water, deep wells have been made in their towns

The establishment of many courts has done good in keeping all the villages in closer touch with the Government. At the same time it is bad in some ways. It brings a separation, jealousy and enmity between one clan and another. At present, when a man from one clan sues a man of another clan and the case is tried in the defendant's area, the chiefs of that court may sometimes be partial and spoil the case. This was not so when we had the central court at Ikot Ekpene. The people would deal with one another as brothers.

This new system has also done good in the way it is encouraging education. Several schools have been built for different clans. There is also a Training College where our best young men can become teachers. These are all paid for and supported by our tax.

When I think of Europeans I notice that they differ, not only in complexion but also in manner, habits and speech. Some are good, kind, patient and strong in judging what is right and trying to understand us and our customs. Others are hot-headed and will not take the time to seek to know us. Possibly it is because they are new to us and are worried by having so many things to do.

The white men are great in their fashion of doing things. They like to do everything in order. They are not like some black men who jump from one thing unfinished to a fresh one, and by so doing may be unable to finish both. They trust very much to writing. I do not think they can remember anything properly if they do not write it down. I have gone many times to meet them for business. Whenever I went they had to write some words before they could remember to do my wish. Sometimes twenty and more men would go and lay complaints before the white man and he would not forget any. They were all written in a book.

They spend much time in arranging things in their offices and houses. In the house one would always see some servants brushing the floor and clearing away something hanging from the roof. At the end of the month these servants go and receive a heavy sum of money. I consider this is a waste for such small work. Why, they could have done such for themselves.

I like very much the way they keep their premises. But it would be impossible for me to grow flowers and leaves in places where I should plant yams and other crops for food. They seem to take interest in what cannot feed them. I wonder why they like to satisfy their eyes rather than their belly. I think they do not know the right use of money. They spend their money for those who cook their food, of which they will also have a share. This is very ridiculous when a man has got a wife, a brother or a sister who can cook for him.

The white men love their wives more than anything they have in life. I have been acquainted with some of them for over twenty years but I have never seen them quarrelling or fighting with their wives. It is a surprising thing to me to note that they are all rich, but they would be seen with only one wife.

In speech they are different from us. They do not all speak together. They have patience and speak one after another without any interruption. But they do not use parables to illustrate their judgment when they want to decide any case as we do. I do not always enjoy meeting them when they come new from their country. They have so many different manners. Sometimes I go to the office or house to meet them. If there is no interpreter present they try to satisfy me with the words: 'Obon, Ndewo! [Chief, I salute you!]' They would have to call the interpreter before they could say any more. They speak very rapidly and I praise the men who have to interpret such a stream of words.

# III

# The Story of Ndansi Kumalo of the Matabele Tribe, Southern Rhodesia

*recorded by J. W. Posselt and Margery Perham*

## Foreword by Margery Perham

Chief Ndansi Kumalo leaves very little to be explained. With his two African companions he visited me at my home where, although everything was strange to him and he cannot speak a word of English, he made a deep impression by his beautiful manners and his dignity. He told us stories of the old days, which were interpreted by Mr. J. W. Posselt, formerly District Commissioner in the Native Administration of Southern Rhodesia. I was so much impressed by these that I arranged further meetings at the Chief's lodgings in London. There, thanks to the patience and skill of Mr. Posselt, and to the Chief's confidence in him, I was able to take down this account of his life.

It is interesting to learn that the Gaumont British Company thought so well of Kumalo's acting in Matabeleland that they brought him over to England in order to obtain further 'shots' in their London studios. Here, as a man and an actor—though in his case there is, perhaps, no distinction—he has won the respect of all who have worked with him. Members of the cast have given him presents as tokens of their liking and respect, a pair of riding-breeches from Mr. Walter Huston (who plays the part of Rhodes), a knife and a pipe from the actresses, while the West Indians, who impersonated his soldiers, presented him with an address of friendship. The following is a quotation from a letter written to me by Mr. Hugh Findlay, of the Gaumont British Corporation. 'Mr. Berthold Viertel (who has a lifetime experience of acting and production, both stage and screen) was sincerely enthusiastic concerning Kumalo's performance. In Mr. Viertel's words, the Chief "has a simplicity of behaviour that in addition to his physical presence brings poise and sincerity to all that he is required to do". Personally, I was present when, at the conclusion of shooting, everyone "behind" the camera, including Mr. Viertel, loudly applauded the Chief for his work. I can assure you this rarely if ever happens in any studio.'

## The Story of Ndansi Kumalo

I am proud and honoured to tell you my story. My father's name was Mhlahlo and he was Induna of the Gaba regiment. My mother's name was Mafase. My grandfather was Zirwaba of the Bedje clan.

We lived in the Matoppo hills. My people came with Mzilikazi from Chaka's country, from Zululand, to Mkwahla (Zeerust). The journey took twelve months. From Mkwahla we were driven away by the Boers and journeyed on here for another twelve months. We suffered much from starvation and thirst on the way. My uncle was killed by a buffalo. The people lived mainly on the flesh of dead cattle and roots. The children were fed on the liquid from the entrails of dead cattle. The deaths were mostly among the women and children. All this my father told me; he was a young man at the time, not yet married. In those times the king allowed no one to marry until they were well advanced in years. My father was a brave man and a hero. On the way up they fought the tribes they met; when they reached this country all the men were one mass of battle scars, here and here and here, all over their bodies. Not many women were taken from other tribes because they had not much food for them. When they were settled in Matabeleland, then they went out and raided for women. My grandmother used to tell stories of Chaka, of how he ill-treated Mzilikazi's father and cut off his right arm. He was forgiven after his arm was cut off and put in charge of his warriors again, but he did not live long. Mzilikazi was well liked: he was a great chief. When he decided to leave Chaka he burnt his own kraal and then fled.

I was born about the time when Mzilikazi died; I was a small boy of four or five at the time when Lobengula was made king. Nothing special happened during my childhood. My duty was to herd the stock; first, as a little boy, the goats, and later, the cattle. My father had a big herd, 200 head, close to the kraal. My father was very severe, we were often punished by being thrashed with switches, very hard, like this . . . The children were always kept at a distance at meal times until their elders had finished. I was in great fear of my father so I behaved very well, and did not get so many punishments as the others. Mother was very bad-tempered, but she was very much more gentle with us after my father died. She reached a great age and died after I had taken my second wife. Many thrashings we got when we did not look after the cattle properly and they got into other people's land. If we neglected bringing back all the cattle and left one, even if we had gone to sleep they would come and pull us out from under the blankets and we would get a good thrashing. But it made men of us. We used to cry bitterly over it, but it did us good. Often we slept out on the veld where we were, afraid to go home. We dare not treat our children like that, there is no discipline nowadays; all we can do is to talk and threaten and plead, but to use a switch—no! They have little respect for us now.

When we were afraid to go home we used to sneak back to the kraal at night and creep in between the cattle and lie among them so as to keep warm. If it was raining we usually went to one of the old mothers and knocked, very quietly, like this, and she would let us in, and at daybreak we would creep out again. The old women were always kind to us children, shielded us and looked after us. We have a saying that an old woman is far more capable of looking after children than a young one.

Hyenas killed quite a lot of cattle: one day they killed 20 head. The remainder broke away and came back to the village and next day the people went out and tried to kill the hyenas. The boys quarrelled and had many fights with sticks; they were jealous about taking cattle to watering places and grazing; there was rivalry, too, between the herds. We were in great dread of hyenas. We spent a lot of time setting traps for birds; we would catch them and cook them on the veld and take them to our mothers. We used to hunt hares and small buck. As young lads, when we grew older, we used to go up to the king's kraal and sing and show that we were nearing manhood and would be of value to him, and we would sing his praises. If the king was in a good humour he used to turn out one of his cattle for us to kill. It was always very interesting to him to see the rising generation ready to turn into fighting men. It was through the young fellows visiting his kraal in this way that the king had a good idea of the numbers that were growing up, and soon the command came to draft them into regiments, after the age of puberty, at about fifteen or sixteen. It was a great honour and we went without hesitation, for it meant that we were men, not boys any more. We spent about a month singing and dancing near the king's kraal; he used to give us lots of food and we were well looked after. We brought our own outfit, our skins and shields. Our parents provided our spears. At the beginning we carried no particular colour; that was to come later.

Our first duty was to tend some of the king's cattle which were put in our charge; we had to go to a special area and look after them. We were detailed to the Shangani area. When we had built the necessary shelters for the cattle these were divided up, five or ten head to two of us. Each was personally responsible. We were allowed to milk the cattle and have the milk. While we were first there, lions killed two of the king's cattle; we hunted the lions and killed them with spears. On one occasion a lion killed two of our party and the king was very angry. 'You mustn't allow lions to kill human beings—you can't have been doing your duty. That must not occur again or there will be serious consequences. I will not punish you this time, but, to let men be killed, someone must have played the coward. I have no use for cowards; I want brave men.' We received orders to leave Shangani and go to Gwelo, still in charge of cattle. Here a cheetah came and killed a cow, and we surrounded the cheetah and killed it. Soon another lion came and killed one of the cattle: on this occasion we followed the lion and despatched it, and it did not kill any of us.

We learnt to fight by practising amongst each other with switches, and then with proper sticks as if it were a real fight. Here on my head you can still see the mark of the wound I got when I was training in this way. In these fights there was no bad feeling. I was a chief's son but it did not matter: it was all fair play and no distinctions. Of course if anybody molested a chief's son outside such a fight, that was a serious matter.

We were not allowed to marry without the king's consent. If a young warrior took a wife he would not be so brave as an unmarried one: he would not attend to his duty. Only the middle-aged men married. Of course we had our own special girls and we agreed that we would marry them when we had permission. But I did not wait for the king's permission. The girl I chose was so beautiful that many men wanted to have her and I nearly lost my life at the hands of jealous suitors. They made violent love to her and tried to carry her off by force, but I protected her. I had my spear, and I was a strong man and able to beat them off. Also, I suppose I must have been handsome then, for she chose me. I put her in the charge of my mother. We had one daughter but my wife died young. I have had other wives since.

At Shangani we spent two years and at Gwelo two years, still in charge of cattle. All this time we did not fight with men. Then the order came that we should go out on our first raiding expedition. There were five regiments. There was the Tgaba, a word which means tin, Amhlope—the white ones—and on the other side Mcijo, meaning sharp point, and Mavene, meaning baboons: we called them this because they were a mixed lot, not pure Matabele. My regiment was the Mcijo, the last regiment ever raised by Lobengula. Memeze was our commander; he was not a striking man but had a good personality and was very capable. We went right across the Zambezi and raided tribes beyond it. Unfortunately we were overtaken with an epidemic of smallpox and most of us were incapacitated by this. We did not get any cattle, only a few goats, but we took away quite a number of their womenfolk and a few men, but most of them ran away from us and deserted their womenfolk. On the return journey the epidemic got worse and worse and there were many deaths; for two months we could not move through the smallpox. Before we reached Bulawayo we received a report that the pioneers had entered the country. We were very distressed to hear the news, all the more because we were not capable of rendering any assistance to our king. We had often seen white men, for they used to come to Bulawayo to see the king. When I first saw a white man I could not make it out and I ran away. When we got used to them we would go with goats and sheep and buy European clothing. Later people used to take cattle and barter for beads and blankets.

We were terribly upset and very angry at the coming of the white men, for Lobengula had sent to the Queen in England and he was under her protection and it was quite unjustified that white men should come with force into our country. Our regiments were very distressed that we were not in a fit condition to fight for the king because of the smallpox. Lobengula had no war in his heart: he had always protected the white men and been good to them. If he had meant war, would he have sent our regiments far away to the north at this moment? As far as I know the trouble began in this way. Gandani, a chief who was sent out, reported that some of the Mashona had taken the king's cattle; some regiments were detailed to follow and recover them. They followed the Mashona to Ziminto's people [Victoria district]. Gandani had strict instructions not to molest the white people established in certain parts and to confine himself to the people who had taken the cattle. The commander was given a letter which he had to produce to the Europeans and tell them what the object of the party was. But the members of the party were restless and went without reporting to the white people and killed a lot of Mashonas. The pioneers were very angry and said, 'You have trespassed into our part.' [This was in 1893.] They went with the letter, but only after they had killed some people, and the white men said, 'You have done wrong, you should have brought the letter first and then we should have given you permission to follow the cattle.' The commander received orders from the white people to get out, and up to a certain point which he could not possibly reach in the time allowed. A force followed them up and they defended themselves. When the pioneers turned out there was a fight at Shangani and at Bembezi.

I was in the Matoppos and had not recovered from smallpox. I did not see Lobengula at this time for we were isolated. We sent a message to the King asking for permission to join with his forces; he agreed and we reorganized our regiment. The King agreed that we might come out of quarantine and told us to go to Gwelo to fetch some of his cattle, but we could not: we were too weak. Only fourteen of our regiment went to try and recover the King's cattle and on the way they heard that they were too late. The white men were there and had seized the cattle. These fourteen incorporated themselves in Imbizo's regiment and fought at Bembezi, and two were killed. The next news was that the white people had entered Bulawayo; the King's kraal had been burnt down and the King had fled. Of the cattle very few were recovered; most fell into the hands of the white people. Only a very small portion were found and brought to Shangani where the King was, and we went there to give him any assistance we could. I did not catch up with the King; he had gone on ahead. Three of our leaders mounted their horses and followed up the King and he wanted to know where his cattle were; they said they had fallen into the hands of the whites, only a few were left. He said, 'Go back and bring them along.' But they did not go back again; the white forces had occupied Bulawayo and they went into the Matoppos. Then the white people came to where we were living and sent word round that all chiefs and warriors should go into Bulawayo and discuss peace, for the King had gone and they wanted to make peace. The first order we got was, 'When you come in, come in with cattle so that we can see that you are sincere about it.' The white people said, 'Now that your King has deserted you, we occupy your country. Do you submit to us?' What could we do? 'If you are sincere, come back and bring in all your arms, guns and spears.' We did so.

I cannot say what happened to Lobengula, but the older people said, 'The light has gone out. We can do no more. There is nothing left for us but to go back to our homes.' All that we could hear was that the King had disappeared alone; no one knew where he went. It could not be that his body, alive or dead, should pass into the hands of his enemies. Our King was powerful and a great king; he was invincible against other tribes. He ruled right up to the Zambezi. He was just; and if, unfortunately, many innocent men were killed it was through the jealousy and cunning of others who sent false reports which the King believed. At the beginning Lobengula was loved by everybody, but later bitterness arose in the families which had suffered loss and there was a good deal of dissension. I remember a tragedy when two of my relatives were killed. They were at the King's kraal and he was annoyed with them. He fired towards them with a shot-gun to frighten them and the warriors took it as a sign to despatch them and clubbed them to death. When news came to their kraal the children fled, but their wives said, 'Let us die with them.' The King sent them a message that it was a mistake. It all arose from a dispute over cattle.

So we surrendered to the white people and were told to go back to our homes and live our usual lives and attend to our crops. But the white men sent native police who did abominable things; they were cruel and assaulted a lot of our people and helped themselves to our cattle and goats. These policemen were not our own people; anybody was made a policeman. We were treated like slaves. They came and were overbearing and we were ordered to carry their clothes and bundles. They interfered with our wives and our daughters and molested them. In fact, the treatment we received was intolerable. We thought it best to fight and die rather than bear it. How the rebellion started I do not know; there was no organization, it was like a fire that suddenly flames up. We had been flogged by native police and then they rubbed salt water in the wounds. There was much bitterness because so many of our cattle were branded and taken away from us; we had no property, nothing we could call our own. We said, 'It is no good living under such conditions; death would be better—let us fight.' Our King gone, we had submitted to the white people and they ill-treated us until we became desperate and tried to make an end of it all. We knew that we had very little chance because their weapons were so much superior to ours. But we meant to fight to the last, feeling that even if we could not beat them we might at least kill a few of them and so have some sort of revenge.

I fought in the rebellion. We used to look out for valleys where the white men were likely to approach. We took cover behind rocks and trees and tried to ambush them. We were forced by the nature of our weapons not to expose ourselves. I had a gun, a breech-loader. They—the white men—fought us with big guns and Maxims and rifles.

I remember a fight in the Matoppos when we charged the white men. There were some hundreds of us; the white men also were many. We charged them at close quarters: we thought we had a good chance to kill them but the Maxims were too much for us. We drove them off at the first charge, but they returned and formed up again. We made a second charge, but they were too strong for us. I cannot say how many white people were killed, but we think it was quite a lot. I do not know if I killed any of them, but I know I killed one of their horses. I remember how, when one of their scouts fell wounded, two of his companions raced out and took him away. Many of our people were killed in this fight: I saw four of my cousins shot. One was shot in the jaw and the whole of his face was blown away—like this—and he died. One was hit between the eyes; another here, in the shoulder; another had part of his ear shot off. We made many charges but each time we were beaten off, until at last the white men packed up and retreated. But for the Maxims, it would have been different. The place where we have been making the film is the very place where my cousins were killed.

We were still fighting when we heard that Mr. Rhodes was coming and wanted to make peace with us. It was best to come to terms he said, and not go shedding blood like this on both sides. The older people went to meet him. Mr. Rhodes came and they had a discussion and our leaders came back and discussed amongst themselves and the people. Then Mr. Rhodes came again and we agreed at last to terms of peace.

So peace was made. Many of our people had been killed, and now we began to die of starvation; and then came the rinderpest and the cattle that were still left to us perished. We could not help thinking that all these dreadful things were brought by the white people. We struggled, and the

Government helped us with grain; and by degrees we managed to get crops and pulled through. Our cattle were practically wiped out, but a few were left and from them we slowly bred up our herds again. We were offered work in the mines and farms to earn money and so were able to buy back some cattle. At first, of course, we were not used to going out to work, but advice was given that the chief should advise the young people to go out to work, and gradually they went. At first we received a good price for our cattle and sheep and goats. Then the tax came. It was 10s. a year. Soon the Government said, 'That is too little, you must contribute more; you must pay £1.' We did so. Then those who took more than one wife were taxed; 10s. for each additional wife. The tax is heavy, but that is not all. We are also taxed for our dogs; 5s. for a dog. Then we were told we were living on private land; the owners wanted rent in addition to the Government tax; some 10s. some £1, some £2 a year. After that we were told we had to dip our cattle and pay 1s. per head per annum.

Would I like to have the old days back? Well, the white men have brought some good things. For a start, they brought us European implements—ploughs; we can buy European clothes, which are an advance. The Government have arranged for education and through that, when our children grow up, they may rise in status. We want them to be educated and civilized and make better citizens. Even in our own time there were troubles, there was much fighting and many innocent people were killed. It is infinitely better to have peace instead of war, and our treatment generally by the officials is better than it was at first. But, under the white people, we still have our troubles. Economic conditions are telling on us very severely. We are on land where the rainfall is scanty, and things will not grow well. In our own time we could pick our own country, but now all the best land has been taken by the white people. We get hardly any price for our cattle; we find it hard to meet our money obligations. If we have crops to spare we get very little for them; we find it difficult to make ends meet and wages are very low. When I view the position, I see that our rainfall has diminished, we have suffered drought and have poor crops and we do not see any hope of improvement, but all the same our taxes do not diminish. We see no prosperous days ahead of us. There is one thing we think an injustice. When we have plenty of grain the prices are very low, but the moment we are short of grain and we have to buy from Europeans at once the price is high. If when we have hard times and find it difficult to meet our obligations some of these burdens were taken off us it would gladden our hearts. As it is, if we do raise anything, it is never our own: all, or most of it, goes back in taxation. We can never save any money. If we could, we could help ourselves: we could build ourselves better houses; we could buy modern means of travelling about, a cart, or donkeys or mules.

As to my own life, I have had twelve wives altogether, five died and seven are alive. I have twenty-six children alive, five have died. Of my sons five are married and are all at work farming; three young children go to school. I hope the younger children will all go to school. I think it is a good thing to go to school.

There are five schools in our district. Quite a number of people are Christians, but I am too old to change my ways. In our religion we believe that when anybody dies the spirit remains and we often make offerings to the spirits to keep them good-tempered. But now the making of offerings is dying out rapidly, for every member of the family should be present, but the children are Christians and refuse to come, so the spirit-worship is dying out. A good many of our children go to the mines in the Union, for the wages are better there. Unfortunately a large number do not come back at all. And some send money to their people—others do not. Some men have even deserted their families, their wives and children. If they cannot go by train they walk long distances.

I was living in the part where I am when a message came that I was wanted in Bulawayo; a car was provided and there I met Mr. Posselt and was told of the making of this film. I was allowed to go back to my village to await orders, and afterwards another car came to take me to the Matoppos. I did not think I was a proper person to choose to play the part of Lobengula because I realized there were more senior men in the country who should have first chance. I was very upset and perturbed because I was not a fit person to play the part of such a great man. Although I consented to play the part I was nervous all the time because there was a great deal of jealousy and it was thought that I might be called on to be a successor to Lobengula. But the people were told that it was merely a play and no trickery. It was very well done; when the warriors came with their headdresses and shields the old times came back into my mind. I was dressed like Lobengula with a headdress the same as he wore.

When I was approached about going to England I was strongly opposed to it; I felt I could not possibly take a journey like that to an unknown country, but at last I consented; the promoters and officials prevailed on me. 'You are a man; if it were a battle you would not turn back half-way.' 'I will go through with it,' I said. For the first time I left my country and travelled to Beira where I first saw ships and the sea, and this thing was marvellous to me. I had no idea of the immensity of the sea; we were on the water for days and nights.

When I came here to this great city I looked this way and that way; there is no beginning and no end. It is all so overwhelming. What a tremendous lot of white people there are in England: more than I know how to describe. And the traffic! It rushes like an African torrent after the rains. Only the torrent dies down, while this traffic goes on and on and on. Then I had the honour of going down to the King's palace and we were given facilities to see him. 'Bayete' I cried, and he returned our salute. He is a great king; my heart was white as I looked upon him and I was filled with happiness. Before leaving we had longed to see him for, after all, is he not our heaven and our earth? We got no more than a glimpse of him, but I could not expect more than that because, after all, I am only an ordinary man. The first sign we had was from the people outside; their eyes seemed to be all drawn one way and we knew that he would come. Our hearts were glad and our bodies felt happy. Our people all know what a great king he is and hold him in great reverence. They will be astonished to hear that I actually saw him, that I was near his palace. Some will doubt it at first, but in the end I will be able to convince them.

Another place that was wonderful to me was Madame Tussaud's. There we saw famous people in living form. I saw the King and Queen and their sons and all the past rulers and eminent people and it made me feel how far we were behind because we have no records of our past rulers and famous men. And then we went to Croydon where we saw the aeroplanes go off and flew in one ourselves. And then we saw the Zoo, and other places, all so marvellous. We saw the film *Sanders of the River*, and in that we saw how other tribes lived. But we could not understand all that was happening. There was a real chief who acted and looked like one, but the other, though a fine man to see, seemed to us to lack something in his bearing and appearance. We did not feel he was a chief. And their dances were not nearly so fine as ours.

One day we went down to see a farm near Guildford. Everything was wonderfully clean; at home we milk into any dirty old vessel. We saw cows milked by machine. But one thing was wrong. The calves were not allowed to run with their mothers. It is cruel to separate mothers from their little ones. Afterwards we were invited into the house and sat down at table to eat with the white people. We were amazed at such kindness. That was the first time in our lives that we have been treated by white people as equals. We were filled with awe. We are happy to think that there are white people far from our own land who care about us.

We must think that your people here are happy, as they are not killing or poisoning each other. But then, of course, we do not know their inner lives and their jealousies. You have no poverty. Where are your poor people? All those we see are dressed in fine clothes, and especially the women. They move about freely wherever they like: we wonder whether they will all get married. You say they may not want to, but can they support themselves upon their own earnings? Then you must have more money in your country than there is in ours. We do not see how all these people can live and feed themselves when they seem to grow no crops.

We went to the War Museum and saw all your terrible ways of killing, big guns, and tanks, aeroplanes and submarines. With your weapons you shoot from far, far away and do not know whom you are killing: that is unmanly. We prefer to fight man to man. These weapons are too dreadful for us. No one could escape them, not by hiding at the back of caves, nor burrowing under the ground, nor by getting below the water. If the white people must make such weapons, let them fight among themselves! It is not a fair way of fighting. No, it is not manly.

All the ways of the white people are marvellous to us. They are too much for us. I think that Mlimu, the Creator, must have willed death, for if it were not so I am sure the white people would have conquered death. Their figures in Madame Tussaud's look at you, but they have no life. There is even one lady [the Sleeping Beauty] who breathes, but, still, she has no life.

I am very pleased to act my part and I only hope I have done it well enough. I had no idea how these things were done; it was wonderful. All the people at the studio work very hard, but there are too many bulls [*i.e.* too many people in charge of the herd of workers]. The microphone is like a hawk that swoops down and takes away chickens, so it takes away our voices. They asked me to speak a few words in English, but I realized from the beginning that it was beyond me: my tongue is twisted and no light has entered my dark head. We thought that we should only be five or six weeks here, but now much more than that has passed and we long to get back. It is cloudy and misty here now: we hardly ever see the sun. I have done my part; I have been away a long time and come very far and my love for my home and family is great. I must make provision for food for it is ploughing time now; we must put in our crops soon or starve. We are anxious now to pack up; once we are on the boat it will not matter. But we shall never forget our journey over here and we shall probably talk about it for the rest of our lives.

IV

# The Story of Rashid Bin Hassani of the Bisa Tribe, Northern Rhodesia

*recorded by W. F. Baldock*

## Foreword by Margery Perham

Rashid is an old friend of Mr. W. F. Baldock, of the Forestry Department of Tanganyika, who records his life. Only one point requires comment. This story deals in part with the occupation of East Africa by the British. The incidents described appear, in the view of two men who knew the country in those days, and to whom I submitted the story, to be substantially correct, though queries were raised about one or two points. It would have been possible to pursue this verification in other quarters and to give results in a number of footnotes. But the main interest of Rashid's story lies in his own adventures and, indeed, in his own view of them, and not in his version of the opening-up of East Africa, the history of which can be read elsewhere. I therefore leave this section without comment and have done no more than replace names by symbols wherever the identity was uncertain or where this course seemed desirable for other reasons.

Rashid's story illustrates, among other things, how the Swahili people of the coast absorbed new blood through slavery and conversion to Islam. Rashid with his endurance and adaptability is a fitting representative of those coastal porters who played such an essential part in the European occupation of East Africa.

## The Story of Rashid Bin Hassani

My name is Rashid bin Hassani, and I was born into the Bisa tribe beyond Lake Nyasa near Nakotakota and Kazungu in Northern Rhodesia. I was the tenth child of my mother; all the children before me had, however, died when quite young; after me my mother bore two more children, both girls. One of these died in the famine that came when she was about four; the other was killed by a spear during the Angoni raid when I was taken prisoner. My father had three wives; of the wives other than my mother, one had a boy and a girl, and one a baby girl, her firstborn. He had three huts, one for each wife, they lived separate lives and cooked separate food; my father ate and slept with each wife in turn for a week; the huts were round with low, mud walls and steep pointed, thatched roof; the doors were low and made of plaited withies, as planks were unknown.

The houses were in a group with other huts to the number of twenty, in a big clearing with other groups of huts to a total of nearly four hundred, including that of the Sultan. The whole clearing was divided into four areas occupied by different clans. It was situated in rolling orchard-like bush country in the valley of the Musora, which is a permanent river ten to twenty feet wide running into Lake Wemba [Tanganyika] in the Babembas' country, our neighbours and relations.

We had a certain amount of stock; to the ordinary man, about four or five head of cattle, ten sheep or goats and masses of fowls, with forty head of cattle to the Sultan. We had not more stock as the Angoni raided our cattle and took them from us. The stock was kept away from the village so that the Angoni who raided at night often missed a head or two, and if they did not catch the cattle by night the herd-boy drove them into the forest or into the swamp on the Musora.

Our main crops were millet—both eleusine and sorghum. Eleusine was the most dependable crop as it grew even in years of bad rainfall. It was planted only in the ashes of the burned orchard-bush or forest, fresh clearings of which were made each year. After the harvest the trees of the bush quickly re-established themselves, as their roots were not killed by the fire, and many of the stumps which were cut two or three feet from the ground sprouted at once. The clearing was done by the men, usually helping each other: a man would make beer and all his friends would help him clear an area and next day they would all help somebody else.

Sorghum was planted as many as five times in the same area on wide raised beds about six feet wide and a foot high. The sorghum was sown on the ridges of these beds and sometimes ground-nuts on the sides. In these millet-fields the beds were made by the men and women working together with iron hoes. Both sorghum and eleusine were attacked by swarms of small birds, and constant watching by children was necessary. By night the fields were liable to raids by elephant and pig and by day by baboons and monkeys. We had no guns to scare or shoot elephants and we frightened them with fire and sometimes shot one with poisoned arrows.

At the end of the harvest some of the grain was carried to the village, but most was taken to islands in a papyrus swamp in the Musora, where all the women and children and most of the stock retreated to hide in times of Angoni raids.

In times of famine people used to eat fruits from the bush and roots of plants that they dug up. Wild honey was a great reserve in times of famine. If food was very scarce a man would leave the village and take his family into the bush and build a grass shelter near a group of fruit-bearing trees and stay there till the planting season.

Hunting with bows and arrows and by pits and nets also helped us over the bad times to the next harvest. Besides elephant and pig there were rhinoceros, hippopotamus in the Musora, buffalo, eland, waterbuck, zebra and greater kudu in the forest and probably other game as well, but I do not remember well as I was only a child.

When I was about nine years old, I remember I was going with another boy about my own age to the millet-fields where my mother was working at collecting the millet already harvested to pack into baskets to be brought into the village. We stopped by some sweet-potato beds and started to dig out red moles so that we could tie them up and pretend they were cattle. My mother was about one hundred and fifty yards away when we heard two screams from her. My companion stood up and said:

'Look at that great dog.'

'Lion,' I replied, as I knew what it was, and we ran; we crossed an arm of the swamp and I started to shout for help and ran towards the village. We met my father running up the path with his bow and arrows, as he thought we had been stolen by some men. He asked what was the matter and we told him that my mother had been taken by a lion. Then two more men came running up and asked my father what had happened. When they were told, they asked him if he had seen the lion and he said

'No, but my son saw it, let us go after it,' but they hesitated and wanted help, so we returned to the village. Most of the men were out fetching millet from their fields but they came running in. Then we returned to the millet-fields and I was carried on a man's shoulder to show them the place. I showed them the place, and near by we found my mother's loin-cloth: I was then sent back to the village. Later I was told that they followed the trail and found my mother dead and her neck and shoulder eaten by two lions: the lions were on the body, and as they left it, one was shot by an arrow and the other got away. They waited till next day and found the wounded lion dead, and the other was never seen again. We did not bury people killed by lions for fear the lions should kill more of us, so my mother was left for the lions and hyaenas and next day there was nothing left. The day she was killed everybody came and helped carry in the millet and that field was abandoned altogether.

After my mother's death, I continued to live in the same hut with my sisters, and my grandmother looked after us. For the next two or four years I lived the ordinary tribal life and learnt to look after myself as my grandmother was old and infirm.

In those days we traded cotton-cloth, beads, axes and hoes with Yao traders who worked in from the coast at Kilwa. They took from us ivory and slaves.

There were also certain families that knew how to smelt iron and make axes and hoes from the iron, and others bought iron from the Yaos and made axes and hoes. The iron-smelters made clay furnaces about ten feet high and eight feet in diameter, converging into a funnel at the bottom, below which was a pit. The clay was well puddled with water and built up quite wet, and the cracks were filled up as they appeared in the drying till the sides were hard dry. Firewood cut in billets was stacked at the bottom of the furnace and other alternate layers of ironstone and fuel were put in till the furnace was full. It was then fired and the molten iron ran into the pit at the bottom of the furnace; when cool the clinkers and stones were removed and the furnace reloaded; at each charge a lump of iron the size of a two-pound loaf was made. One lump in every nine was taken to Mtisa, the Sultan. Each lump of iron was put into a charcoal fire blown with goatskin bellows, cut up into pieces and beaten with a hammer into hoes, axes or arrowheads; the bad parts of the metal and pieces of ash and charcoal were burned off in the fire or flaked off as the metal was beaten into shape.

We had no proper beds, but occasionally men made fixed beds of sticks stuck in the ground with poles on the top and then more cross-sticks, on which was spread a skin or a mat plaited of split hippo grass. The women made cooking-pots and water-jars out of clay and burned them; some people did not know how to make them and bought them; the price was a fill of the pot with grain.

The full dowry paid for a girl was five hoes, four goats and a full load of tobacco, as well as some small symbolical and ceremonial gifts.

Marriages were arranged by the fathers when the boys were fourteen years old and the girls often only about four or five. A beer drink was arranged and a pot sent to the Sultan as evidence of the betrothal. A few beads were bought by the boy's father and given to the boy, who went with his friends to the girl's home, saluted the girl's mother and father and hung the beads round the girl's neck. Then they grew up side by side. The boy's father started to pay the dowry with occasional gifts of a hoe, joints of meat and loads of grain in times of good harvest. During this time the boy gave the girl any cloth or beads he could lay his hands on. When the girl came of marriageable age there was a dance for all the women and young girls, after which the bride was shut up in her hut for a year and did not see any men except her father. The mistress of the ceremonies, a kind of godmother, then instructed her in her duties as a wife and mother.

When the dowry had been paid and the girl's hair was long and her skin light from confinement in the dark, a final payment of a load of salt was made and the wedding proper took place.

A big dance and feast was held for the whole district. The bride with a small axe with metal inlaid in the handle, and her hair all dressed, plaited, oiled and decked with cowrie shells and with masses of beads round her neck and waist, wore nothing except a bark-cloth or cotton skirt. The bridegroom wore a loin-cloth and a quiver on his back, and bracelets of brass and ivory on his arms, with his bow in his hands. Thirty young unmarried youths followed the bridegroom and thirty girls the bride: they danced all day facing each other and holding hands and wriggling their shoulders and chest muscles. In the evening the bridegroom snatched the axe from the bride's hand and went for a young bull that had been prepared for the occasion. The bull had been tied up for two days without food and its tail and hind quarters pricked and inflamed with raw pepper. The bull was let loose at the bridegroom, who dodged its charge till he eventually succeeded in killing it with a blow of the axe between the eyes. Occasionally the bull was too quick or too strong and knocked the bridegroom down [a lasting disgrace], when one of the bride's brothers dashed up and shot the bull with an arrow. The older men and women sat further off and drank beer and helped eat the bull. When the meat was eaten, the bridegroom escorted the bride to his house and she was taken inside by all the girls, and young men danced outside half the night.

Generally a young man had no house of his own and the pair lived in a lean-to against the bride's mother's house till she was pregnant, when a house was built for her, and when the child was born she then started living in her own house with her own pots and hoes and other evidences of a separate establishment. The house was built on the strength of a beer drink with the help of their friends and relations.

A girl had the right to refuse to be married. Her father then had to repay the dowry, which he had generally used, so considerable pressure was put upon the girl unless she had a lover who could pay or agreed to pay the dowry and settle the matter that way. Girls usually married their betrothed, as they had received many presents and small favours from their young men: only if the young man was very notoriously unfaithful or lacking in his attentions and gifts did the girl refuse.

When a man died he was put in a round coffin made from a hollowed tree trunk or pieces of bark. He was not buried till all his relations had arrived; in the case of a Sultan this might not occur for a month.

Slaves were owned by the tribesman. They were either born as slaves or bought or made slaves as punishment for a crime or as compensation for the fault of one of their clan. Occasionally a man who was very hard up would sell himself into slavery to get food, but this was rare and only done by outcasts from their clan, as men of a clan always lent each other food in times of stress. Slaves married slaves and their children became slaves; the Sultan and other headmen had many slaves, and as these had children the numbers were always increasing.

Petty theft was uncommon, as members of a clan were

generally willing to lend or give what nowadays is often stolen. Petty theft was settled by restitution or payment in stock or grain. Even murder was sometimes compounded, usually by payment of a son as a slave. The only kind of tax generally paid was the gift to the Sultan of one tusk of any elephant shot.

Sometimes when food was short, organized raids for food by peoples from a distance were carried out. A man would find the whole of his store of food looted in the night. He then went to the Sultan who investigated the matter. The Sultan called up his witch-doctor and told him of the theft. The witch-doctor made a fire on which he placed a large pot of water and added his medicine of a mixture of herbs and forest fruits and finally his medicine stone. The water was boiled and then allowed to cool. Meanwhile a large concourse of people had gathered to watch.

The medicine man then put his hand into the water and felt for the stone, and when he felt it he held it up for the people to see and everybody knew that the thief was not of the Sultan's people. The medicine stone was then replaced and the witch-doctor asked if the thief came from some neighbouring sultanate, and if he felt the stone and held it up everybody knew that the thieves did not come from that sultanate.

This went on until, when the witch-doctor put his hand into the pot, the water bubbled and boiled and he could not feel the stone which had hidden itself in the pot; the people then knew where thieves came from. The Sultan sent eight or ten men to this other Sultan with a message that his country had been named by the witch-doctor as containing thieves. The second Sultan sent his own messenger to the first Sultan to ask whether the message was true and, when it was confirmed, he allowed the witch-doctor to come and smell out the thieves.

The witch-doctor came and brewed up his medicine and put the stone in the pot. Then in his right hand he took a zebra's tail and in his left half a baobab gourd in which he put the medicine stone. He waved the zebra-tail in a certain direction, asked the stone if the thieves came from that direction and then smelled at the stone. If he smelled nothing he knew that the thieves had not come from there. He tried different directions till he smelled the stone and then knew in what direction to go. He started off and at every crossroads or fork in the path he consulted the stone. When he arrived at a village the headmen and all the village were called up.

The witch-doctor brewed up his pot of medicine, put in the stone and each man in turn had to come and stand with his face over the pot and cough. If he coughed he was allowed to go, but if he failed he was examined by the Sultan further as to where he had been when the theft was committed. The water was boiled up and his arm smeared with medicine and he had to get the stone out of the pot. If he succeeded he was guiltless, and the man who had accused him had to pay him compensation, usually a goat for a false accusation.

If a man's child or wife or old mother died suddenly he would suspect black magic and ask where the dead person had last eaten food, and sometimes he would accuse the last host of having bewitched the dead person. They would then squabble and quarrel and eventually go to the Sultan. The witch-doctor was called and he boiled up his medicine pot until it bubbled and frothed, and then he put the stone into the pot and if the accused man found it and fished it out he was innocent and the accuser had to pay heavy compensation—five head of cattle or a slave, as an accusation of black magic was a very serious one. If, however, the man accused failed to find the stone he was seized and string tied tightly round his fingers till it cut the flesh to see if he would confess; his elbows were drawn together till they met behind his back; pieces of bamboo were split and sharpened and fixed in a kind of collar which was then put round his head and forehead and pulled tighter and tighter till his eyes were ready to drop out of his head. He then named his associates, and all were sold as slaves to Yao safaris that came to trade guns, red cloth and beads for ivory and slaves. A gun, a barrel of powder and a box of caps went to the Sultan and the rest of the price was paid in beads that were distributed to the rest of the people of the district.

The accused might be taken out of the village into the forest with five or six men to guard him and everybody watching and himself made to cut firewood; this was stacked and a crib raised above it; he was put on the firewood and more wood above the crib. Then they made fire with sticks (they did not use fire from the village) and lit the small sticks and bark as kindling near his legs. When the fire burnt hot, it loosened his tongue and he confessed that he had bewitched the child, saying I did this and this. All his relatives, his whole clan, even if it were sixty people, were seized and sold as slaves.

We liked and respected our witch-doctors as they freed us of our enemies—those who practised black magic.

We had no formal religion, but we knew there was a God and had a word for him in our language. We were afraid of the spirits of our ancestors: if we did not mention their names and sing their praises or have beer drinks often enough in their honour, they would come and annoy us and we should be ill. We built miniature houses for them outside our villages or houses and put small earthenware pots in them in which we put offerings of meal or beer. If a man was ill he could propitiate the evil spirit by a big beer drink and dance. If a lion roared night after night we knew that the dead Sultan was angry (for some lions are sultans) and we poured beer on the Sultan's grave and slaughtered several oxen and held a big dance.

At the time that I was about twelve years old and was scaring and snaring birds in the crops, the Angoni, whose country was some way off, raided our country. I had heard of Angoni raids, but there had been none that I could remember. I was told that my grandfather was killed by the Angoni and many other people at the same time. This raid probably took place about two years before I was born. My father at that time escaped to the swamp of the Musora, but he was nearly caught on account of a dog that I can well remember, called Mlengebera, the whisperer. My father and others were hidden in the swamp with the women when he missed his dog, and thinking that the Angoni had left as they had fired the village, he said he would go and look for it. He took his bow and arrows and returned towards the village calling the dog. The Angoni had hidden themselves near the village and when the dog left the village they followed. My father ran off to the Musora, pursued by the Angoni, swam the river and shot at the Angoni from the reeds on the bank till all his arrows were finished, when he made his way through the swamp to the others, taking two Angoni clubs that had been thrown at him as evidence that they were still in the village.

When I was captured it happened like this.

When evening came I went as usual to my grandmother's hut to get food and to sleep. I was asleep on a skin on the floor, when I was awakened by her. 'What is that?' She shook up the log, that lay smouldering as usual in the centre of the hut, till it burst into flames. As she did this there was the noise of shields rattling on doors all round us and ours was burst open: half the doorway was blocked by a shield of buffalo hide. The old woman ducked to run out of the door and an Angoni stabbed her in the ribs and she fell almost without a sound. I realized that these were Angoni that I had heard of and I thought I would run away: when I was clear of the door, I was swept by the warrior with his shield against his thigh and held there as his property and so that nobody else should stab me. My little sister started to scream and cry and another warrior grabbed her by the arm, held her up, and killed her with a blow of his throwing spear; he was afraid she would give the alarm in other parts of the village. I was too frightened to move or cry out. It was just getting light. All men who tried to come out of the doors were killed, but many burst through the walls of the hut and got away: these went off to the Sultan's.

I could see outside each hut two or three bodies were lying and one or two Angoni warriors standing waiting. It was quite quiet as anybody who screamed was stabbed. My father I never saw and I do not know if he escaped or was killed; I believe his second wife was killed but I never saw her body; her elder child I saw taken away as a slave, but in another party, and I never spoke to him again. His youngest wife I saw standing with her baby at her breast and many of the younger women also. My captor went off to the next part of the village and to the Sultan's. The other prisoners and I were immediately taken off about two hours' walk to the Angoni camp in the bush; there were more than twenty of us, four tusks and all the axes, hoes and everything of value. When we got to the Angoni camp we saw the smoke of our village behind us.

The male prisoners were bound and fastened in pairs to wooden yokes; the women and children walked free but were tied up for the night to stop us running away. When we reached the Angoni camp we found thirty other prisoners from other Bisa villages and cattle from our village already there including two of my father's. The Angoni had already taken two other small villages without any resistance. We all stayed that night in their camp and they gave us food; they drew water from the Musora as there was none in the bush nearer their camp.

Each Angoni warrior had a shield of buffalo or ox hide, a stabbing spear and three small throwing spears with very sharp points and feathers on their butts, one or two clubs and sometimes a sword. They wore no clothes except a huge feather headdress; their shields were painted like those of the Masai. The Angoni had no definite warrior organization or warrior class like the Masai, nor were they organized in definite fighting companies like the Masai.

The Babisa had only bows and arrows and small axes, but no spears or shields. Poison for the arrows was made from the bark of trees, which was boiled in special pots, and the men did not sleep with their wives for two months after making it.

The Angoni, having decided on a raid, made a main camp near the borders of their own country and the warriors and women gathered in it; the women went on the raids to cook the food. They then moved rapidly four ordinary days' march in two days and made a camp in thick bush and were careful of their fires so that no smoke showed. They then sent out scouts to locate the villages to be raided and the paths to them; they also noted the position and number of any doors in stockades round villages or cattle kraals. After a couple of days they would move into the fields round a village at sunset, and close in quietly all night, till at dawn they were waiting outside the doors. As it became light they would burst open the doors and take the village by surprise. If the Babisa saw the Angoni scouts, they warned all the villages and tried to find out which village the Angoni intended to attack: then everybody collected at that village, and in the evening the village would be abandoned and all the men would hide in shallow holes in the cultivated ground while the women and children were hidden in the bush. The men lay all night out in the fields and waited for the Angoni to pass inside them. When the Angoni were standing up and preparing to attack the village, the Babisa would shoot them with arrows from the rear or open side unprotected by the shield. Owing to their shields the Angoni were not easy to hit, and if you missed and an Angoni saw you, he would rush you and stab you before you could fit another arrow, unless your companion shot him from the uncovered side as he rushed. Our bows were poor and had only a short range.

The day after I was taken prisoner we were moved off to a camp which the Angoni had built of thorns near the Sultan's stronghold. The Angoni had not attempted to take the Sultan Mtisa's village by surprise and all his men, women, children, stock and ivory had been taken into his stronghold. This stronghold was on a steep rocky hill called Mkinga. The sides were in places almost precipitous and there was one narrow path up it which could be held by half a dozen men armed with loose stones. On the top of the hill was a plateau and in it a big cave in which the grain and ivory were stored, and the mouth of which could be blocked with a big stone. There was no permanent water on the plateau, but a spring at the foot of the hill; this spring the Angoni warriors seized, and they called to Mtisa, 'Have you any water'? 'Yes, rain water in the rocks.' We were in the camp and saw and heard all this as the camp was under the hill. The Angoni leader, named Kiliaonga, then called out, 'Shall we show you something?' 'Yes.' 'We will fetch it.' Mtisa then began to curse them and said, 'What do you thieves mean by coming and stealing my men and cattle?' We could see him sitting on a rock at the top of the cliff on the edge of the plateau. The Angoni came back to the camp and brought out his two daughters who had been living in another village which had already been captured. When he saw them, he stood up and seemed very surprised and shocked: he moved to another rock. Kiliaonga asked, 'Do you want your children?' 'Yes, I do.' 'Bring some goods.' 'I have none.' 'Bring some ivory.' 'Yes, I will bring the tusks tomorrow.' 'No, wait till our chief comes.' 'Who is he?' 'Mpeseni.' 'Mpeseni, is he there?' 'No, he is not, wait till he comes.' The Angoni leaders passed through the camp and disappeared into the bush, ostensibly to fetch Mpeseni. At 5 o'clock they came back and said, 'Bring the ivory tomorrow.' Mtisa replied, 'I will bring the ivory now. My children will be hungry.' 'No, we will give them food; are they not a sultan's children?' 'We will eat together tomorrow' [as a sign of friendship and submission]. The Angoni returned to their camp and the children got meat and good food to eat and were told not to be frightened, as tomorrow they would go to their father.

In the night some Angoni warriors made their way up to the plateau and hid between the cave where Mtisa had shut himself in and the big rock where he came to speak with the Angoni below. In the morning he came out of the cave; the stone was not replaced, and he stood on the rock to speak to the Angoni not knowing he was surrounded by hidden warriors. The Angoni, unarmed, came up the path with his daughters and the ivory was carried down. When his children were near the top, the Angoni called, 'Are not these your daughters?' He stepped down to meet them, and there was a sudden shout and we saw him seized and his followers killed. They seized his gun and tore off his powder flask. He was very angry and swore at them and told them to let him alone and he would come and see Mpeseni, their Sultan. They brought him down to the camp and told him that he would be taken to Mpeseni. He replied 'Who is this Mpeseni? Do you think I will go to him?' They argued with him till sunset but he refused to go and said they had better kill him as he refused to go. They then cut a pole about as thick as my thigh and eighteen feet long, sharpened it to a very sharp point and buried the other end in the ground; round this pole they built a stage on four poles six feet high; they then seized him and lifted him up: some held his arms and others his legs till he was sitting on the point of the pole, then they all pulled together: at the first heave, the pole passed up into his stomach; at the second as far as his chest, his head fell back and shook once or twice and blood and entrails ran down the pole; at the third heave, the point of the pole came out of his throat; he made no sound and his children uttered no sound; everybody watched in amazement but dared do nothing. When he was dead the warriors uttered one great yell. They left his body on the pole. So died one of the finest men I ever saw. He was far larger than anybody else in the tribe and had great authority. His daughters were taken to Mpeseni who took them for his wives.

When Mtisa was seized the stone was replaced at the mouth of the cave and the women and children and those who happened to be inside escaped.

Next morning we moved off to the Luangwa river, near the Basenga's country; the next day we slept at a Senga village, and here I was sold as well as many children too young to go far. My father's younger sister who was a good-looking girl was sold to the Sultan, Marama. The man who bought me was called Kilole, and it was then millet harvest. At the next planting season he sold me to a Yao safari, and with me went fifteen others. This Myao's name was Chamba and he treated me well; he gave me food and cotton cloth to wear. He took me eventually to Kilwa and sold me to a Manga Arab, Bwana Saidi, who lived in Zanzibar. He also bought six other slaves and hid us in his house for two days for fear of the European steamers which looked out for slave traders. At the time there was only one European in Kilwa, a French Father. We were taken on board a small open boat by night and hidden under cloth and a coconut screen in the bottom of the boat. We must have made a fast passage as the first night we were run into a mangrove swamp and hidden: the next night we were landed in Zanzibar and hidden in a coconut plantation at Fuoni, where we remained seven days. Each day Saidi brought clothes and took two of us into the town and to the market and handed us over to the market-master, an Arab, called Saidi Ram. I stayed three days with Saidi and then I saw a man wearing a turban come to the market and say, 'Bibi Zem-Zem [the sister of Said Bargash, the Sultan of Zanzibar] wants some slaves, go and pick some out.' Perhaps twenty of us were picked out, taken to her house and lined up. Here I was terrified and thought, 'Here I shall be killed and eaten.' Out came an enormously fat woman with gold ear-rings and gold nose-rings. I thought, 'She is as fat as that from eating men.' I did not then know much Swahili but she said, 'Where are the slaves?' in a very high voice. She picked out ten, saying 'That one, that one, that one,' and counted up ten. Then she said, 'How much do you want for these?' I was bought for 40 reales [60 rupees] and others for 60 reales. When the deal was completed she told a man to take us to her shamba. There her headman, Nakoa Athmani, beat a drum and called all the slaves together from their houses on the shamba and said, 'Anybody who has not got a child and wants one, can choose one from this lot spawned by the old girl.' A woman named Mtondo Msanja from the country south of Kilwa came and carried me off and the others were similarly taken. When her husband came home he was told, 'I have got a child.' He was called Hassani and that is why my name is Rashid bin Hassani; my tribal name was Kibuli bin Mchubiri. Here I remained three years, was circumcised and taught the Mohammedan religion and to read the Koran. I was adopted as his son but did no work in the shamba; he worked with a hoe in the coconut shamba and on the cloves. On Thursdays he worked on his own shamba of rice, maize and cassava for food, and Friday was his day of rest.

After three years Bibi Zem-Zem sent word to the plantation to look for slaves to work on a house. Five of us were produced and built houses for Indians and got eight pesas [pice] a day, but this Bibi Zem-Zem took. Each day we were fed and got one pice for ourselves.

During this period I got married to a slave of Bibi Zem-Zem. We were married with Mohammedan rites and my adopted father paid the dowry. The girl was a slave born in slavery. She bore me one child—a girl. I had my own house and continued to work at odd jobs but I kept all my wages and was merely under Bibi Zem-Zem's protection.

When my child was about five years old I saw one day an amazing sight. There were Goan shops that sold wines and cognac and this day I saw Swahilis spilling money and throwing about rupees. We asked where they got their money and were told 'You are all fools here; you will only get women; go abroad and you will get money. We came from Uganda. We went with a European from Smith

Mackenzie's. Have a drink first and then we will go along.' We sat and drank two or three days and were given money; these men were like Europeans. Eventually we went and saw three Europeans at a table; one had no left hand. Some of us were written on for a safari to the mainland. We were to get 10 rupees a month; half we drew and half was paid to our masters. That same day we went on board a steamer called the *Juba* and went to Mombasa. There was then no railway. We remained in Mombasa a month till five hundred porters had been collected. We had with us on this safari a man called Nadikombo who had been as headman on a safari to Uganda with Captain Lugard. He had induced a hundred and fifty of them to desert, had seized guns and money and had raided and harried from Usoga through Kavirondo Lumbwa, Sotik, Masai, Kikuyu, Ukamba, Teita, Voi, Usambara, Uzigua, to Pangani, where he crossed over to Zanzibar. There he was caught and condemned by the Sultan to carry a load back to Uganda with a chain round his neck.

On this first safari, which took a year, we had no adventures.

On my second safari with Bwana Y. we lost a hundred and twenty porters out of a hundred and sixty when attacked by the Lumbwa and Sotik; we were taking loads of wire, beads, cloth and cowrie shells.

In those days there were only three up-country bomas, at Machakos, Kikuyu and Kampala in Uganda. On this second safari we went to Nairobi; no boma, no town, just a stream in Masailand. When we left Nairobi we went with Major X. and Bwana Y. through Masailand south of where the railway now runs, but we found no water for four days, had a very bad time and had to return to Nairobi; thence we went through Naivasha to Kisumu; this was the first safari to reach Kisumu. On the way back we left Mumias and Kavirondo behind and went northward through Lumbwa country with Bwana Y. We were a hundred and sixty porters and had not bothered to build a stockade but were sleeping in the open on the ground. About 1 a.m. we were attacked by the Lumbwa; those who lay still escaped, those who tried to rise were killed by spears and swords. The first shot was fired by Bwana Y., who had his arm cut off as he was trying to reload; his boy grappled with the Lumbwa, wrenched the sword from his hand and killed him with it. The Lumbwa did not wait to fight but dashed through camp stabbing and hacking. I was sleeping in a small tent with three others; two were stabbed as they tried to rise and one fell on me. I got up and grappled with a Lumbwa who cut me in four places on the chest and ribs with his knife before I threw him off, when the fourth man in my tent shot him dead; this was only the third shot fired, and the Lumbwa then ran.

In the morning there were only thirty of us unhurt and ten more or less badly wounded. Y. had bound up his arm and told us to collect the dead. We piled them up and spread a tarpaulin over them.

Y. told us each to take a cooking pot and a box of cartridges to every four men. We abandoned the trade goods and started off; after half a mile we found we were surrounded and the Lumbwa were sticking spears into the dead in our camp. Bwana Y. got scared and halted the safari, telling his boy to make tea. He sat on his chop box and after a cup of tea pulled out a whisky bottle and started to lower it till Sergeant Z. took it out of his hand and put it back in the box. Bwana Y. looked at him but said nothing. He then looked all round with his glasses, loaded his elephant gun and Martini rifle and again sat on his chop box. Meanwhile the Lumbwa were closing in all round. Bwana Y. eventually took up his gun, took very careful aim at a man wearing a lion's mane headdress, fired, and hit him in the heart as he leapt into the air, so that he fell dead. This was the Lumbwa chief.

We then started to retire, leaving two men to guard our rear and others firing into the bush in front. As we went we met herds of cattle being driven about the country. We fired at the herdsmen who promptly bolted; if we met any women they lay on the ground and I can remember seeing several parties lying stark naked on the ground or running in the distance. We made some of them drive the cattle with us, but if a man appeared in front we fired and the cattle stampeded. When night came we made a double boma of thorns: Bwana Y. and the rest of us in the middle and a mass of cattle outside so that the Lumbwa could not rush us in the dark. The Lumbwa tried to get at us once in the dark: they put their shields on the thorns of the fence and got among the cattle, but a sentry saw them and fired, the cattle stampeded and knocked over the Lumbwa and they did not attack again.

Next day we made our way to the Mau forest and through it, as the Lumbwa would not follow us into the forest. When we came out of the forest the Lumbwa were still hanging around and occasionally tried an attack, but if you fired a shot and hit one man in ten the rest ran and so never pressed an attack home.

At last we saw a great cloud of dust in front of us and out of it came the Masai, perhaps two hundred strong. One of us who spoke Masai told them that one of the Europeans had been attacked and wounded by the Lumbwa, and as the Masai were friends of the Europeans they should help us. The Masai then started a war dance and sent back for ten oxen which they killed for us. Some went back after the Lumbwa and chased them back to their own country.

When we got back to Kikuyu we found that the boma had been burned and that Bwana Tayari had gone to Nairobi. At Naivasha we met Major Smith and Martin and went with them to Nairobi.

I did a third safari to Uganda, but nothing of note happened on it. Each safari there and back took a year and I had a year's rest between each safari.

All this time I was still a slave of Bibi Zem-Zem and she took half our pay. We were paid off wherever we were engaged. At the start of each safari we had 15 rupees in advance and our owners another 15 rupees. When we got back it depended upon our owners how much we got, but the generous ones took half and gave us the other half; for a trip to Uganda we got 120 rupees, or 10 rupees a month. On these safaris we each received two lengths of cloth, a cooking pot, a blanket and a short Schneider rifle.

At this time an Arab called Bwana Mbaruk who lived at Jasini near Mombasa and who had refused submission to Said Bargash and his successor Saidi Khalifa, against both of whom he had fought, was fighting with the reigning Sultan, Saidi Ali. Saidi Ali had a gunboat, the *Glasgow*, with a captain called Dick and a Parsee Engineer. Saidi's askaris, who were trained and led by General M., drove Mbaruk out of the country south of Mombasa and fell back to the north. At Takaungu was a European, Bwana Makutubu, in charge of some more of Saidi's askaris, and when Mbaruk attacked Takaungu and threatened the fort there, Bwana Makutubu sent a telegram to Mombasa for reinforcements. Saidi's officers [Comorians and Swahilis] forcibly enlisted a company of askaris of whom I was one. That same day we were given uniforms and Martini rifles and were taken on board the *Juba* and to Mombasa. Some of us did not know how to handle arms but others had been on safari to Uganda. Next day we sailed to Takaungu and landed unopposed as Mbaruk had retired to Kuruita, and fortified a position there about two days from Takaungu.

We stayed a month in Takaungu drilling by day and doing sentry-go by night. There were four watch-towers on the corners of the fort where sentries were posted, and every hour they called 'All's well'. If a man did not answer when called because he was asleep, another man was put in his place and he got 25 with the kiboko. From Takaungu we went to Mtondia, half-way to Kuruita, and stayed there six months: it was drill, drill, drill all day and sentry-go all night. Our hair turned red from dust and our clothes black from sweat as there was no time to wash.

One day I was sent with a letter by Captain Wick from Mtondia to the Captain near Kuruita. When near Kuruita I saw three men carrying guns cross the path I was following through some millet-fields. I ran into the millet and hid behind a large double-headed ant-hill; these men saw me and came after me with several others and I was surrounded; they approached creeping through the millet-stubble [about 4 feet high]. I saw three close to me and one further off so I started on him as he was standing up on another ant-hill: I got him first shot, the 400-yard sight up; the other three close to me I also shot, but a fifth that I could not see kept on firing at me and hitting the ant-hill, so I slipped off into the millet and returned to the last village. I said to the people of the village, 'Do you suppose I am such a fool as to go through this country without a strong charm? You heard the firing and I am safe. I warn you that if you do not come with me I will shoot you all.' They agreed to follow me and we went back to the millet-fields and picked up four muzzle-loading guns. I told the people to keep their eyes skinned and to tell me at once if they saw anything and if a shot was fired at me I would shoot them. I did this because I did not want to run into any more of the enemy. I went thus to the post at Kuruita and was received by the Captain. He turned out half the garrison and we went straight back to the millet-fields but could not trace my assailants, who were Mbaruk's men. We threatened to shoot the villagers unless they showed us where Mbaruk was encamped, but it was no good as they did not know. For this work I was promoted Corporal.

Next day Captain Wick joined us and we went to Tezo hoping to catch Mbaruk there, but he had left that morning. We returned to Mtondia, but shortly afterwards heard that Mbaruk had returned to Tezo and fortified the place. Tezo was only three hours from Mtondia. To Mtondia came three ships, two were British with white crews and the third a transport. The bluejackets were landed; their commander was bald and rode a horse; he had plumes in his hat. Captain Wick told us the Europeans would go to Tezo and we should go to Bambo to surround Mbaruk.

We started at dawn, found the camp deserted and the stores intact. We burned all the houses and stores and then returned to Mtondia, where the Europeans went on board their ships. The warships waited three days while scouts were sent to find out where Mbaruk had gone: he was reported to have gone to Lamu and the ships left. Later we heard he had fallen back on Kuruita Ya Juu, three days from the coast. I went on a patrol with Captain Wick to Mwengea, two days from Mtondia; at Mwengea we came up with Mbaruk and fought him from 9 till 3 when he retreated and we captured his stock. He ran into the other company under the Captain and a fierce fight followed; he fell back on Marunga and thence he went to Kasigao, through Usambara and Uzigua to Dar-es-Salaam where the Germans had established themselves. That was the end of the war and Mbaruk lived to an old age in Dar-es-Salaam.

We returned to Mombasa and I remained there as an askari. About this time we heard of the death of the Sultan Mohamad bin Sweni and that the Europeans had refused to allow his son Saidi Haridi to become Sultan of Zanzibar as he was too young. He refused to give up his authority and the English sent a warship that sank the *Glasgow* and shelled the Sultan's palaces.

His chief adviser, Salehe Mlambajini, a Comorian, told him to go to the French consul; but he refused to help him, so he went to the Germans at Shangani who sent him in a warship to Dar-es-Salaam. He was succeeded by Sultan Hamud.

At this time they started the railway from Mombasa.

While I was at Mombasa I took another wife, a Kikuyu, but she was childless.

While I was at Mombasa also Bibi Zem-Zem died and under her will all her five or six hundred slaves became freemen. There were three of us askaris who had been her slaves and we got leave to go to Zanzibar, but the funeral was over when we got there.

I was an askari for three years, and when my time was up I went to Voi and ran a duka, selling cigarettes, potatoes, dried fish, etc.; but I saw no profits. In those days Voi was railhead.

I travelled by train for the first time from Voi to Mombasa to see my wife. In Mombasa I was recognized as a sergeant and enlisted again for the war against the Nubians [Sudanese] who had rebelled under Bilali Amin and murdered their officers when told to go and fight round Lake Baringo. They went across the Lumbwa and Kavirondo country and captured Usoga boma under Bwana

Grant: they made him and five other Europeans, including two women, prisoners. On their march they killed nobody and were under strict discipline; no looting was allowed but they killed a few oxen for meat. When they reached Usoga they could not cross and waited at the boma.

We left Mombasa and went to Voi, beyond which there were only construction trains as far as Tsavo. From Voi we marched by forced marches and with relays of fresh porters daily in fifteen days to Usoga. When we got there we found the Nubians in the boma and a big camp of Europeans from Uganda, of whom Bwana Jackson was the leader about two miles away. We were called the Uganda Rifles, but the names of the officers I have forgotten as we were out such a short time.

The day after we arrived three Nubians came unarmed from the Usoga boma to meet Major Jackson. The Nubians were offered a safe conduct back to their country as they had done no harm beyond killing a few cattle and had always been well behaved: the spokesmen accepted but went back to their leaders for confirmation. That night sentries were posted all round the camp and we slept in the middle round the Europeans' tents. Early in the morning at the first streak of dawn Bwana Jackson's boy went out through the sentries and saw the Nubians lying in wait all round the camp. He was unseen, and slipped back to warn Major Jackson that the Nubians were waiting to surprise the camp. Bwana Jackson dressed hurriedly and had all the men fallen in and posted at four paces' interval round the camp. The Nubians must have realized they had been seen.

Then three Nubians came armed out of the dawn and Major Jackson went to speak to them. They demanded to be allowed to keep their arms, but this was refused. Then the Nubians and the Nubian interpreter started getting angry with each other and insults flew till the leader of the Nubians, called Maburuk, a large fat fellow, threw up his rifle and shot Jackson through the shoulder. As he fell, a European fired at and knocked over Maburuk, who was hit in the loins, but he killed two more natives before he was finally shot dead. Then all the rifles woke up: we fired, the porters fired, the Europeans' boys fired and the Nubians fired. We were all lying flat on a grass plain with the Usoga boma in the background and the grass about a foot high. One European we called Bwana 'Tooth' [because of his gold tooth] kept on shouting, 'Lie flat, lie down,' and if anybody raised his head he was shot at once. The firing started at sunrise and went on till 11 o'clock, when the Nubians had had enough and retired by rushes to the boma, covering each other with rifle fire. When they reached the boma the firing ceased. We spent the rest of the day collecting the wounded and burying the dead. Many Swahilis and Nubians were killed, but no Europeans. We buried them ten or twenty in a grave, Swahilis and Nubians all mixed up. There was a doctor who attended the wounded, but many of these died. I dug graves.

Next day the Baganda, who had come in masses and were camped in the banana groves about two hours away and were waiting to see who would win the fight, came and begged permission to be allowed to attack the boma. They said they could rush the boma and bring out the Nubians alive. That day they cleared out the bananas between the boma and the arm of the lake so that they could surround the boma completely.

Next day the Baganda attacked the boma; some were armed with Turkish rifles with falling-block actions, others with muzzle-loaders and others with spears, and small shields with a boss in the centre and a goat's hair fringe;

they attacked at 8 o'clock, charging across the plain with drums beating and pipes playing. We merely watched. The Nubians were outside the boma, which was a stockade of trees; they did not realize that the Baganda were intending to attack them, but thought they were our porters doing a war dance for amusement, until the Baganda started to fire. Then for two hours it sounded like a heavy thunderstorm on a tin roof as it was nothing but rifle shots. When the Nubians realized that the Baganda were coming on in larger and larger numbers they retired inside the stockade where they had two quick firers. They also put their rifles through the stockade and, when the Baganda tried to rush it, they shot them down two to every bullet they fired. Many Baganda were killed but the rest took no notice; eventually, however, they drew off about 11 o'clock.

That night the Nubians left the boma and got across further up the river where it was narrower, in canoes and boats which were brought there for them by a Muganda named Mlamba. We occupied the boma and found the bodies of five Europeans, two ladies and three men. Messengers were sent to Entebbe to bring canoes and boats.

We waited a week before we crossed, and in that time came a hundred and fifty King's African Rifles under one European from Mombasa and the askaris from Takaungu and Zanzibar. We took two days to cross, and the Europeans went on to Mwanga's [whose men had attacked the Usoga boma under Kamanyiro] and asked why the Nubians had been helped across. He replied that it had been done by Mlamba without his orders and that he would kill Mlamba for it.

He was told he would not be punished, but he must either capture or stop the Nubians. The K.A.R. followed after the Nubians, hoping to overtake them in the Unyoro country, and by forced marches they came up with them on the fourth day, although the Banyoro had made no effort to stop the Nubians. We, the Uganda Rifles, followed behind on the flanks to keep an eye on the natives in case the Nubians doubled back. The country was thickly inhabited and we went by sections keeping in touch with each other. I was Sergeant-Major of the right flank guard. On the twenty-first day we heard that the K.A.R. had captured half the Nubians and two native officers and thirty of their women. We all stood by in case we should be called upon for assistance. We lost our officer, Captain 'Tooth', and the European Sergeant in Unyoro.

We heard from Mumias that a Kavirondo had started a rebellion. We started out a hundred strong under Bwana McCrusty to put down this trouble in Kavirondo. We crossed the lake and entered the Kavirondo country at Mumias, where we waited three days. We heard that ten men had been sent out to buy cattle against our return journey and that they had been killed and the cattle stolen. We met with the Administrative Officer and the second day out met the people who were supposed to have murdered the porters. The report was, however, untrue, and due to spite, as it was the Masai who had been responsible for the murders. These Masai were a branch of the Masai, called the Uasingishu, who had been driven out from Naivasha and had taken to cultivation like the Kavirondo. We were led by loyal Masai through the country and collected all their cattle. The disaffected Masai ran away, but when we had rounded up their cattle they came in to make terms and produced five warriors, who had done the murders, the porters' guns and a bale of cloth and load of beads. These men were chained up.

We returned to Naivasha where I spent a year building the boma.

I then took a draft of twelve sick askaris to Mombasa. Railhead had reached Nairobi, but was not open to traffic beyond Sultan Hamud. There was, however, a construction train full of contractor's labour, so I cleared them out of one truck and we got in. An Indian came along and told us to get out, but we refused and I knocked him down. A European then came along and gave us leave to go to Kilima Kiu where we slept, got another train to Sultan Hamud and then a proper coach to Mombasa.

Next day I was told to go back to Naivasha, but refused, as we got too much kiboko from the European Sergeant 'As you were'. I was locked up for a week for refusing to obey orders. I was ready to go anywhere else but not to return to Naivasha. As I continued to refuse I was discharged.

I went back to Voi and restarted my duka, but after a month I got a letter from Bwana Maji Moto [hot water] at Ndii to bring fourteen men to make into police. I got fourteen men and they were enlisted; Bwana Maji Moto wanted to make me his boy and when I refused I was also signed on as an askari. I remained there three months and then the boma was abandoned and the detachment broken up. I went to Taveta with Mr. Hope and built a boma there. I went three times to Moshi to see the Germans and Mr. Hope used to play billiards. I was his orderly. I remained four or five years at Taveta as a police askari and became a corporal.

At this time there was a Teita who had evaded capture by the police and Europeans and who had raided cattle and held up Swahili safaris. His name was Mwikambi and he had fifteen followers.

We were on patrol at Mwatata with Bwana Reid and I got drunk and was put in handcuffs to cool off. In the guardroom I told the men on duty about my Uganda safari and the Uganda Rifles. I was overheard by Mr. Hope. Next day I was sent out with two other policemen to try and find this Mwikambi as he had just lifted twenty-two head of cattle from an Arab living near Mwatata and thirty head from a native Teita village. The second day we reached a Teita village in sight of this Mwikambi's village which was on a high ridge in the Teita hills. We got there about 11 o'clock, had a good feed and got hold of the village headman who said he would show us the way to Mwikambi's village. We rested till 3 p.m. and then went through the bush, not following the footpaths, having taken off our uniforms and wrapped our rifles up in sleeping mats. We arranged with other Wateita to go to their homes to feed and to meet just before sunset below Mwikambi's village. We duly met, being seventeen men in all, including the three of us police and the Arab. We slept till 3 a.m. and then made our way up the hill which was slippery with rain. We surrounded Mwikambi's huts and I put one policeman at the door of his compound and told him, 'Shoot in the air if they run, but do not shoot unless you have to.' I went inside the compound with Mwakidunda, the Teita who knew the village, and I pulled open the door of his hut and called him, but one of his wives answered sleepily and said he was in the next hut. I went to the next hut, put a box of matches ready near the door and knelt ready with my rifle. I called him and, when he came out, fired into the air, and he lost his head and dashed back into the hut. I struck the match, rushed in and seized him. The Wateita came and tied him up. We also caught eight other men and tied them up with the thatch rope. We took his women and children, his cooking pots and fowls and went down to Mwakidunda's village. We sent out the Teita and collected his cattle from the two bomas in the bush where he had hidden his stock.

Next day we drove everything off towards Mwatata. I had Mwikambi tied to me with a rope and his arms fastened behind his back. We tied up the other eight men one behind the other, and one policeman came behind and the other looked after the cattle. We got back to Mwatata on the second day about 9 o'clock and found Bwana Reid waiting on the road for us as the news had got in front of us. Mwikambi was put in the guard-room and his women in the Sergeant's house. We counted up the cattle and there were 260. The cattle were returned to their owners if they could establish their claims. The two askaris got a heifer each and the Government took the rest. Mwikambi died from haemorrhage of the chest due to the strain on his chest by being tied up with his arms tight behind his back. His followers and women were let go.

I think this happened about 1903-4, as in the next year I heard you could get hunting licences in German territory, and was a hunter five years and then a forest guard for five years before the war broke out. When my five years were up I went into the German territory and settled on the north-east end of the Usambaras where I lived with an Msambaa. I had no wife. For two years I took out shooting licences at ten rupees. I was allowed to shoot anything except elephant, giraffe, ostrich and zebra. I lived by selling the meat. I usually shot rhinoceros and oryx which were, and still are, the commonest animals there.

When I had been here two years, Bwana Sakarani [drunkard] came on a shooting trip with his wife and camped near my hut. He told the headman to find him a hunter and I was fetched. He asked me if I was a hunter and I said 'Yes', so he told me to fetch my gun. I brought him my gun which was a muzzle-loader; he looked it over and asked if it was loaded, and when I told him it was not, he took it by the barrel and smashed it against a tree and split the barrel. He went into his tent and brought out a German army-pattern rifle which he gave me. I became his hunter and went on safari with him. I went round his plantations scaring baboons by day and pig by night. I got thirty rupees a month.

I remained there for three years till Bwana Sakarani went to Europe; then one day I went to see his wife and to take the horns of a rhino I had shot. It was in the rains and the horn had got rotten round the edge; she got very angry and slanged me up and down and boxed my ears, so I went and chucked the rifle and cartridges in the courtyard and went back to Mnazi where I bought a muzzle-loader.

Shortly afterwards I intended to go back to Lushoto to get a fresh licence, when I heard that Bwana Sakarani had returned. I knew he would be after my blood, so I went across to Gonja in South Pare, along the Pares to Kampi ya Simba and then across to the south end of Lake Jipe, where I found a friend and spent a few days fishing. One day as I came out of the lake from fishing I met two policemen from the Mwatata days. We started to talk but they arrested me for having a gun. My friend had sent word to the boma that I had brought a gun into the country. I did not know that the law about natives carrying guns had been altered as it was some years since I had been in Kenya. I was taken to Taveta and then Mwatata, where my gun was taken from me and I got one month in gaol. I should have got more but the police sergeant spoke up for me and also my old officer at Tetu. When I got out I went to Kitobu near Moshi, but just outside German territory, and made wicker fish traps and caught a lot of fish which I sold. I then found an old friend on Kilimanjaro near Moshi, who had a good shamba with a fine furrow [for carrying water to his land]. Another friend and I with his two daughters decided to go over and join him, so we crossed the boundary by night in case we should be caught by the boundary police. We settled down till one day I went to Old Moshi and met a European on the road, a Government Surveyor whom I had seen with Bwana Sakarani. He recognized me and told me he wanted me to work as a forest guard in the Rau Forest. I did not understand what the work was and thought he wanted me to be his orderly. As he was a surveyor it would have meant being always on safari, so I refused. I went down for a week to the Mbuguni near Arusha Chini to fish, and when I got back to the shamba at Msaranga I found this European there and he induced me to sign on as a forest guard.

I remained five years as a German forest guard in the Rau. Soon after arriving I married a wife from Zanzibar. She had previously been married to a European's boy and had lived in Dar-es-Salaam, Tanga and Lushoto, where she left her husband. She did not become pregnant till just before the war, which was remarkable, as she was by then getting old and was thought to be barren; she died in childbirth. I had another wife at this time, an Mchagga who had also been married before and who had a child by her first husband. I had a child by her, a girl whom you can remember and who was accidentally killed by a gun going off.

I was a fool about these women. When a man has two wives they should be kept in different houses and only meet casually on the road or in the shamba. I had specially married this second woman to get a child, as I knew she had borne one child and I hoped she would bear me one too. The day after she was delivered I went off to get her some butter, and was away in Pare for seven days. My first wife looked after her, but she was jealous and knew that if I died the child would inherit my property. She therefore used witchcraft to kill the child and her mother. She went and picked a big basketful of unripe beans which are anyhow bad for a woman just delivered. She made my second wife shell them and then cooked them herself. She also took the bullet out of a cartridge and put the powder into the pot, gave it to the mother to eat and went off into the town. The mother became very ill and would have died, had not some Chagga women passed and heard her moaning. They knew there was a Chagga woman living there, but at first they were afraid to go into a Swahili house. [Rashid, as a Moslem and a detribalized African, lived like a Swahili.] But eventually they went in and found the mother lying on the ground and the child in another corner. They cleaned up the mess and called in another Swahili woman and sent for the girl's mother from Old Moshi. She came and brought butter and cooked it up with raw pepper and the girl recovered. Two days later I took her to the European doctor in Moshi and he put her right, but he refused to allow her to suckle the child and it was fed on cow's milk out of a bottle. She never became pregnant again.

The truth of the gunpowder came out, as I asked several old men, including the Sheik of Moshi, and they examined both wives. The mother said the beans looked black and tasted bitter but not the bitterness of salt; unknown to her they mixed up some gunpowder with water and they gave it her to taste and she said it tasted like the 'salt' in the beans. The older wife died in childbirth: it was a judgment of God upon her for trying to murder the mother and child.

Later I took another wife, but this marriage was not a

success. To get a child it is necessary to take precautions with your wife. Among us it is usual to pick a girl for a wife when she is very young and start paying dowry for her and then her father and mother look after her and do not let her have a chance of getting away with young men. I made this arrangement with an Mzigua who lived near Moshi and gave presents to the girl until she was nearly ready to be married. Then her father, who was a native herbal doctor, died and, as I had paid 500 rupees in dowry in cattle and cash, I wanted to marry her; but she refused. We went to the Liwale, and as I had paid dowry in full I was entitled to take her, as she could not get anybody to repay the amount. I therefore was married to her by the Liwale and she lived in a hut behind my house. I went to her house every night for a month, but she would have nothing to do with me. She was cooking my food, and I was afraid she would poison me, so I returned to my other house to eat but she still refused me, so I went to the Liwale for a divorce and stated that she had refused to sleep with me for a month [adequate grounds for a divorce]. I had to swear that I had not slept with her and I added it was because she refused. She was asked why she had refused and she said I was old and had not killed an ox, nor a goat nor a fowl to make her a wedding feast, but only fleas; she lost control of herself and slanged me up and down and all the elders in court hung their heads for shame at the torrent of abuse and insults. When she had finished the Liwale asked what I had to say. I said I was through with her and tore up the marriage certificate and the judgment for 500 rupees dowry, and asked for a divorce. I then told her to clear out. She is now living at Mkuyuni and not even a dog would want her as she is a mass of sores. This also was a judgment of God upon her for disobeying her father's dying wish that another

Mzigua should be her father and arrange her marriage: she refused to comply with his request and to marry me as he wanted.

I did nothing during the war in the way of fighting as I was getting old. Major Hope was the first English Administrator in Moshi and he wanted to make me Liwale, but I refused as there was too much sedition. For two years I continued living in my house and then I started being paid again as a forest guard by the Administrative Officer till a forest officer came in 1920. I am now too old to be a forest guard and am living by the waterhole on the edge of the Rau Forest.

You ask me whether the state of the people was better when I was a child or now? The best answer is the way I have just come from Moshi to Dar-es-Salaam to see you: I have come with nothing but a stick and I shall return with nothing but a stick. I left my house and property in complete confidence, and I shall find it as I left it when I get back. When I was a child my father went to the shamba with his bow and arrows and took us with him; he dared not leave us even for a day for fear we should be seized and sold as slaves. I have heard young fools complaining about tax, which they regard as oppression by Europeans, and saying that the old free state was better. It is true you were free to live where you liked and go where you liked, but it was much more a question of living where you could and going where you dared. I tell these people you may be inconvenienced by your tax every year, but it is better than finding yourself on the end of a spear or sold as a slave to be inconvenienced till the day of your death.

I have worked many years for the Government as a rifleman in the Uganda Rifles, as a Kenya policeman, as a German forest guard, as a British forest guard; but I still pay tax and get no pension. I have worked more than twenty-five years spread over a period of more than thirty-five. My best hope is that you will return to Moshi, as I shall then never be short of a friend.

# V

# The Story of Nosente, The Mother of Compassion of the Xhosa Tribe, South Africa

*recorded by Monica Hunter*

## Foreword

The Xhosa are a Bantu tribe living in the eastern part of the Cape Province of South Africa. They first encountered Europeans—colonists moving westwards from the Cape—in the beginning of the eighteenth century. There was a struggle between Xhosa and colonists for land, and after a series of wars, culminating in the war of 1877 mentioned below, the Xhosa were finally broken and scattered. A great part of the country in which they lived is now occupied by Europeans. The Xhosa are crowded into small reserves. To earn money to pay taxes, supplement the food grown in the reserves, and buy European trade goods, all the men, and many women, go for periods to work in European towns. All through Xhosa country there are European-owned stores, mission-stations and schools, and the mode of life is changing rapidly. Nosente tells something of the old life, and of the new conditions.

# The Story of Nosente, The Mother of Compassion

I am an Umgqwashe [a clan] of the Gcaleka house of the AmaXhosa. I was born in Nyara, in the Transkei. In those days there were many cattle. The food of the Xhosa was meat and milk. The fields were small. People dug them with sharp pointed sticks. We lived in round beehive huts with grass covering the roof, and coming right down to the ground. Women wore skirts of ox-hide, and antelope skins as a head-covering. The chiefs wore leopard skins.

When first menstruation came I was secluded in a hut in my father's kraal. [A kraal is a group of huts occupied by a patrilineal kinship-group, consisting of a man, with his wives and children, and wives and children of sons. Kraals are scattered through the country at irregular distances of some hundreds of yards, to several miles.] On the day on which I went into the hut a goat was killed, and I was given a special piece of meat from the right foreleg to eat. I stopped drinking sour milk, for while a woman is menstruating she must never drink milk, or the cattle will become thin and ill, and she too will be unwell. My mother and her sisters, and friends, and all men were forbidden to come into my hut. I was looked after by my father's sisters and the girls of my home. Girls from neighbouring kraals came to visit me, that they should learn something. After I had been in the hut for a month, I came out for some weeks, and then I was secluded again. On a certain day my father killed an ox in the cattle-fold. At the time of killing boys were fighting with sticks, and the women were singing and rejoicing. Someone fired a gun. Again I was given meat from the right foreleg by my father's sister. Many people came, and the women danced the *umgqungqo* dance which must be performed when a girl has menstruated. Girls came too, and they danced dressed only in their bead aprons. Men lined up in rows in front of the cattle-fold, and danced the dance of men. Women ran and beat the ground with sticks before those who danced well, praising them. Many fires were made. In the morning roast meat was eaten; in the afternoon boiled meat was eaten. To each petty headman with his people was given a portion of meat. Before sunset cattle were driven from all the neighbouring kraals. The young men took them to a distance, then raced them back past our home. They swept down on us. As they passed the men shouted praises of their oxen, and women made trilling shouts. After that day I came out of the hut. I went to wash in the river. The grass on which I had lain in the hut was burned, and the floor of the hut was smeared with cowdung [the usual method of cleansing it]. A fire was lighted, and I jumped across it.

While I was still a girl, not yet married, there came the war of Ngcayecibe [1877]. The Xhosa young men said, 'Our beer is finished. The beer of the AmaFengu is not yet finished.' [The Fengu were a tribe whom the Xhosa despised and detested. They had arrived in Xhosa country as poor refugees, fleeing before Tshaka, and after living some time with the Xhosa, had secured the sympathy of the British, and had been given territory that the British had taken from the Xhosa.] People came out. The country was dead. There was fighting. We women lived in the forest. During the whole war we were there. We ate nothing but meat. After the war we were scattered. When peace was made we were given a place in this country, the Ciskei. [Nosente looked doubtfully at some Fengu present when she told this part of her story.]

We saw many stores when we came to the Ciskei. At my home I had only seen one.

When I was at Middledrift [in the Ciskei] I was seen. In those days young men when they wished to marry travelled about the country, looking at the girls. One young man saw me, and he sent messages to my father asking that he might marry me. My father called his brothers, and they talked with the messengers. They talked about the cattle that that man should give to my father. After a time we saw strange cattle in the cattle-fold. We were told that they had been sent to graze in this country, and that my father was looking after them. I had never seen that man. I did not know that I was to be married until one day people said, 'You will go to be married today.' [This is by no means a universal Xhosa custom. Most frequently the man has spoken to the girl before he approaches her parents.]

I was afraid, but I could not help myself. It was the decision of the elders. I was a very ignorant girl then. All the time since those men had first talked with my father, the old people of the kraal had been getting baskets, and mats, and blankets. They asked for baskets from my mother's brothers. My father sold a goat, and bought other baskets and mats from those who make them, and he bought blankets, and a hoe from the store. But I did not see any of these things. The old people did not tell me that I should be married lest I should run away.

Seven cattle were brought to my father before I was taken to be married. Word was sent to the home of that man to tell them that the bridal party would arrive on a certain day. My sisters from the kraal [father's brothers' daughters] accompanied me, and a sister of my father who was a widow, and another who was divorced, and two men, adherents of my father, to whom he had lent cattle. The other girls and my father's sisters were all carrying baskets, and mats, and new blankets. We went on foot. At dusk we arrived at that kraal. We sat down behind the huts. After we had sat a young man came to ask us for what we had come. The men replied that we were strangers travelling, and that we sought a place to sleep. We were given a hut swept and freshly smeared. When we came to that kraal the people pointed out my husband to me, saying. 'That one is your husband.' A goat was brought and killed, 'to bring us off the mountains' [*i.e.* to welcome them]. Half the goat we cooked, and we ate in our hut. The other half was left to the people of the kraal.

The next day I went early to the river with my father's sisters and the other girls. There we washed, and rubbed ourselves freshly with fat, and with red ochre, and my father's sister put on me the new long skirt which she had brought, and many bead ornaments. The other girls also were dressed in long skirts. [Married women wear skirts to the ankle, unmarried girls, skirts to the knee.] We were given handkerchiefs for our heads, and were warned that none of us should go uncovered, for we must show respect in this kraal as brides.

In the cattle-fold men killed an ox. Meat was brought to us, and I was given to eat first. Many people came to feast. Men and women danced the *umdudo* [wedding dance]. In the afternoon I was taken to 'walk in the courtyard'. I stood with my sisters before the men of the kraal. My father's sisters took the blankets off our breasts, and we stood that the men might see us. Then I was given a spear, and told to throw it in the kraal. The women of the kraal were running to and fro shouting, 'Here people plough, here people weed, here people grind, here people draw water, here people are diligent.' After I had thrown the spear, I went with my sisters to draw water and collect firewood. We left the wood and water outside the great hut. At the same time the men from my home were giving presents from the goods they had brought to the parents of my husband and to his sisters.

The next day the people from my home went away. Before they left they exhorted me saying that I should be diligent and humble in this kraal, that I should cook for all the people of the kraal, and behave myself seemly, so that when they came they should hear no evil of me. My husband's people gave me a new name, calling me Nosente, the Mother of Compassion, because they avoided the name by which I was called at home. I do not know why they said Mother of Compassion. They called me what they liked.

The home of my husband was a big kraal. By the time I was married my husband's parents were dead, but he had six brothers, and they all lived together in one kraal. There were six huts, in a semicircle facing the cattle-fold. Each wife had her own hut. The wife of my husband's eldest brother lived in the great hut opposite the gate of the cattle-fold.

When I was a bride I had to be very diligent, and respectful to all the people of my husband's home. I got up very early in the morning, and cleared the ashes from the fire, and went to fetch water. Every day I went to gather firewood, and wild green plants for food. I ground meal for porridge and beer, and cooked and swept, and smeared the floors with cowdung. Only I could not sweep or smear the back part of the great hut, for the back part of the hut is the men's part, and it was the hut of my husband's elder brother. In my own hut I could go all over. I could not go near the cattle-fold, or cross the courtyard between it and the huts. Even at night we must not cross the courtyard, and if a wife goes out she must cover her head, for, it is said, the ancestors [*i.e.* ancestral spirits] of her husband are there. When a bride goes from one hut to another she makes a wide circle round the back of the huts, that she may be far from the courtyard and the cattle-fold.

I could not call the names of my husband's elder brothers, or of his father, who was dead. I could not say words like their names. A bride when she first comes does not speak much. She listens to the other women talking and hears what they call things. All the women in the kraal should avoid those words which wives may not use, for if a daughter of the kraal call her brother's name [as she is entitled to do] then a bride may hear, and call what she should not call. When she makes mistakes her husband's mother and sisters reprove her, and tell her what she must say. Sometimes if a bride does not behave nicely, and neglects to do the things which she should do at her husband's home, it is said to her, 'You call your husband's father's name', and then she must go back to her own father and get gifts to bring back to her husband's home, to 'wash' with. She may bring a goat, and it is killed, and the people of the kraal eat it. But her people tell her that she has done wrong, and that she must not act in such a way again.

I could not eat milk food in my husband's kraal when I was first married. Then one day a beast was killed, that I might eat. My husband's younger brother handed me sour milk, and meat of the beast which had been killed. I ate them together. After that I could eat the thick milk of my husband's cows.

Each wife living at my husband's home had her own field, but we worked together in the fields. People were beginning to use ploughs drawn by oxen then, and the men ploughed the fields. We women weeded with hoes we bought from Europeans. When the weeds were many we took millet, and soaked it in water until it sprouted, then ground it with more millet, and made beer. People saw the smoke when we were cooking the beer, and we told them that we were going to weed such and such a field, with beer, on a certain day. They came with us to the field at sunrise, bringing their hoes, and many people hoed our field. We sang the hoeing song. We carried some beer to the field in baskets, and clay pots, and people drank. Then when the sun was hot they left their work and came to drink at our kraal. We too went to hoe the fields of other people and to drink their beer.

At harvest the grain was brought home, and stored in pits dug in the cattle-pen. The grain was put in, and a stone put over the mouth of the pit, and the mouth was sealed with dung, then the cattle trampled upon it and hid it. Each wife had her own pit. Each in turn cooked food from her field, and all the people of the kraal ate together. I cooked tonight, and my husband's brother's wife cooked tomorrow.

In autumn we repaired our huts, cutting grass, and repairing the thatch, and replastering the walls. When we came to this country after the war we saw people making huts with mud walls and grass roofs. People said, 'Look, there are good huts!' and we made them also. The old huts with grass walls were low and caught alight very easily, then people sleeping in them, men, women and children, were burned. When there was much work to do thatching and plastering, we sometimes made a little beer and called our friends, the women who lived near, to help us with the work, then afterwards we drank the beer. The men came to drink also although they had not worked.

Now people make square houses with iron roofs.

After I had been married a short time I became pregnant. I told the wife of my husband's brother. She showed me the plant which I should put in a pot of water. Every day I drank of that water. [A pregnant woman drinks an infusion of a plant as a laxative. Different families use different plants. A woman must always use that of her husband's family.] Every day I still went to draw water and fetch wood, and I worked in the fields. When labour pains began I went to my hut. The women of the kraal came to me. Then when they saw that the child did not come they sent a boy to call Nomanga, whom people said was skilled as a midwife. After she came the child was born. I took it and washed it. Next morning early I put some leaves of the tree *isifuto* on the fire at the back of the hut. After washing the child I swung it in the smoke of the fire, singing as I did so,

*Hotshi! Hotshi!*
*Lomtana akule,*
*Abemdala apike into azaziyo.*

[*Hotshi! Hotshi!*
*May this child grow.*
*When it is old may it deny the thing it knows.*]

This I did every morning and evening for a month, that the child might grow strong. I called the child uPote, the twisted one, because he was born with heavy labour.

After ten days, when the navel cord had dropped off the child, I came out of the hut. I went to the river to wash myself, and I smeared the floor of my hut. I ground corn and made beer, 'to wash the hands'. After that I again cooked for people, and men might enter my hut. Before that they could not enter, lest, it was said, they should be 'soft', and weak in battle.

When I had come out of the hut my husband killed a white goat to bless the child. [This, and the killings mentioned at initiation, and marriage, are all to secure the blessing of the ancestral spirits, upon whom health and prosperity are believed to depend.] With the skin of the goat I bound the child to my back when I was working. But the child grew heavy to carry, and I had no little girl to care for it, so I went to my father's home, and I asked that my younger sister should come to live with me to care for the child. She lived in my hut, and every day when I went to the fields she kept the child. The other girls of the kraal were also keeping children. They bound them to their backs, and they went together to visit girls in other kraals, and to gather wild plants and berries in the veld.

One day my child fell ill. It coughed very much, and when it breathed there was a noise. After three days my husband said, 'I am going to beat sticks' [*i.e.* inquire of a diviner]. He called two of his brothers, and they travelled for half a day, until they came to the kraal of a diviner whom men said was sharp. They sat down in the courtyard of the diviner's kraal. Before they had yet spoken the diviner greeted them, saying, 'Greeting, men who have come to inquire about one who is sick.' This he said because he was a sharp diviner. He told the men to sit down and take the coverings off their heads. He sat opposite them and began to divine, saying:

'You come about one who is sick.'

*Men clapping:* 'It is agreed.'

*Diviner:* 'It is an old person who is sick.'

*Men clapping softly:* 'It is agreed.'

*Diviner:* 'No, I am only playing with you men, it is a child that is sick.'

*Men clapping loudly:* 'It is agreed. Put it [that point] behind you.'

Then he told them that the child, when it was playing in the veld, had met a short boy. He was like a boy, but he was hairy. He was *Tikoloshe.* The diviner said that that *Tikoloshe* had caused my child to be sick. He said that *Tikoloshe* was sent by the wife of my husband's brother who lives in another kraal. She was jealous of me because she was married before me, and she still had no child. But although the diviner told us that it was she who had sent *Tikoloshe* we did not accuse her openly, for there was already a magistrate in King William's Town.

After some days my child got better. I warned him that if he saw a short hairy man on the veld he should tell me, but he never spoke of having seen *Tikoloshe* again. [Children commonly say that they have played with other children on the veld, which grown-ups cannot see. This is said to be *utikoloshe.*]

In those days there were many festivals. At the time of harvest boys were circumcised, and they lived in their own hut out on the veld. On the day they entered that hut a big man killed an ox at his kraal, and there was feasting. Other men made feasts while the boys were still in their hut, and the initiates danced the *ukutshila*, the dance of initiates. Initiates from different districts came and danced, contesting with one another. Men praised those who danced well, and women ran and beat the ground before those whom they favoured. On the day the initiates came out of their hut there was a great feast, with beer and meat, and the 'mothers' of the initiates [*i.e.* their own mothers, and contemporaries of their mothers] gave presents to their sons, that they might 'see' their sons. Girls also gave them bead ornaments. There were many meat feasts [ritual killings made to propitiate the ancestral spirits] and beer drinks, but I was still a young wife, and did not go to meat or beer. Only old wives of the kraal, and a sister of my husband who was divorced, went. It is not our custom that a young wife should go about to festivals. Now young wives stay at beer drinks all night, and it is their 'mothers' who go home to cook and care for the children, but that was not the old custom.

One day my husband's elder brother said that we should grind beer to sell, because there was no money to pay the taxes of the men. It was not formerly the custom to sell beer, but since Europeans came many things are sold. A whole bag of millet we soaked, and spread in the sun to sprout. We called the women neighbours to come and help us to grind, and we asked for pots from many people. There were two huts full of women working for three days, and we cooked many pots of beer. The pots filled a big hut. On the day when the beer was ready people came from far. They bought a basket full of beer with a sixpence. Those who had come back from the mines [where they had earned money working for Europeans] bought for their friends.

When they had drunk men began to sing and dance. They danced in a line, and they were led by a young man with a concertina, which he had brought back from the mines. Then I first saw a concertina. The dust rose from the floor of the hut as they danced and the sweat poured down their bodies. Men danced alone praising themselves for their exploits in battle, and each woman danced her own dance. [Each woman has her own private dance, which it would be very bad form for a neighbour to copy, just as with Europeans it is bad form for one woman to copy a neighbour's dress. 'But if a woman were travelling and saw a dance she liked, when she went home she might dance it, if her home were far away.'] Nomanga, who was the little wife of Mabandla, had been accused by Mabandla's mother of causing pains in the legs of Mabandla's mother, by witchcraft. She had left her husband and returned to her own people. When she danced she sang:

*A marvellous thing,*
*A marvellous thing,*
*There was a wife who was accused of killing her mother.*
*There was a wife who was accused of killing her mother.*
*A marvellous thing.*
*A marvellous thing.*

People clapped loudly [the audience claps the time of the dance] but Mabandla looked at her by the eyes. [Women often 'dance a quarrel'. The majority of their solo dances are dramatizations of quarrels at their married homes.]

On the next day, when people had drunk much, Mbeya handed his pipe to Somponos' wife, that she might take oil from the stem to chew, because she lacked tobacco. Somponos saw them, and hit Mbeya, because he thought that Mbeya was talking privately with his wife. Mbeya's brother was near, and he hit Somponos. Other men took their sticks and fought. Those who lived near Somponos fought with him, those who lived near Mbeya fought with him. Women ran to the ridges and shouted the war cry, that other men should come to help their men. The head of one man was broken with a stick, and afterwards he died. Afterwards the police came from King William's Town and caught many men, taking them before the magistrate, who fined them for fighting. The magistrate said that we were living in the country of Europeans now, and should no longer fight.

After some time we left the kraal near King William's Town, and came to live in the kraal of my husband's eldest brother at Ntsalamanzi. It is the custom that when men have been married some time they should be given their own place in which to live. My husband's eldest brother had been given his own place, and after we had lived at his kraal for some years my husband was given his own place also. When my husband was owner of the kraal then I was *inkosikazi* [chieftainess] of that kraal, and I could walk across the courtyard and go all over all the huts, but I still could not approach near to the cattle-fold.

Then I went with my husband to visit the son of my husband's elder brother, who was working in Port Elizabeth. We walked all the way [a distance of 148 miles by road]. We finished the journey after one week. We stayed six months in Port Elizabeth. My husband worked for Europeans, and I also was hired to do washing and ironing. What I did not like there was noise and bustle. All the time people were passing backwards and forwards, backwards and forwards, talking and making a noise. Many people were drinking and they fought one another. The tramcars and carts of Europeans rushed along the streets, making a noise. There was no tranquillity. The houses were dirty and ill built, and set down anywhere. They were not as they are now. There everything was bought with money—houses, and firewood, and milk, and mealies, and everything.

While I was in Port Elizabeth I heard people preaching Christianity. I was not converted there, but when I came back to my home I saw that it was good that people should pray to God, and I was converted. After that my husband and I were married in church.

I bore six sons and one daughter. After uPote, there was Tolbart, who was born at the time of the coming of the locusts. One I called Simon, because when he was small he was already humble, and one I called Flans [France] because when he was born my brother came back from France. [He went there with the Native Labour Corps during the war.] All my children went to school. UPote passed Standard VI, and his teachers said that he should go on and become a teacher, but he did not like to do that, and he ran away and went to work in Port Elizabeth. All the others passed Standard V or VI. My daughter died in the influenza epidemic in 1918. My husband also died. UPote, who was working in Port Elizabeth, died there. Another son went to work in Johannesburg and died there. Another went to work in Cape Town and died there. Two are here at home. The elder is not working for Europeans. The younger goes to work in East London for a time, and then comes home.

The elder one living at home is married to a girl from Gqumahashe. When she was brought by her people a goat was killed, 'to bring them off the mountain'. The next day an ox was killed for the feast, and she was married in church. Before they went away her people gave her advice, saying that she should show respect to her husband's home and conduct herself humbly; that she should cook, that when guests arrived in the kraal she should give them food, and that there should be no one in the kraal to whom she did not give food; that she should no longer go about with young people, but with old people, that she might learn their manners; that when she laughed she should not raise her voice loudly, but that she should laugh softly out of respect. We of the kraal also gave her advice telling her these same things. Then the men of her home presented the gifts they had brought to us, the people of the kraal. They had brought dresses, and shawls, and dishes, and such things.

Now since we are 'school people' my daughter-in-law does not avoid parts of the hut, and the courtyard, as I did when I was a bride. She does not call the name of my husband, or of my sons older than her husband, or words like them, but she may write the surname of the family when she writes a letter to her husband. School people do not kill that the bride may eat the milk of the kraal. I gave sour milk to my son's wife, and after that she drank it. She lives in my hut and cooks with me, but she has her own hut to which she goes with her husband at night. She has four children. Now when children are born all the old customs are not followed by school people. Men may enter the hut of the mother of a newborn child before she comes out, but some still do not like to enter. School people do not kill a goat just when the mother comes out of the hut, but the baby is baptized in church, and on that day a baptism dinner is made and a goat is killed for the feast. At the baptism dinner of the eldest child the top tier of the parents' wedding cake which they have kept as their 'proof' [*i.e.* proof of a legal marriage] is eaten.

My daughter-in-law and I work in the fields. I weed much. For a time I worked in the kitchen for Europeans. Now I wash and iron. My daughter-in-law is also hired to sew for Europeans.

[I asked Nosente whether she had been present at a recent festival to welcome an UmXhosa of the neighbourhood who had returned home after taking a medical degree in Edinburgh. She replied as follows.] Yes, I was there. I was not cooking. [Cattle and sheep had been slaughtered, and a number of women were preparing the feast.] I was there listening when the speeches were made. I was thinking of the old people of Lovedale [a neighbouring mission and school of the Church of Scotland], and of the work of Scotland. Our sister Scotland has worked for us indeed. I was rejoicing to be there, and to hear the words of the chiefs and of the Europeans.

[In reply to a query, Nosente summarized the changes she observed in Xhosa life.] The difference between life now, and life when I was young, is that now there are poverty, and sorrows. When I was young nothing troubled me. Now the difference is great. Now children do not live with their parents as they used to do. They are scattered. Only two or three children are with their parents. The mother wonders how the others are. She wonders whether they are ill or what. There is heaviness. Children no longer honour their parents as they used to do. Times have changed.

# VI

# The Story of Amini Bin Saidi of the Yao Tribe of Nyasaland

*recorded by D. W. Malcolm*

I Amini bin Saidi, an Myao of Fort Johnston, of the Mohammedan religion, can neither read nor write, but I am learning to do both. I think I am about thirty-one years of age for I was a child without sense at the time of the Majimaji rebellion in Tanganyika, while at the beginning of the Great War in 1914, although I had not started to pay tax, I had begun to work.

My tribe, the Wayao of Nyasaland, are a very great tribe and a clever tribe too. We originated on the east of Lake Nyasa but went over to the west and south after the wars with the Waswazi who beat us. The Waswazi came from Rhodesia, and, as they came round to the east side of the lake, we went round to the west, whence they had come. The Waswazi or Zulu are now called Angoni, and a large number of them live in the Songea district of Tanganyika, as well as in Nyasaland.

My grandfather Mnembe was the sub-chief under Mataka who was the first, and perhaps the only great war chief of the Wayao. The tribe is now ruled by one chief and one Nduna or sub-chief. It has always been so. The chief has great power and the present one is well liked, though his uncle, who was chief before him, was a bad man.

My clan lives at Fort Johnston and has been there for a long time. It is a big clan and is primarily agricultural.

The principal food crop is maize. There are no stories of wars in which we took part except the fighting with the Angoni in which many of my clan were killed. Many also were sold as slaves by the Angoni. Two of my uncles were sold at Lindi and have never been heard of since. Slavery was a bad business because even friends would sell each other to buy clothes. I hear that slavery is not quite dead even now in some countries.

My father, Saidi bin Mnembe, now lives at Fort Johnston and has three houses in the town. He has two big shambas [arable fields] and three wives. I am the only living child of his first wife. When he dies, if I have no money at the time, I shall claim inheritance after the Swahili custom, but if my cousin does not allow my claim I have no power to press it, as I can only inherit from my maternal uncle according to tribal law. My father used to be a cotton-ginning mechanic and got 25s. a month from Mr. E. in the country of Lichenza, the other side of Blantyre. He has now got about twenty-nine head of cattle, but they are not very valuable in Nyasaland. They are worth about 15s. to 20s. a head and milk fetches only about a penny a bottle.

The first thing I can remember is being sent to my cousin to be taught the Koran. I only stayed two months because he cursed and beat me so I ran away home and said to my father, 'I do not want to read because I am cursed and beaten every day,' and he allowed me to stay at home.

When I was a child I was a fool and always went about with my mother. I was very fond of her and did not like to let her out of my sight. My father, and even my mother, were very annoyed with me for following her about all the time; my father therefore sent me to be initiated so that I might get some sense and be ashamed to be always with my mother. I cannot remember clearly the details of my own initiation, for it was long ago, but I will describe what a Yao initiation is like, for they are all the same, and I have since attended six as guardian to the sons of my friends.

When a male child comes to the age of puberty his father collects other boys of the same age and then calls the 'Ngaliba', an old man. They all go off into the bush with perhaps thirty onlookers, men who have been initiated. The fathers do not accompany them. The old man, Ngaliba, goes first and hides himself in a known place, then the children are taken to him one by one with their eyes bandaged so that they may not see. When they arrive at the place where the Ngaliba is, he takes a sharp hook and pulls forward the foreskin and then cuts it off with a razor. The child is held by one or two men. Then the man who brought him [his guardian or tutor for the duration of the ceremony] holds the skin so that it may not slip right back; he has to do so for about an hour until it stops bleeding. Then the man takes a black cloth and binds up the wound; a white cloth is not used because it may stick, but a black one will always come clean away from the wound even if it is left on for a week.

The children are then left with one man each in a temporary grass hut for a month. The cloth is left on the wound for twelve days and then taken off. On the day that the black bandage is removed each boy's mother brings one hen. During the first twelve days the children are not allowed to wash—not even their hands before meals—but on the thirteenth day they may bathe again.

When the month is over, news is sent to the town that the guardians wish to take their children back. The fathers then go to buy sugar-cane, bananas and rice, and if the father is rich he buys from two to four goats and also a drink made from millet called togwa which is not intoxicating. The fathers then send news to the camp in the bush that they are ready. When the children are about to return to the town they are all put inside the grass hut and the door is shut. The hut is then set on fire two hours after sunset, with the children still inside. When the children find that it is getting very hot they break through the walls and escape. They run a little way and then fall flat down on the path. The fathers then bring a huge sheet and cover them all up and the boys go to the town under the cloth on their hands and knees.

When they get to the town there are very many people to see them arrive and there is a big dance to make them welcome; four or five drums are used and the singing and dancing go on from the late evening until dawn. In the morning the children go with the Mohammedan teacher to the river where they are baptized into the Mohammedan faith. They return at the third hour of the day, when each father pays the Mohammedan teacher 6d.

On approaching the town their mothers come to meet them on the way and make a great many 'vigeregere' [trembling screams]. When they reach the town the boys stand on a mat on the verandah of the headman of the town. The fathers and mothers then put by the feet of the children money and food which is taken by the guardians. Lastly the boys are taken inside the headman's house and given food, for they have not eaten since they were left in the burning hut. During the month in the bush the boys are beaten with hippo-hide whips. They are not allowed to cry; if one of them cries he is put by himself and told: 'You are good at crying—you shall therefore cry from morning till night.' If he stops crying he is beaten some more, and so on, until he has no tears left.

To be initiated at the same time makes no bond of friendship and no tie, but in my tribe we have blood brotherhood, of which I will tell later. Initiation ceremonies are secret; even our own women have not seen them, but those who have been initiated may always come.

Even after my initiation I still followed my mother everywhere, so my father told me to work. I therefore took service with Mr. M. and split mica for him for fifteen days in Fort Johnston, but on the sixteenth day my mother came to say goodbye as she was going to stay with relations in Liwanda; I gave up the work without even waiting for my pay and went with her, for which I was very severely thrashed by my father on our return from Liwanda. For the next six months I remained at home and only did a little work on the farm. I was then taken by force by my father to learn the work of cotton-ginning with Mr. E. I did one year in the ginnery at 2s. 6d. a month. Then Mr. E. made me an office boy and I did four months at that work for 2s. 6d. a month, and then he got married and made me into a house-boy. I worked as house-boy for eight months at 5s. a month, after which I left as Mrs. E. had to return to Europe and I was afraid to go on working for Mr. E. as he was very fierce and used to beat the boys with a whip when the work was done badly. He was very just but still I was afraid.

Whilst I was working in the cotton-ginnery there was a black man who came from America and built a big church near Blantyre. He had a black wife from America. He sent men to kill a European and his wife on a neighbouring plantation. There was a very big case about it and many people were hanged.

I went home from Lichenza in company with my brother and another man and two small girls. Just before we reached a town called Makanganikilo, two hours before dawn, we met six big elephants and one baby. The mother elephant attacked us and got hold of the load my brother was carrying and dashed it to pieces and tore up the clothes that were in it. I fell into the ditch at the side of the road and lay quiet. Just afterwards my brother fell heavily on top of me and I thought I had been caught by the elephant and was about to be killed. After some time we started to crawl and went along the ditch on all fours until sunrise.

When I got home I had a month's rest, and during that month the war started and I saw a motor-car for the first time. I had gone down to Blantyre and the car was there. I asked what it was and how it could go by itself. I was told that it was a war-machine and therefore thought that when the war was over there would be no more cars in Nyasaland! I heard it growl and saw a man in it. I thought that he made it cry out and go. I did not know that it made the noise of its own accord.

I next took service with Captain B. as his personal servant at 6s. a month. After a few days at Fort Johnston we took ship to go to Manda, a port in the Songea district of Tanganyika Territory. This was the first time that I had ever been on board ship and it was very rough. I was very sick. I thought I would die as I could not eat anything, and anything I ate I spoiled by bringing it up again. For two days from Fort Johnston I ate nothing. When I saw my companions eating I was nearly sick; indeed my only work on board was being sick. I also thought that the ship must sink, for there were many people on board, and it was a big thing and heavy, with nothing to hold it up.

Just before we sailed from Fort Johnston I saw an aeroplane for the first time. I did not know it was made of iron or that there was a man inside. When it alighted I saw it was made of wood, cloth and steel, but when I saw the gun in it I knew it was another implement of war. When it first growled in the sky I ran into the house because I did not know what it was and was very afraid. When I saw that many people were outside I went out again, and as they were going to see it I went with them but stood a long way off at first! I never thought that I should travel by air but I have recently accompanied my master in an aeroplane from Bagamoyo to Dar-es-Salaam.

When the war started many, many Europeans came to fight. So I thought 'This war will never finish because they can never all be killed.' But when it did finish all the Europeans were gone like grass after a fire. The Europeans who had been in the country before the war told their servants to stay as the soldiers would soon be gone but we did not believe it and went to take service with the officers on account of better pay. I did not know why they fought, but the war was a very bad thing.

From Manda we marched to Malangali, and on this march it was very difficult to get bread. I used to make it for my master out of cassava flour and baking powder, mixed with water, baked in a cooking pot in a hole in the earth, with fire on top, but it was very nasty.

At Malangali we met the Germans and captured about sixty white soldiers and forty black. The fighting was fairly heavy and many people were killed, especially Europeans. For two days servants and porters had no food and on the third day Colonel B. killed three donkeys so that we could have something to eat.

When I first heard a big gun go off during the war my ears were blocked up and I was deaf. I told my friends at night and they told me to put cloth in my ears. I thought at first that I would be deaf until I died as for three days I could hear nothing. The Germans had one very big gun, its name was 'Umekwisha Kula' [you have finished eating] and the meaning of that was that the English had finished eating country, and this year they would all die. But we had a gun too and one of our officers pointed our gun and the shell went into the barrel of the German gun and blew it up, so we captured the Germans with a bayonet charge.

Captain B. was detailed to return with the prisoners, so we went back to Nyasaland, where I was paid off at Zomba as my master had to go to Europe because he was ill. I did not return to the war but stayed in Fort Johnston. For the next two months I remained at home, and during that time a famine started. It was a very bad famine and, although the Government did a great deal to help, food was very expensive—one cupful of machine-ground flour for 1s. Many people had to go practically naked because they had sold all their clothes to get food, and many people died of starvation. Once I went for a two days' journey from Fort Johnston to Liwanda and on the road there were three dead porters. They were as thin as grass and their loads were on the road beside them. We did not die because my two brothers were working as boys in hospitals Nos. 1 and 2. Also after two months at home I got a job with Mr. A., a transport driver, and our pay kept the family alive.

At about this time there was a man who, because of famine, went to steal mealies from another man's farm, and the owner shot him with a poisoned arrow at night and was afterwards hanged for murder. I saw him hanged. The Government let him pray before he was hanged. He died immediately. We natives think that hanging is useless. Suppose I kill someone; I am hanged, and tomorrow you will hear that someone has again killed a man. The reason is this; when a man's heart has become very swollen and he wants to kill, he will kill, without thought of

God or Government. We all think that it would be much better to thrash a murderer, or indeed any criminal, say fifty or sixty lashes, with a kiboko [hippo-hide whip]. He would never forget it and he would always go about telling of it.

During the famine my mother died after three days' illness whilst she was away staying with some friends.

After eight months I left Mr. A. as the pay, 6s. a month, was too little. My next job was with Dr. D. a veterinary officer, at 12s. a month and I went with him to Tukuyu district. The most noticeable thing in this place was the amazing propensity of the natives, the Wasokili, for stealing. We had to sleep in the kitchen and one night the Wasokili came and removed all the cooking utensils and all our clothes as well. I woke up first and lit the lamp which was under the table, and as soon as my eyes were accustomed to the light I saw that we were naked and that there was nothing left in the kitchen. We were unable to go and tell our master as we were ashamed, and also we did not dare to go and wake him up. However, he woke up and shouted for tea. So I shouted back, 'You cannot have any because there is no tea and no kettle and your servants have no clothes and therefore cannot come to you.' Dr. D. then came to the kitchen and was very much amused because the only thing the cook had on was his white cap in which he had slept and which had been overlooked by the thieves. He then gave us some strips of calico and reported the matter to the police; but nothing was ever recovered. I have heard tell that if a European leaves the window open in that country the Wasokili take a long pole, put a hook in the end of it, and fish for his clothes until they get them all! And yet, although they seem to go to great lengths to get clothes, they usually go about naked.

Whilst I was at Tukuyu I tried to ride a donkey. It threw me off and nearly killed me so I did not ride it again. I just led it.

I worked for Dr. D. for one year, and then one day my elder brother, who was cook, got ill. He was told by Dr. D. to make bread, but on account of his illness I made the bread for him, and Dr. D. found me doing it. He thereupon hit my brother, and my brother who was very sick hit him back and was promptly sacked. As I was still young, I feared to work alone so far from home, therefore I ran away that night and caught my brother up on the road, leaving my pay and testimonials behind me. We went into Tukuyu, where Major W. gave us passes to go on the ship to Fort Johnston.

When we reached Fort Johnston I did not get any more work for a year. During this year, 1918, I got married for the first time. For the marriage itself there is no unusual ceremony; one just pays the dowry and takes the girl to wife. But when my wife became big with child, then, as is the custom of my tribe, my parents and her parents gave a dance together for women only. These women dance and clap their hands; no drums are used. Then an old woman explained to my wife all about childbirth in front of all the other women, all of whom were mothers. They then ate a lot of native porridge and the dance lasted from sunrise till sunset. That night my wife and I were taken into a hut by the old woman. Inside it was quite dark except for the glow of a small fire. The old woman then explained to me that during the time my wife was carrying my child before its birth I must never sleep with any woman other than my wife. If I did so and then returned and even spoke to my wife, my unborn child would be destroyed and perhaps my wife killed. So that if I once slept with another woman during my wife's pregnancy I must continue to do so and never show myself at home until after the birth of my child. This old woman later helped my wife in her confinement.

In due course a girl-child was born to me, and for seven days after its birth my wife and the baby had to stay within the hut as the custom is. Then on the eighth day the same old woman came, with some native medicine which she gave to my wife, who had to drink it whilst sitting in the doorway with the child on her knee.

As my child was lying there all her hair was shaved off, because the first hair of children is a different sort of hair and cannot be worn outside the house. Always the child yells very much because it hurts a lot. You see, its hair, which is like cotton and very soft, is scraped off with a bit of iron sharpened and kept for that purpose. When all its hair has been removed the old woman gets some beeswax and puts some on the top of its head because in small children the bones are not joined and their brains go up and down because they have not any sense yet. The wax on their heads is to protect small children's brains from the sun like a tiny hat.

When a female child comes to the age of puberty the women hold a dance. The same women come to the dance as were present when her mother was initiated into the duties of parenthood. The dance is held during the last three hours of daylight. The child then remains in the house for six days. About three old women teach her during the six days; she is taught that she must wear a new sort of clothing and that it must be washed and dried out of sight of anyone else. This is the last ceremony for a woman until she is big with child. Succession is matrilineal. Therefore in the old days a man did not pay dowry; he just came and lived with his wife's people, and, having built a house, became one of the adherents of his wife's clan.

All of us have a method of birth-control. There is a root which grows in the bush which must be cooked. The woman then drinks the water. The bark of the root is then stripped off and made into a string which the woman wears round her waist with two little pieces of wood threaded on it. Having done this it is impossible to get a child. But if later she should want to have a child she must return the belt to the witch-doctor, and in the morning her husband must take flour to the doctor and tell him that he wants his wife to bear children. All three then go to a tree, and the doctor asks the woman, 'Would you like to bear a child now?' and the woman says 'Yes.' The doctor then invokes those who have died, and, taking the flour, covers it with a cooking pot. In the morning the doctor goes to the place alone and finds that the flour has been disturbed; he then returns and gives the news. Then if God helps, you will get a child. This has been done for ages and even the most enlightened of us believe in this method. We practise birth-control because when one is travelling children are a nuisance, and because some women do not like to settle down and take the first step towards old age.

When once a man has been married and has had his food cooked for him he cannot live alone afterwards. Women are not all the same; some want a husband so that they can get money and clothes, and others because they love. If a man marries a mercenary woman the moment he stops working she will want a divorce because she knows she cannot get any more out of him. We know that when a woman is cross she doesn't love any more and she begins to be disobedient, which is very bad. If a woman loves a man she obeys him in everything and will not go to see even her mother without getting permission. There is nothing more to be said about women.

I got my next job with Mr. Livingstone [a descendant of the great doctor] who came with six other Europeans under him to take cinematograph photos of lion and other game. He took me on as boy to Mr. C. at 15s. a month and we went to Fort Jameson to look for lions, elephants and leopards. When any animal was caught in a trap we all went to watch the Englishman taking photos of it. This job lasted for seven months and in the eighth month we went to Tabora.

At this time there were many Akidas, but the people did not seem to like their rule and many took their grievances straight to the Boma [District Office] and many more went secretly to their old tribal chiefs where they felt more certain of getting justice according to their tribal custom.

From Tabora we went to Dar-es-Salaam, where all the servants were paid off. We were given money enough to get us home to Nyasaland, but we wanted to look for more work and did not go. I lived in Dar-es-Salaam for the next six months without work and I was very poor indeed. During this time I undoubtedly suffered the greatest hardships of my whole life. Even the war was nothing like it, nor the famine in Nyasaland, for I could not even go home. I wrote home to ask my father for money, and he sent me 20s., which was not enough to feed me and get me home. One young man who was working for the Government Printer helped me; he gave me food and a place to sleep in and so saved me from starvation. When I got a job I tried to give him a present, but he would not take it as he said that I also was an Myao and he would take nothing. He is a Christian and would not hear of my doing anything for him.

At the end of this terrible six months I got work at the Police mess at 35s. a month. I showed Mr. R. my chits from Nyasaland at 15s. a month and explained to him that I must have more money in Dar-es-Salaam, as in Fort Johnston food cost nothing for we cultivated it ourselves. Here in Dar-es-Salaam there was food and clothing to be bought and room-rent to pay. So he said he would try me at 35s. a month. There were thirty-five Europeans and I was the only table-boy and bar-boy. I worked for three months and then gave notice, as I found the pay too little for the great deal of work I had to do; however, he increased my pay to 50s. and let me have two boys to help me at noon and in the evening. I stayed two years, and then the mess was closed by order of the Medical Officer of Health and the officers went to feed at the New Africa Hotel. I stayed three days in Dar-es-Salaam and was then called to the K.A.R., where I got 40s. a month and stayed for one and a half years, and then my master was sent home by the Colonel, and I was out of work again. I stayed in Dar-es-Salaam ten days and was then called by a boy who said his master had only four months to do before leave, and that as he had no head-boy I must come and help, so I worked as head-boy for Dr. S. for four months at 45s. a month. At the end of that time I sent my wife her divorce, as I heard she was not happy. I wanted her to join me in Tanganyika, but she did not wish to leave her home. My little girl belongs to me, but is still living with her mother.

I then lived in Dar-es-Salaam for a month without work, at the end of which time I was sent for by Mr. H. and sent as head-boy to Mr. D. of the Secretariat, where I worked for one and a half months at 45s. and then left of my own accord. I went over to Mr. H. who had worked under Major W. at Tukuyu and knew me because my cousin worked for him there and I had often been over to his house; he said he would look out for another master for me. I went back to get permission to leave Mr. D.'s service and was offered a rise, but I did not want to stay. The same day Mr. H. sent for me and sent me with Mr. M. to Mikindani. I got 40s. a month and stayed with him for two years. I left because the cook was always picking quarrels. He was jealous because I was put in charge of the store and everything. Mr. M. said that it would be a good thing to get rid of the cook and I should find another who did not make quarrels. But I said that as the cook lived in Mikindani it was better that I should go, as my home was far off and I feared that if he lost his job he would kill me, I being a stranger.

It was here that I married my second wife, Salima binti Feruzi, and bought a house which I still have. When I give her her divorce I will give her the house as the remaining portion of her dowry.

During my stay in Mikindani I entered into a blood-brotherhood according to the Yao custom. Actually it is a blood-sisterhood and I call her sister. The ceremony consists of drawing off some of one's own blood and some of hers; then each drinks the blood of the other. Then witnesses are called in and they eat food. As between blood-relations all property is in common. My blood-sister's name is binti Hamisi and she married the teacher Rufu in the Songea Native Administration school, but he gave her a triple divorce one day when he was drunk so now she has gone back to Mikindani. If she gets married she makes trouble, but not for me. When I have occasion to rebuke her, she listens to me.

I went back to Dar-es-Salaam with the money that was given me and after a month Mr. H. again got me employment with my present master, who took me to Bagamoyo. From Bagamoyo we went to Songea. On the way my employer shot a pig and the Wapogoro porters ate it. Likangaga got the head and it made him ill, so the porters sang 'Likangaga has had a quarrel with a pig. . . . The pig has won.' Another old man had a little dysentery which he attributed to a hole in his stomach which must constantly be plugged with porridge!

During the eighteen months I was in Songea man-eating lions killed about fifteen people all over the District. They actually went on to the verandah of the District Office one evening and frightened the guard, so that no one walked about much after dark.

In November 1930 we went to Mahenge and then Kiberege and Dar-es-Salaam, after which we came to Morogoro, where this is being written down for me.

I first learned to ride a bicycle in Tabora when I was with the cinematograph expedition. I fell off twice, but I was not afraid of it, because it could not kick like the donkey I rode in Tukuyu. But I think now that a bicycle does not know his master, for you buy one and in the end he will hurt you. I looked after my bicycle in Songea very well indeed, but in the end he hurt me very much!

I like to wear European clothes because only a man who has done a lot of work and made money can wear them. Therefore they are the mark of success. Of course one could wear stolen clothes, but to walk with fear on one's back would be more trouble to the heart than a heavy load.

Of all the games and pastimes of Europeans I was most astonished at the cinema. It is very good but even now I do not understand how it works. I see people come and drink and play and walk about, then, suddenly, they are gone, and the place to which they have gone is not known. Also when I first heard a gramophone I was certain that there was a very small man inside who was speaking. My father and many of his generation are still of this opinion.

I know which clothes to put out for tennis and golf, but I do not understand the games.

Now I must tell you of the starch of the Portuguese. Our country borders on theirs and I have been there once. All the Europeans appear to wear nothing but white clothes which are starched from a very high coat-collar right down to their white shoes. Their clothes are starched so stiff that they are like leather. In this country only male house-owners pay tax, but if a woman has no husband she is taxed. And if the women are late paying their tax they are taken off to the District Office and sold by auction. I have seen this with my own eyes. If the woman has a brother he may buy her back from the man who has bought her, if the man is willing to sell! Also in this country I have seen the bastinado given on the hands and feet with a stick shaped like a cooking spoon. If the sentence be twenty strokes ten are given on the hands and ten on the feet. The victim is afterwards carried away as he cannot walk or crawl. Of course, things may be different now as I was there some time ago.

There is a Yao song—the Song of the Crocodile—which goes like this: 'Oh you crocodile, you have shot the child of your friend with a bow. . . . Whom will you talk with? . . . Oh you crocodile, your heart is hard as iron.' The reason for this song is that in my country the witch-doctors turn into crocodiles and go down to the drinking places and having killed their enemy take him to their house. They cannot live long in the water and a crocodile from the deep lake cannot eat a man—it only eats fish. Our witch-doctors do not turn into lions but in the Portuguese country they can turn into lions.

If a man has an enemy he can go to a witch-doctor and buy 'mbigi', which are small sticks threaded on string which are carried and put in the house. Then he must go into the bush at night, put first some grass on the earth and then the mbigi on top, then take a tail which the doctor has given him, and say to the mbigi: 'Go hence and kill my enemy.' Then he strikes the mbigi with the tail and at once they turn into a lion, crocodile or snake as required, which goes off and kills the enemy. The mbigi are no longer on the grass when the owner lifts the tail. Take, for example, lion mbigi. They each turn into a lion and go and wait by the road. Twenty people may pass and will not be killed, but when the enemy comes the lion will kill him and carry him to the little pile of grass and wait there. Then when the owner of the mbigi comes the lion changes back into an mbigi, and, if the owner is himself a wizard, he will eat his enemy; if not, he will carry him and throw him into the lake, after which he must return the mbigi to the witch-doctor. Of course, the mbigi-lions are quite different from the witch-doctors who turn into lions for their own purposes. If your father and mother and relations keep on dying and you know the man who is causing their deaths, you cannot go and kill him for murdering them because you may not be able to prove it, so you must go and get him lion or crocodile medicine so that people will say he died by an act of God.

Speaking of God, I do not see any difference between Mohammedanism and Christianity except the outside ceremonies. After all, do we not all pray to God? Does it then matter much which great Prophet we follow? There is, however, one thing in Mohammedan law which is better and that is plural wives, and I think that always the Africans will prefer it thus. It has always been the rule; if my wife objects very strongly to my marrying anyone else she has no right to do so, and should she make a lot of trouble she would have to be divorced. A woman cannot have a man to herself; many women have no children;

many children die, and so perhaps, if the rule were one wife only, I might die without a child! Our fathers had many wives; that is why we are many.

Nyasaland is a better country than Tanganyika. I only stay in Tanganyika because the pay is better. If I were to go home to Nyasaland without having arranged with my master to work again for him, I would not come back to look for work, for I would fear to be out of work and experience more hardships like the time when I was unemployed in Dar-es-Salaam. I like my work as a boy and I like to work always for the same master. It is not good to work first for one European and then for another, because each European has his own habits and so, if one changes often, one must always be learning new ways. Moreover, one does not get work easily. I like to work because I am accustomed to it, and if I sit at home it irks me for at the end of the month I do not get money and my friends do. I would prefer now to work as a lorry-driver because in my heart I want to know a lot of different jobs, for to know only one is bad. But I see that it would mean starting again at the bottom so I cannot do it. I hope to work for a long time yet if God permits and at the end I will buy some cattle and go and settle down at home. My father likes me to work but he would be very angry if I did not try to come home every two or three years.

I think that it is well for Africans to be taught and to try to learn all that the Europeans have to teach. For if we were left in ignorance we would suffer many hardships, but a man who has brains and works hard may make a name even when everyone is civilized. Our old people who have not learned anything or worked—even now they are only fools. But when a man has learned a lot, let him not think he can learn no more, for anyone can go on learning till he dies, and even then a fool is buried.

# VII

# The Story of Parmenas Mockerie of the Kikuyu Tribe, Kenya

*written by himself*

## The Life of an African Teacher

It was in 1900 or 1901 that I was born at Chui in Njumbi, in Fort Hall, Kenya. My father, Mockerie, and mother, Wagithatu, never attended school. I do not know the exact date of my birthday as they did not keep it. They brought me up in the country, and I always thank them for the way they wished me to live. When I was eight days old my mother took me to our farm and dug up some sweet potatoes and plucked some first fruits of the fields so as to find good luck for my future career. This is Kikuyu tradition. She realized that my satisfaction in life could be a reality if she thus started my career in farming. I cannot remember any occasion in my life when my parents threatened me by beating, as they loved me extremely well. When I was ten years old they gave me a plot to cultivate and on which to plant crops which I could call my own property. I grew potatoes and bananas on my plot and exchanged them for knives and spears, thinking that I would join the young Kikuyu police force one day. My father had been a captain of this police force during his youth before the advent of the white man, and his adventures, which he used to relate to me and my mother, stimulated my desire to join a police force to defend my country. During this time I could not realize that the Kikuyu Young Men's Defence Force had been superseded by the police force which has been created by the European Government. He, too, could not understand the machinery of European power. To make me fit for my future career he had to take me to men's camps which were held every year. I had to sleep away from home for eight days. At these camps I had to learn the discipline imposed upon young men by the old people. Every day I had to go to the river to draw water for camp purposes. After meals in the mornings I had to run about a mile and practise a war dance in order to learn the custom of the young men's police force.

Kikuyu society is based on nine clans, and every clan has a special item to contribute towards the welfare of the society. My clan is Mwithaga. Its occupation was to manufacture medicine for curing coughs, and to produce the rain-makers. My grandfather, Githendu, had six wives who had a large family. My grandmother, Nyamugoiri, had two sons, my father and Mutuambui. Both of them married one wife, only, and did not follow in the footsteps of my grandfather. Mutuambui lost his wife and refused to marry again, preferring a life of celibacy. His trade is to manufacture medicine for healing coughs and to produce 'salt-licks' for domestic animals from his own mine. When Paramount Chief Karuri of Fort Hall was in power, my uncle was his chief agent in supplying him with 'salt-licks' for his livestock. My father interested himself in the leadership of our clan and in village life. My uncle wanted to train me in organizing his salt mine. But going hunting in the wild places distracted me from following his advice. When I was thirteen years of age, I started to lay traps for leopards and lions which had eaten cattle, goats and sheep in our village. While I was setting traps a hyena came towards me. He is the most cowardly animal that I have ever seen. I frightened him to death with a handful of soil by throwing it in the air and in the leaves of trees. I did this in order to make the leaves rattle whilst the soil was falling down. The rattle caused the hyena to run away as he thought I was with a number of people. When he ran away I climbed a tree which was near by. At once a leopardess and her young one came under the tree. I aimed at the young one and killed it with my poisoned arrows. This made the leopardess furious, so she roared at the foot of the tree with an awful noise. She gave me a good opportunity to shoot her through one of her eyes with my poisoned arrows while she was moving round the tree wishing to attack me. She fell dead. I went home and told the villagers how I had killed their enemies. A group of people rushed to the spot to view the dead animal. One of the villagers looked up where I had been sitting in the fork of the tree and saw a big snake resting upon a broad branch. This startled the people. They wondered whether I had noticed it. Fortunately, the snake did not do any harm to me, neither did I notice it when I was on the tree. When father heard this adventure he sharpened my spear still more, but I realized that the spear was too heavy for me to carry and preferred to carry arrows as they were light. I was anxious to kill a lion as this animal was a nuisance to our village. I continued my setting of traps. I joined a group of boys who were setting for fowls like partridges and doves. While we were pursuing antelopes we came across a big lion who was very hungry and was seeking antelopes to devour. My desire to kill a lion was achieved when I shot him with two arrows and brought him to the end of his life. My companions were terribly frightened as they had no intention in their lives to kill the king of animals.

I began to eat partridges which I caught. My father became very angry with me because I ate wild animals. It is the tradition of our clan that no member of Mwithaga should eat wild animals. We had the right to eat only meat from cows, sheep and goats and no other animals. The reason is this: our clan was supposed to make rain and heal coughs among the Kikuyu people, and if some members of our clan were to eat wild animals they were liable to lose their powers. This I thought was merely superstition based on groundless propositions. I became almost an outcast and then began to go to school. I started to read and write my own language probably when I was thirteen or fifteen years of age. I first attended a missionary school at Gitugi and then at Kahuhia in Fort Hall, where later I became a head teacher. My family loved me afterwards when they found that a great number of young people of my age in the village had eaten wild animals and when they found that superstition was no longer binding the young people. My parents objected to my going to a missionary school, as by so doing I had to abstain from associating with them in the social life of the village. Things such as communal dances, drinking parties, and several social items performed by the village community were considered incompatible with Christianity, and my parents were opposed to any mode of life different from that of the tribe. As I am their firstborn I should have to undergo three stages of initiation and attend big feasts in which my parents would make themselves well known among the people in the neighbourhood. They were afraid that if I did not undertake the initiation ceremony they would lose the right of giving advice to other people who would like to perform these ceremonies. Despite their discouragement I continued my schooling until I went to Nairobi and attended night-school; there I worked at a garage and then as a clerk for hiring bicycles. Previous to this I was employed by a European as a house-servant. I walked barefoot on grass land in the city and a broken piece of bottle cut sharply across my sole, and I had to attend hospital for a month and a half before it got better. Afterwards I decided to wear shoes, but my European master prevented me from entering his house wearing shoes in the same manner as Europeans. I gave up the position as house-servant because I was not allowed to wear shoes. I was afraid to walk any longer barefoot as I did not like pieces of bottles or thorns to pierce my feet.

In 1921 I went to study at the Church of Scotland Mission at Kikuyu. I became a pupil-teacher and was apprenticed for three years. My teacher was Mr. G. Greive, now the Principal of the Allied High School at Kikuyu. During my apprenticeship I was appointed by Dr. J. Arthur, the Principal of the school, as head boy of one of the dormitories. At the end of my apprenticeship I was appointed head teacher at the Kahuhia Central School, which is run by the Church Missionary Society, and remained there from 1925 to 1931. In the beginning of the year 1931 I went to Makerere College in Uganda to take a Teachers' Refresher Course. I began to associate with Baganda. Later I met a few Kikuyu from Kenya, in Kampala, and they could take me about the town. I visited the Lukiko (Parliament) and was extremely surprised to find that Mr. Speaker of the House was an African, and the whole body of the House was entirely African. Administrative and financial departments are under the direction of Africans. In Uganda and Tanganyika African Local District Councils are presided over by Africans, and also they hold the office of Treasurer, but in Kenya things are quite different. African councils are presided over by the white man and Africans have no direct control of public finances. When the African financial minister of the Baganda Kingdom took me into his office and showed me how the British Government had allowed the Baganda to control a part of their taxation, without the help of a white man, I was greatly surprised. While I was in Uganda I was taken to large estates possessed by big chiefs. Many poor people live on these estates as tenants and they have to pay yearly rents to their landlords. I learned from some Baganda that some of these estates were unjustly held by the chiefs. When the British Government became protector of the people of Uganda, it allowed chiefs to appropriate these estates.

In April 1931 my course of study was interrupted by the Kikuyu Central Association, an African society among the Kikuyu tribe in Kenya. It appointed me to proceed to England as its delegate and represent the people of Kenya before the Select Joint Committee on Closer Union in East Africa, which was then sitting in London, and was hearing evidence from East African witnesses. There were nine African official witnesses from Uganda, Kenya and Tanganyika. Besides these official witnesses, the Kikuyu people under the auspices of the Kikuyu Central Association delegated Mr. Johnstone Kenyatta and me as unofficial representatives to the Select Parliamentary Joint Committee.

Travelling from East Africa, I embarked at Mombasa, the Kenya seaport, on the *Mazzini*, an Italian steamer. It was my first journey to Europe. It was strange to me to find the boat sailing day and night in the vast sea. The first day that I was in my cabin on the boat I saw a warning notice showing what people should do with life-belts in case of an emergency. I began to read the notice and had a short lesson on it every day. On the boat my hair and beard grew long and needed to be cut. I approached a European barber and he told me that he could not cut my hair in his shop as he was afraid to lose European customers on the boat if they found a black man being shaved there. He said that he would come to shave me in my cabin. On the boat there were other Africans from Italian colonies on the coasts of the Red Sea. They consisted of soldiers and porters. They conversed in Italian among themselves. This was strange to me as I had never heard porters in the British Colonies speaking English, as they are not given the opportunity of learning it.

On May 20th, 1931, I landed at Genoa and travelled to Paris by train. Here a crowd of African men and women who had come to see the French Colonial exhibition added something to the beauty of Parisian streets. At the exhibition, African villages were built, and every African trade, art and culture was represented. When I was passing to and fro in the exhibition grounds I saw a group of African soldiers doing military shows. As I never had been to Europe before I expected to find this sort of thing in London. I made an inquiry about the attitude of French people towards African people in the French Colonies in Africa. I could hardly believe there were African Representatives in the French Chamber of Deputies in Paris, and that an African native of Senegal had been appointed Under-Secretary of State for the French Colonies, because in East Africa, in the British Colonies, the African people have no direct representation on the local legislatures, which consist of white men only.

On May 22nd, 1931, I arrived at Victoria Station in London. It was summer-time. The weather was cold and rainy. The first thing I had to do after my arrival was to buy warm clothes and an overcoat, as the cold weather had beaten me. I used to wear cotton clothes in East Africa, and I could not imagine that woollen clothes were so important in England if one wanted to keep fit. The crowded streets of London, with men and women dressed in overcoats in summer-time, could hardly convince me that people in England had ever enjoyed the bright and sunny weather which Africans and other tropical inhabitants enjoy almost the year round. It was in the summer of 1933 that I realized that sometimes there is similar weather in England to that of Central Africa. During that time I spent a few days in England pouring with perspiration due to the heat.

My mission to England disappointed me extremely, since the Parliamentary Select Committee did not receive us officially as we hoped they would do. But I had the hope that truth would win in the end in spite of the disability placed upon African people in political problems. I could not imagine the reason why the Parliamentary Select Committee refused to allow us to give evidence before it. This refusal was not a new thing; it was an opinion held by some white people that Africans who hold independent views should be ignored. The Kikuyu people, realizing this attitude, became disillusioned by African representatives appointed by the Government to give evidence before the Committee and wished to be represented by their own delegates. However, we were able to secure the help of some British sympathizers who are not conservative in their outlook with regard to imperialism, and who wish the African people to progress on the same lines as white men. I learned when I was addressing meetings in London, Birmingham and Colchester that there were some people in England who have the welfare of Africans at heart. But imperialistic views dominate too many English people. Consequently, it becomes very difficult to deal with problems relating to the land which was expropriated by the white settlers in Africa, who subjected the Africans who formerly owned the land to the position of wage-earners under capitalistic exploitation.

My anxiety regarding my stay in England for further education increased when I decided to study at Fircroft Working Men's College, one of the group of Selly Oak Colleges, Birmingham. I had no personal friends in Birmingham and wondered how I could manage to live in a big city with a great population without a friend. Fortunately, I met Dr. and Mrs. Duncan Leys and their little boy, Colin, who are very interested in African problems. Their acquaintance removed the feeling of loneliness which I experienced before I came to Fircroft. At Fircroft College I started to learn about English society, of which I had no previous knowledge. The thing that surprised me most is the feeling of friendship between the white and coloured people at the Selly Oak Colleges, particularly at Fircroft. I was associated with the social life of the College and made many friends among my fellow students. I stayed at Fircroft as a resident student from October 1931 to Easter 1933, and then became a resident student at Ruskin College, Oxford.

One who, like myself, comes from a country without such educational facilities as those provided in the Oxford Colleges, with a big student population, would lose no time in observing what is going on in these colleges. One of my great desires was to see whether there were Africans in them. Fortunately, I met Mr. Mayanja, a native of Baganda, who has just graduated as a Bachelor of Arts; Miss Aina Moore from West Africa, who was studying at St. Hugh's College; and also there were several Africans from other parts of Africa and the West Indies. It was a great pleasure for me to meet Miss Stella Thomas, an African lady who had just become a barrister. African women in East Africa would hardly believe that an African woman could pass in law during this stage of African development.

Education to fit African men and women for professions such as is given in Oxford and Cambridge cannot be obtained in Africa at present. The environment and the scope of educational stimulus, which is obtained in the African village community, is limited. For this reason a great number of African students must come to Europe for higher education, although it will cost them much. During my stay in Oxford and other parts of England I could not change my belief that the right thing for the African Government to do for African people would be to give liberal scholarships to African students who desire to become teachers, lawyers, doctors and engineers and allow them to pursue their studies in Europe. The Western sciences cannot be followed successfully in Africa where libraries are lacking and the environment does not give facilities for higher education. At the same time there should be higher education for Africans who are not able to go abroad. Scholarships should be provided without any suggestion that Africans should be educated gradually as certain educationalists have emphasized. Gradualism is disaster when it is applied to education. It aims at enslaving the minds of the people, and at preventing them from the realization of truth. Parents who do not feed their children sufficiently cause them to be weak mentally and physically. When a pupil has been to school and grows up as a citizen, and does not understand the principles of his relations to the community and State, there must be something wrong in the teachings of the school. I would rather prefer Africans to know the truth early than late. This can be completely achieved if the scope of their education is not limited. During my visit to schools in England I found that education is not limited. Children are given every opportunity to have sufficient education. The same spirit which is held by educationalists in European countries should be maintained by educational authorities in Africa. Modern civilization and its complicated science have been evolved, not to benefit only a section of the community or one class, but to benefit human beings in the world without respect of race or colour. So any human being who restricts these benefits from being enjoyed by every creature is cursed.

While attending a meeting of the League of Coloured Peoples in London I had an opportunity of seeing Mr. Paul Robeson, the negro who is well known as an artist and singer among the white men in Europe and America. His lovely voice aroused me when I heard him singing on the wireless in England. After a few days I read in a socialist newspaper, the *Daily Herald*, that Mr. Paul Robeson would like to see Africa as a Republic with a negro President. This would be a sign to show that the negro race has reached the stage to show to the world that it has something to contribute to the world. If there had been such a Republic, Mr. Paul Robeson would have been made a Peer or Lord of Africa, as his contribution to society is similar to that of those who have been made Lords by the British Government.

In the nineteenth century, when white men began to realize that negro people were human beings and not subhuman as some white men had thought, they fought amongst themselves in order to set free the negro slaves in America. Those whites who died for the cause of black people wished to recognize the negro race in society. But the intention of these gallant whites seems to be disregarded during this generation. As an instance, I will relate here how I entered a refreshment house in London and I was told that I could not be served as black people at this house were not served. It is very often heard that there are some parts of America, and Africa, where black men cannot travel in the same carriages with the whites, or eat at the same hotel. This shows that besides the white men setting the negro slaves free there is something more they have to do. That is the removal of racial prejudice. If this were achieved, the coloured man would be recognized in society. To remove this prejudice the Governments in Africa should raise the education of African men and women to the level of that which is given to the children of white men. I am convinced that if Africans are given opportunity and their way of advancement is open they will make their own characteristic contribution to world culture.

In the summer of 1932, I spent my vacation in Denmark and visited a number of High Schools, and I also visited bacon factories and dairies. The dairies are very clean and well managed. I could not imagine that I would meet any African in Denmark. A Danish friend took me about Tivoli, a place of pleasure at Copenhagen, in the evening. Promptly I met an African, a well dressed and tall man, who was a native of the Congo. He speaks Danish fluently, and a little English, and has been thirty years in Denmark. He married a white woman and has six children: when I asked him how he was treated by the Danes, he said that they treated him nicely.

'How did you come to Denmark?' I asked him.

'A Dutchman brought me to Holland, and he died. I was employed by a German, and when we came to Denmark, he disappeared, and I had no money to get back to

Holland. Subsequently a Danish firm employed me, and here I have been for thirty years.'

Next day, when I was strolling through the Danish Parliament in Copenhagen, an Abyssinian who was a singer in Copenhagen attracted my attention. I introduced myself to him.

'How did you come to Denmark?' I asked him.

'A German prince engaged me as a chauffeur from Egypt, and brought me to Germany nine years ago. I left his service because his German servants were always bullying me: I became an artist at Vienna, and a Danish hotel manager employed me to entertain visitors at his hotel in Copenhagen. I tried to go to London to visit my fellow countrymen who are students there, but when I got to Dover the British Government would not allow me to enter Great Britain, although I had sufficient money to keep me there,' he said. I asked him whether he had an Abyssinian passport with him, and he showed it to me at once. He could speak and write German fluently: his knowledge of Spanish, French, Italian, Danish and English was not far from perfect.

Whilst I was in Copenhagen, I was told that at Elsinore there is a castle where Danish kings used to torture their prisoners. I visited it, and found that a large part is used as a museum, and the other part is a long dungeon where prisoners were kept. It could hold about three hundred persons if they were packed like boxes of articles stored in a barn: from the roof leaked water, artificially placed to wet the prisoners. It has no windows, and is very dark, so that not one prisoner could see another. I can say with certainty that this torture place for a white king's enemies was much more cruel than anything used by Africans before the Western powers established themselves in Africa.

As I am writing this in England in August 1933, I cannot end without a reference to the events which have taken place in Germany during my stay in Europe. When Hitler came into power, his Government tortured the Jews and banned the negro jazz bands, yet when the World Economic Conference met in London, a German delegate presented a manifesto to the conference demanding back the German African colonies which Germany had lost in the war. Hitler's Government dislikes the negro race, yet it makes a claim to a share of African territory. German administrators in Africa before the war were cruel and inhuman: Africans were tortured like beasts. How can Germany govern a people whom she hates?

I have now finished my time for study in Europe. I must go back to my own country, and work among my own people. I am full of hope, though I do not know what the future holds for them or for myself.

# VIII

# The Story of Martin Kayamba Mdumi, M.B.E., of the Bondei Tribe

*written by himself*

## Part I

### My Life and Work in East Africa

I was born on 2nd February, 1891, at Mbweni, Zanzibar. I am the first son of Hugh Peter Kayamba. He is one of the sons of Chief Mwelekwanyuma of Kilole, son of Kimweri Zanyumbai (Kimweri the Great) King of Wakilindi. The Wakilindi are a ruling clan, who ruled over the Wasambaa and other tribes in the coastal areas of Tanga prior to the German occupation of these countries. The first Mkilindi named Mbega came from the hills in the Handeni area. He was a famous hunter and through his hunting prowess and generosity was chosen by the Wasambaa to be their ruler. Chief Mwelekwanyuma was appointed by his father as Chief over the Wabondei and the Coastal section from Pangani to Vanga.

My father was born at Kilole Bondei, the seat of his father, about 1865. He was first a Mohammedan. My father joined the Universities Mission to Central Africa in 1877 and was educated at the U.M.C.A. Schools at Umba and Magila. He was sent to England in 1882 and was educated at Bloxham School, near Oxford. In 1885 he returned from England and became a teacher at St. Andrew's College, U.M.C.A., Zanzibar. He married my mother, Faith Kalekabula, a teacher like himself, in 1890. My sister, Mary Elizabeth, was born on 23rd December, 1893. My father in 1892 was sent to the Bondei country to evangelize and was made a Reader. He resigned from the Mission in 1895 and joined the Government service at Mombasa as a clerk in the Uganda Rifles. He fought in the Mbaruk war and received a medal. My father worked for the British Government till 1926 and was last engaged as the Akida (Headman) of Mombo in the Usambara district. I was baptized on the eighth day after my birth by Rev. Sir John Key at St. John's Church, Mbweni. Miss C. D. M. Thackeray and Margaret Durham Mdoe were my godmothers, and Alfred Juma was my godfather.

My mother was a very strict disciplinarian. She made me pray daily before I went to bed and when I woke up, and before and after taking meals. She taught me to give alms in church by giving me two pice every Sunday to put in the alms bag in church. She made a rule that I should be indoors at 6 p.m. and go to bed at 7 p.m. and wake up at 6 a.m. sharp. She used to wake up at 5 a.m. herself. She enforced the rule until I got married. She was very particular about my life and behaviour. She was very quick at chastising me. I received more thrashing from her than from my father. But she loved me dearly. She died on 28th August, 1912. From 1895 to 1896 I was educated at the U.M.C.A. Boys' School, Kilimani, Zanzibar, as a day boy, then I went to the Church Missionary Society School at Mombasa. In the school we were boys of various nationalities. There was one European boy, who was my great friend. There were also Indians, Arabs, Baluchis, Comorians and Swahilis. All lessons were taught in English. I was fortunate to pass all my examinations at the first sittings. In 1899 when I left Mombasa with my parents I had already reached the top form.

In 1899 my father resigned his service at Mombasa and went to Zanzibar, taking us with him. At Zanzibar I was sent to Kilimani School. Miss D. Mills was in charge of the school, and Miss E. Clutterbuck was the schoolmistress, assisted by African teachers. Bishop F. Weston (he was a priest at the time) was our Chaplain. The discipline at Kilimani was very strict indeed, and I must confess both Miss Clutterbuck and Miss Stevens were sterner than any of my headmasters. Boys used to get whippings every day. Sometimes mothers of the boys quarrelled with them for whippping their children or detaining them in close confinement without food and water. The Chaplain also was very strict. From the Life of Bishop Weston [*Frank, Bishop of Zanzibar*, by the Rev. H. Maynard Smith, S.P.C.K., page 38]: 'From time to time he examined the secular work of the school and sometimes he was asked to inflict corporal punishment. This he did with as much vigour as all else. . . .' The boys were more afraid of the schoolmistress at Kilimani than they were afterwards of their headmaster and masters at Kiungani College. At Kilimani I was again fortunate in my lessons and in one year I got to the top class.

In 1901 my father went to the Bondei country and took us with him. I was sent to the U.M.C.A. school at Magila. I was there for about six months. In 1902 my father returned with us to Zanzibar. Bishop F. Weston, who was at the time the Principal of the Kiungani College, asked my father to send me to Kiungani College as my friends in England were paying for my education in the U.M.C.A. My friends were Mesdames C. N. Goldring and Weston. On 1st February, 1902, I joined Kiungani College. I was placed in the III Class. In the July 1902 examination I passed and was promoted to II Class. In the December 1902 examination I passed and was promoted to I Class. My age was then 12 years. Being a small boy, I was not made a teacher.

The discipline was very strict at Kiungani. Bishop Weston was very strict and good to the boys. He treated us like his own children. The food that was supplied to the boys during his time was exceptionally good. The welfare of the boys was his first and foremost consideration. He used to tell us: 'I do not want to be called a miser.' If the cook did not cook our food well, he ordered it to be cast away and he cycled to the town to get us bread and relish. In school one could never wish a better teacher. He taught all his subjects clearly and lucidly. In discipline he was very rigid. He never cautioned an offender without whipping him. Every evening after our dinner, guilty boys were watching with anxiety who would be called first to receive some thrashing. It was a rule that after the second school bell had rung there should be a complete silence. One day, just after the second school bell had gone a mango fell down and I impulsively shouted to a teacher, 'A mango has fallen down!' The Bishop was walking towards my direction going to the classroom, and he heard me shouting. He instantly ordered me to go to his room at 12 noon after school time. When I got there all to my grief and unexpectation, he gave me ten with a cane. I expected to be warned as this was my first offence in the college, besides that I was a stranger, but I was whipped. Boys who failed in examinations always received thrashing as their prize, and this was done every month because we had monthly test examinations. In the book of the Life of Bishop Weston, page 45, he writes to a friend: 'We are as a training school far more efficient than we were a year ago; and I have hopes and schemes for a still greater development and improvement. I introduced one new feature into the prize giving which fairly staggered the school. After declaring that my Majesty was pleased to approve of much that the boys had done, I proceeded to inform my subjects that there were some whom the examination had proved to be mere idlers and wasters. For them also I had reserved prizes—of a different sort—which would be distributed later in the day! Oh, that you had seen the faces of the slackers! So I left them from 4 p.m. until after dinner—in awful horror and dread expectation. At 8.15 I was about to ring for the first victim, when in came a lazy youth to explain why his marks were few. As I had no designs on him I cheered him up. Later, ping! my bell rang, and up rushed a real prize-winner, all agog to know who would be called! "Call Petro," says I,—and downstairs he ran into the arms of an expectant throng. Up came Petro, fearful and sad. One boy, one brute, one cane—and six of the very best. "Call Martin" [another boy called by the same name as myself; he was his godson]. Enter my godson. One godson, one godfather, one cane—and six of the very best. "Call Antonio." Enter the fat boy of the school. One fat boy, one thin headmaster, one thinner cane—and six of the very best. "Call Jack!" Enter the harum-scarum of the school with many excuses. One protestant, one pope, one cane—and six of the very best. Meanwhile below were several sinking hearts, which only beat normally when Jack was heard to go weeping to bed, calling no one to take his place. And these new kind of prizes I have promised shall be given after each examination, much to the annoyance of many small kids.'

The discipline which Bishop Weston instilled in the boys of the college was of real value to them in after life.

It was the intention of Bishop Weston that I should eventually work as a Mission teacher. Personally I did not think that this was my vocation. My mother was taking a great deal of pains to bring me up in a real Christian way. My father was keen that I should receive the best education available in our Mission schools. When I was at home my father always gave me some homework and not infrequently I got a severe lashing from him for making mistakes in my lessons. One advantage I had in my school days—both my parents were teachers and took a great deal of interest in my education.

In December 1904 I was made a teacher. As I did not like the work I did not associate much with my fellow teachers. Of course, most of them were much older than myself. I was strictly instructed not to mix up much with the boys. One day I took a boy off his duties in contravention of the order and I was severely reprimanded by the Acting Principal. I angrily offered to resign the post of a teacher, and that same evening I was reduced to an ordinary schoolboy. Bishop Weston was in England on leave when I was reduced in rank. On his return from leave he tried his very best to persuade me to take up the rank of a teacher again, but I refused and selected to leave the College to work as a clerk outside. In February 1906 I left Kiungani College and went to my father at Mombasa.

There were not many settlers in Kenya in those days. There were a good number of European commercial firms at Mombasa. The hinterland was not so much improved as it is today. The tribes were living in peaceful occupation of their land. My father put me in the Telegraph Department to be trained as a telegraphist. After a month I was ordered to proceed to Voi Station to work in the post office there. My mother refused because she thought I was too young to be left alone, so I had to resign from the post office. My father then got me into the Public Works Department to be trained as a draughtsman. On 1st June, 1906, I joined the Drawing Office under Mr. Dodd, Architect, and was trained as a tracer. I made a good progress in this work and Mr. Dodd was very good to me. After six months I was transferred to the Store Department to work under the Chief Storekeeper, Mr. C. W. Gregory, who had just arrived from South Africa. My work there was good and Mr. Gregory made me in charge of outside stores. After some few months I resigned and started my own business. My mother and godmother were against my doing trading business. When I started the business my mother was in Zanzibar, and when she returned she objected to my doing the business as I was very young. In the end I had to give in and I ceased trading.

On 6th September, 1907, I was re-engaged in the Public Works Department as assistant store clerk in the Executive Engineer's Store at Mombasa. Mr. McGregor Ross, who was the Director of the Public Works Department, was very kind to the African Staff and took a great deal of interest in their work and welfare. He made personal visits to sick African employees and arranged for the doctor to go and see them in their houses.

On 11th February, 1908, I married Mary Syble, a teacher of the Girls' School, U.M.C.A., Mbweni. My wife was a pupil-teacher of the girls' boarding school and was herself a boarder. I first knew her when she came from Pemba to the Girls' School, Mbweni. She was a very small girl at the time. I met her again at a wedding at Mbweni and engaged myself to her in 1905. On January 9th I was transferred to the Public Works Store, Nyeri, as a store clerk. On the same day after my departure a daughter was born to us, named Constance Faith Mary. At Nyeri I had to act as sub-storekeeper for six months as two European sub-storekeepers, as a result of ill health and old age, died a few days after their arrival. On the arrival of the third European storekeeper I was transferred to Fort Hall Store as a clerk in charge of Fort Hall Public Works Department Station. I worked there for a year. Mr. C. C. Cresswell, the Executive Engineer of the P.W.D. there, was very kind to me. He treated me very well and proposed to build me a nice house. At Fort Hall he built me a nice little corrugated iron sheet round house, the first of its kind in that part of the country. He trusted me in my work of responsibility. He gave me the charge of the Fort Hall store and P.W.D. Station there. On 29th December, 1910, I was stationed at Nairobi as tools and plants clerk in charge in the Executive Engineer's office. On 25th February, 1911, we got a son named Hugh Godfrey. On 15th April, 1911, I resigned. As the Director of P.W.D. stated in my certificate, 'I was becoming a very useful clerk when I elected to resign for the second time.' I was dissatisfied with the salary I was getting at the time, which was not equivalent to the responsible duty I was discharging when in Nyeri, Fort Hall and Nairobi. The Asiatic staff who were doing the same kind of work or less were paid better than the African staff.

I proceeded to Zanzibar, where I was employed as a private tutor to two European Government officials. In August 1911 I secured an employment in the Public Works Department, Uganda, as a workshops clerk. I left my wife and children with my parents at Mombasa and proceeded to Entebbe, Uganda, alone. The Uganda natives have their own native Government under the Kabaka or King; they have their own native Parliament and Treasury and courts; it is one of the most advanced native Governments in Africa. A few days after my arrival in

Uganda I got shocking news by telegram that my wife died at Mombasa. My heart was entirely broken and, although I liked my work in Uganda very much, yet I soon realized I would not be able to remain in that country alone after such tragic news. I had left my wife in a very good health at Mombasa and she took me to the railway station at Mombasa to see me off. I was really staggered by the sudden news of her death. She died eleven days after my arrival in Uganda.

In the workshops there were many Baganda apprentices, trained as carpenters and blacksmiths. I was very happy amongst them, and made several best friends. Prince Joseph of Kampala was a great friend of mine and so was Sosene Muinda, who is now a big chief near Kampala. I was afterwards transferred to the Store Department as a store clerk. On the departure of the Chief Storekeeper to England on leave, I acted as issuing clerk.

A friend of mine, Mr. J. Walker, a native of Sierra Leone, persuaded me to join the International Correspondence School of London. I chose the commercial course, for which I had to pay about £20 in instalments. I passed several subjects and the lessons were of immense benefit to me. I am sorry to say, owing to the intervention of war in 1914, I was cut off from communication and could not complete my course.

On 28th August, 1912, my mother died at Mombasa. It became impossible for me to remain any longer in Uganda owing to these two deaths of those very dear to me. I had already got an employment in the Government School, Zanzibar. On 20th September I resigned my post in the P.W.D. Entebbe and returned to Zanzibar via Mombasa. I was sorry to leave my service because the Director of Public Works was very much interested in my progress. I had worked under him at Mombasa and Nyeri, and he knew me since I started my work in the Drawing Department at Mombasa. He arranged to put me as an apprentice in the Drawing Section. He asked me to write to him about work again as soon as I had finished mourning at home. I am sorry I could not do it.

In the Government School, Zanzibar, there were over two hundred boys of various nationalities. The principal nationalities were Indians, Arabs and Swahilis. The headmaster was a Parsee; under him in the English classes was a Goan, and I was the third teacher. There were also several Arabic teachers under the Arabic schoolmaster. It is wonderful that this conglomeration of nationalities and teachers was always friendly. The school was and still is a very important one in Zanzibar. Boys belonging to the royal family and high Arab families were being educated in this school. As I am a Christian and this was a purely Mohammedan school, I was required not to teach the Christian religion or talk about it in the school. It is surprising that in this school there never were religious controversies even though it was the centre of Arabic and Koranic culture. There was no distinction among us except of rank, and Arab teachers never shunned me. We were always very friendly indeed. I cannot understand why this is seldom possible outside such an environment.

A certain teacher belonged to a noble Arab family, and had been educated at Beirut in a Roman Catholic College; his father had spent a considerable amount of money for his education. One day he told me that in the Beirut College he used to go to the college chapel. I at once stopped him talking about this as it was against the school order given to me. Another day as I was going to a classroom to teach I met him on the steps, and he said to me that he liked the Christian religion. I was thunderstruck and really I was on the horns of a dilemma. To prevent him from talking about Christ and his religion was to act against my religion; a soldier of the Church Militant would never retreat from such a situation, yet to encourage him to follow Christ was to break the school law. The only course remaining to me was to walk away without saying a word, and this I did. Whether he read what was written on my face or not, I do not know; but in the evening on my return from the football game I was struck to find all my furniture in one of my rooms had been removed to another room and new furniture had been substituted. I asked my servant who had done it. Suddenly to my great surprise I saw the teacher entering the room. I asked him what was the matter. He replied that he had fallen out with his father because he refused to go to the mosque to pray. I was perturbed; his father was a great friend of mine and I found it rather difficult to reconcile the situation. I could not send him away because I did not know where he would go to. There was no alternative but to force him to go to the mosque to pray, as he was ordered by his father. So I made it clear to him that I would not have him in my house unless he went to pray in the mosque, and asked his father for pardon. He argued. The next day I went to see his father over the matter. He was evidently very sorry to see me. The news of his son's stay at my house had already reached him. He took me to his inner room and told me he was very sorry and much upset about his son. He was surprised that I, who was a great friend of certain big Arabs and was much trusted by them to enter their houses and be introduced to their families, could break faith with them by enticing his son to become a Christian. I explained all the circumstances to him as they had occurred and undertook to return his son to him. I told him I had sheltered his son because I was afraid he would go astray. On my return home I spoke strongly to the teacher and made him return to his father. This brought me peace. I think I was right in the step I took. I could never make myself believe that a boy who was so unthankful to his father could make a good Christian. What actuated him on the spur of the moment to adopt a Christian faith was obscure to me. On the other hand I thought that if he really meant to become a Christian my action would not deter him. On this I was right, because he never talked about it to me again. I had had several experiences of the sort before of people who imagined they were called to become Christians and eventually discarded the religion after gaining their worldly aims.

The schoolboys were good, and we had a variety of types; the discipline was very strict. For lashing an Indian truant the headmaster was sued in the court by the father of the boy. But the Government defended the headmaster. A circular was issued to parents after that, to the effect that schoolboys were subject to school discipline and punishment and parents who wished their boys to remain in the school had to agree to this. My time in the school was always full. I was in charge of the football game; and had to coach, at their homes, Arab boys who were backward in their lessons. I also had to give Swahili lessons to Europeans after school hours. I liked the schoolwork and had many friends in the school and outside. My boys were getting on well.

On 9th January, 1914, I resigned the post in the Government School and went to the Bondei country to visit my relations and if possible do some trading. I thought I needed some more money to better my prospects. I got a passport from the German Consul at Zanzibar for myself and my daughter, and sailed to Tanga. At Handeni I took out a trading licence for which I was charged the 60 rupee fee paid by Indian traders for a similar business. The German District Commissioner at Handeni, after inspecting my certificates of service, said to me I was an intelligent man and should therefore pay the same fee as Indians. Natives paid 36 rupees for the same kind of trading licence. For the bigger licence I was asked to pay 100 rupees, other natives paid 60 rupees.

I made two trips in the interior, trading. On my second trip, whilst returning to Muheza, in the train at Korogwe I heard a rumour that there was war between the British and the Germans. Natives were talking about it. It was 2nd of August, 1914. On my arrival I hurried to the U.M.C.A. Station at Magila and reported the matter to my friend Mr. Russell. He did not believe me and said it was impossible for the British and the Germans to fight because they were friends and relations. I replied that I thought there was something in the rumour, and returned home. Then I heard the German troops were already on the move and Rev. Spanton, the Principal of Kiungani College, Zanzibar, who had come with his college boys from Zanzibar on vacation leave, had been arrested by Captain Hering and sent to Tanga under escort. This was the beginning of troubles.

The natives were much excited to hear about the occurrence of war between the British and the Germans. Some of them thought they had prophesied its occurrence. Why and how they thought so it is difficult to explain, but there were some who even predicted its outbreak that year. The news of its outbreak did not appear to be very astonishing and in a few days it was a commonplace talk. I could not get my way to Zanzibar or Mombasa, where my father was, and this was really bad for me and my daughter. Brother John (Rev. Williams), who had gone to Tanga to try and get a dhow for Zanzibar, was unsuccessful. All roads to Kenya had been closed. German troops were already at Tanga and Moshi. I then heard that English missionaries and planters had been arrested and escorted to Morogoro for internment. Rev. Keates and a few mission ladies were left at Magila Mission Station. My daughter was very ill at the time. She had a bad sore foot. I took her to Magila Mission for treatment. A false allegation was fabricated against Rev. Keates that he was signalling to the British men-of-war near Tanga from a hill near Magila by means of fire. It was the beginning of the persecution of the African Christians belonging to the U.M.C.A. I found my safety was jeopardized. Rev. Keates, mission ladies and African teachers of Magila were escorted to Morogoro, Kilimatinde and Tabora.

On 12th January, 1915, my turn came; I was sitting at the farm of my relation when I was called to the village, which was about fifteen miles inland from Tanga. Jumbe Omari of Umba, who was my nurse when I was a small boy, came to see me with a message from Akida Sengenge of Ngomeni; I was required by the District Commissioner at Muheza. We walked there together. The District Commissioner asked me what I was doing and if I intended going anywhere. I replied I was trading and produced my licence, which he took from me. I said I had no intention of proceeding anywhere. He asked me where I had come from and when. I replied I came from Zanzibar, and delivered my passport from the German Consul, Zanzibar. I was informed afterwards that certain persons had reported to him that I was a spy and had come into the country one month before the outbreak of the war from the Zanzibar Government. This was disproved by my passport from the German Consul, Zanzibar. He asked me if I was a British subject and could speak English. I replied in the affirmative. He then said I would be sent up country to stay there till the end of the war as I might create trouble in the place. I said I was not going to make any trouble and I had my trade property apart from my personal property, and what would happen to it? He said I would get it after the war, but I had to be sent up country to stay there till the war was over. I was then escorted to the prison. As I had only 20 rupees with me I asked my relations to send me another 80 rupees, in two instalments of 30 rupees and 50 rupees because I was afraid the German African soldiers might rob it from me if they knew I had money. They brought me 30 rupees and before I received the second instalment I was handcuffed with another Bondei Christian, named Geldert Mhina, and was escorted to Handeni. At the Muheza Station the German Assistant District Officer of Tanga abused us and said we would surely be shot because we were passing news to the British.

At Korogwe we had the most terrible time. As soon as we got there, it was about 2 p.m., we were put in a prison gang and despatched to carry sand till the evening. We used to work with criminals from 4 p.m. till 11 p.m. From 8 p.m. to 11 p.m. we carried ammunition boxes from the train to the Police Station. We had our meal only once a day, at 4 p.m.; the meal consisted of boiled maize. We were kept with criminals and treated as criminals. After six days we were escorted to Handeni together with the wounded British soldiers of the Lancashire Rifles who had been captured in the battle of Tanga. The British soldiers were carried in hammocks by the native prisoners of war. On the way the British soldiers were well treated. We were joined by the Korogwe English missionaries, including Bishop Birley and Brother John, with African teachers of the U.M.C.A. We marched together to Handeni. There we met in prison over one hundred African teachers of the U.M.C.A. and Rev. Canon Petro Limo, an old African priest. These were afterwards sent to Kondoa Irangi, where they were brutally treated in prison. Some of them died as the result of the most atrocious treatment meted out to them by the German officer of Kondoa Irangi and his African prison warders.

Our gang was sent to Kimamba. Some of us were made to carry the loads and hammocks of the English missionaries. I was fortunate to obtain a job of safari cook. I got myself engaged in this work in order to save myself from carrying loads and hammocks for nearly eleven days. I had never carried loads before in my life. I knew nothing about cooking as I had never done this work in my life, but I had to make the best of it. Having tasted European food while at Kiungani College and having often been dining with Miss Thackeray, etc., I had to form some idea as to how this food was cooked. It was a difficult job. For two days the cook of the German officer was doing the whole cooking and I was watching him. On the third day I was ordered to do everything myself. I do not know how I managed it, but somehow or other I made some sort of food which was fairly eatable. I remember one day I boiled three ox-tongues for three hours and yet they were as hard as a bone. I did not know the trick of getting them properly boiled. But to my surprise they were passed as eatable. I sometimes wondered if the food cooked by me could be eaten by anybody else other than missionaries. They probably knew I was not a cook and made concessions accordingly. I must have caused them bad stomachs, but I did not hear of any complaints. If I had cooked for the German officer I would surely have received some knocking for bad cooking.

When we got to Kimamba my work ceased. I contracted an acute dysentery on the way and at Kimamba my condition was worse. But I was cured by a German doctor at Kimamba. On our way to Kimamba the German African soldiers who were escorting us were treating our gang very badly. They made us run and lashed the stragglers. Bishop Birley very often had to rebuke them for this. It was the road of the Cross. At Kimamba we entrained for Tabora and the English missionaries detrained for Mpwapwa. On our arrival at Tabora Railway Station we were despatched to the Prisoners of War Camp. There we found Indian soldiers who had been captured at Tanga and Jassini, about two hundred of them, and some African teachers of the U.M.C.A. who had been sent there before us. These are the teachers who were together with Rev. Keates. They related to us that when they got to Tabora they were sent to gaol and kept with criminals. They were so very harshly treated that they thought not one of them would survive. They were made to hoe from morning to evening without lifting their backs, and whenever they tried to do so they were severely flogged. They were all in chains and slept with chains round their necks. They did everything in chains. At last their condition was so bad that they had to choose between life and death. One day when they were returning from their daily toil they met the German Chief Secretary on the way with his wife. Apparently his wife was French. The leader pulled the whole chain gang and approached the German Chief Secretary in spite of the threats from their escort. The Chief Secretary asked them what was the matter with them, and they told him they were brought from Muheza by the Government and they did not know why they were not tried but were put in gaol with criminals and treated worse than criminals. He said he would go into the matter and they would hear from him later. The result was they were transferred to the Prisoners of War

Camp and were promised a better treatment. They saved us and everybody who came after them.

The camp was guarded by German African soldiers. There was a separate camp for European prisoners of war. First we were detailed to carry building stones from a certain hill to the European camp, about a distance of two miles. We were made to run all the way with stones on our heads, an African soldier in charge was lashing those who were behind. He had a special order from the German officer to drive us and lash us. This order was given in our presence before we started the day's work. The time was really terrible for us and I remember a day when I was so exhausted that I was on the point of fainting. We had our meal once a day in the evening and had to cook it ourselves after we had been exhaustively fatigued and were very hungry. What frightened us most was the news that a Greek had been sentenced to death for having signalled to the British troops at Moshi by means of fire. He was shot. We were very dejected and could not tell what our fate would be.

During the first days we were not supplied with relish and had to live on bare cassava. We had to sleep on the open ground. Our drinking water was filthy. Buckets which were used for W.C. were afterwards used for our drinking water. It was not surprising when dysentery of the worst kind broke out in the camp. One-third of the Indian soldiers and about one-sixth of the native prisoners perished of it. On certain days we had to bury as many as six persons in one day. There was not a day that we did not bury someone. It was a camp of death.

A German doctor was appointed to the camp and a hospital was built near the camp. It was always full. The diet was then altered and two German officers were appointed in charge of our camp. These gentlemen were very good to us. I was first made one of the headmen of the camp. My duties were to supervise my fellow prisoners at work and in camp. Headmen had more than this to do. It fell to our lot to represent the grievances of the African prisoners to the Camp authorities. I was afterwards made a head mason. I learnt this work in camp. We had to build a brick house for German officers, and as my work was good I was soon promoted to the rank of head mason.

In the camp Geldart, my mate, and myself were in charge of camp construction work, and we built a very nice camp. Our clothes were worn out and we were not supplied with clothes or blankets by the German authorities. We had to contrive some means of obtaining clothing. Our food was brought in Americani bags, and we had to turn the bags into shirts and shorts. I was then transferred to the camp hospital as a hospital assistant. There I worked with Dr. Mohammedin and Dr. Kudrat Ali of the Indian Kashmir Rifles. They were both good men. Dr. Mohammedin was always helping his people very much. Dr. Moesta, a German Medical Officer in charge of the native hospital in town and our camp hospital, was exceptionally good. He did all he could to help the patients and poor people and I often saw him spending his own money to help them. He treated us very nicely indeed. Another German medical officer who was formerly in the man-of-war *Konigsberg* was also very good.

I was afterwards transferred with another African prisoner, Samwil Msumi, to the native hospital in town. My work was to look after patients in the wards and give them medicines and to help in the operation room. Samwil Msumi was doing microscopic work—colouring blood preparations, etc., for the doctor to examine by microscope. Dr. Moesta took the trouble to train us to examine germs found in blood, etc., of patients by microscope and to diagnose diseases. We could do this work eventually. He gave us a good medical training and we became very useful to him in the hospital. He often worked from 6 a.m. to 7 p.m. and was never tired. He visited each in-patient twice a day and examined personally every patient who came to the hospital for treatment. He could speak several European languages. Every one in our camp liked him.

The condition in our camp was ameliorated and the diet was improved. The work for prisoners was not so exacting as before. The buildings in our camp had to be extended by us, as we were getting more prisoners in the camp and the accommodation was insufficient.

I was very anxious to see my daughter, whom I had left at Magila with a bad foot. There was no sign of the ending of the war, and we did not know what our fate would be. We first thought the war would take only three or six months to end, or at most three years. Periodically we got news about the war through the Africans. It was wonderful how Africans could pass from mouth to mouth news about the war in Europe, which was perfectly correct. The news travelled so quickly that even cable and wireless could hardly compete. We heard about the approach to Paris by the German troops, the joining of the Turks on the side of the Germans, the death of Lord Kitchener, the arrival of General Smuts and his troops at Mombasa. Although the defeats of the German troops were kept strictly secret, they were soon known to the prisoners in the camp. How and by what means the news was obtained it was difficult to tell. Some of us were incredulous until the news was proved to be true on our release.

When the Belgian troops were near Tabora, some of the African prisoners were taken as porters for the German troops. In the hospital I met a British doctor who had been captured; I was ordered to take him to our camp for a visit. On the way I had a long conversation with him and I explained to him our position. I have seen a book written by him about the war in which he mentioned our meeting at Tabora. A German missionary was working in the hospital and was very kind. He took me one day into the doctor's room when no one was there and told me that he was very sorry that two friendly Christian nations were fighting against themselves and that we African Christians were persecuted by a Christian power. He then started weeping and said he hoped God would soon bring all this to an end. We then parted. He was always kind and good to every one and never said a harsh word. He was very sorry for Archdeacon Woodward of the U.M.C.A., who was at the time in the European Prisoners' Camp at Tabora. It was arranged for the Roman Catholic priest to visit us once a week and preach to us, and we had to go to the Catholic church on Sundays. Bishop Leonard of the Catholic Mission, Tabora, was very good to us. Afterwards Archdeacon Birley (the present Bishop) was allowed to come to our camp under escort to hear our confession. On the first day the German European soldier who escorted him to the camp wanted to hear what the African Christians confessed to the Archdeacon. He bade him that they should speak audibly for him to hear. Evidently he suspected that they were telling him something in connection with the war or he was passing war news to them. The Archdeacon retorted that he could not divulge what was said to him in confession, what he heard in confession was sealed and couldn't be given out to anybody.

So such was our state in prison. We had neither bodily nor spiritual peace. On a certain occasion on Sunday after we left church we went to the market, and whilst returning to the camp with our escort we passed the European camp where the Commandant of the Prison Camps had his office. He saw us passing and asked us where we had been. The escort replied that we were coming from the market. He said he would come to the camp to hear the case. Directly we got to the camp we reported the matter to the officer in charge of the camp. He said we should not have passed near the European camp. He had no objection to our going to the market, but he knew the Commandant was not good. We did not know that the Commandant would find fault with our going to the market. In a moment the Commandant arrived at the camp and saw a prisoner peeping through the hospital window. He ordered him to be given five lashes. We were all brought before him and he inquired as to who originated the plan of our going to the market. There was some dispute between two prisoners, each one of them contending that the other started the plan. The Commandant could not waste more time over it, and in fact he did not mind who got the punishment; it was sufficient to him that someone got it. So the last speaker of the two was ordered to be given fifteen lashes. The Abyssinian Sergeant administered the strokes. When he got to three strokes the Commandant thought he didn't lay the strokes firmly, so he ordered that a strong man should do it, and a cruel Indian prisoner snatched the hippo stick from the sergeant and hit the prisoner with all his might.

When the Belgians were near Tabora, Dr. Moesta, who was in charge of the Civil, and Prisoners of War, Hospitals at Tabora, got permission from the Governor for me and Samwil Msumi to remain with him in the hospital when our prison mates were removed from Tabora to an unknown destination. On Tuesday, September 19th, the Belgians entered Tabora at 12 noon. In the morning Dr. Moesta asked me to select twelve of my friends to remain with me at the hospital. It was a special favour, but most difficult to put into action for the simple reason that I had many friends in the camp, and to select some and leave the others to suffer was the worst betrayal of friendship. Those who were to be removed from Tabora courted death at every minute and to let one be removed was tantamount to condemning him to death. I did what was humanly possible in such matters. One of my friends whom I could not save was actually crying when he was leaving me for the bush. No sooner had they left than Dr. Moesta came to me again and said to me I could select as many of my friends as I wished to remain with me in the hospital. Alas! It was too late, I could not do it as they had already gone.

African teachers were left behind with the European missionaries. We could not work in the hospital as it was contemplated because the Belgian African soldiers burnt the hospital near the camp and looted the property of the patients. They also burnt our camp. They pillaged some of the native properties and took away with them some of the wives and daughters of the natives. It was unsafe for women to walk about. They committed several atrocities in the native town. The whole town was thrown into chaos. We had to go to where the English missionaries stayed. I saw Dr. Moesta the next day and I told him I could not work in the hospital owing to the state of affairs at that time. The whole town was in chaos. Business was disorganized and the native inhabitants were panic-stricken. Food was commandeered by the Belgian military authorities. It was unsafe for natives to walk about in the town. The Belgian native soldiers were a terror to the native inhabitants of the town. Wherever the Belgian troops passed in the country there was desolation and privation.

On the 1st October, 1916, I left Tabora with the European missionaries and African teachers to go to Kisumu, where we were kindly received by the Kavirondo Christians. This excellent reception was arranged by Bishop Willis of Uganda. From Kisumu we went to Nairobi. Here we were well received by the British Red Cross Staff. At Nairobi I suddenly became very ill indeed. My old friends took me to their house and nursed me until I was well again. They nearly gave up all hopes of my recovery. I then travelled to Mombasa and was very glad to see my father, sister, brother-in-law and son.

When I reached Tanga I applied for work at the Political Office. The District Political Officer engaged me as interpreter as from 1st February, 1917. I had to work for the Police and in Court. There was much work in the Political and Police Offices at the time because the country was not quite settled up from the effects of the war. However, the work was good.

On 6th October I married pupil-teacher Dorothy Mary Mnubi of the Mbweni Girls' School, Zanzibar. Her parents are Zanzibarians and her home is Zanzibar. Her father, mother and eldest sister had been to England and received some education there.

In 1918 we had to work to raise money for the British Red Cross. Europeans, Arabs, Asiatics and natives all contributed handsomely to the fund. I hired the Tanga Cinema and raised 373 rupees for the fund. My wife put to auction one native dish cover which was worth a shilling and it fetched 40 rupees. A fête was arranged and several thousands of rupees were collected for the Red Cross. Tanga was animated by the Red Cross work and over 35,000 rupees was collected for the fund. The Africans were very keen on helping and I can certainly say that Tanga was never so happy as in those days. The natives liked very much the new regime because forced labour, flogging and oppression from German native soldiers had gone and they were anticipating a rule of justice and fair play for all subjects. The work in the Political Office was good and the officers were doing their best to help the Africans by every conceivable means. We had the arduous work of collecting porters and detecting the deserters from the military. In 1918 I was transferred to the Political Office as interpreter and clerk. In 1919 I was promoted to a correspondence clerk and typist in place of an Indian clerk. On 15th August, 1919, I got a daughter named Louisa Beatrice Mary.

On 11th November, 1918, it was Armistice Day. Everyone was very glad to see the end of the great war was drawing nigh. From 19th to 21st July, 1919, we held Peace Celebrations. A big feast and sports were made to celebrate the occasion. There was a great rejoicing everywhere on that great day.

On 1st September, 1923, P. E. Mitchell, Esq., M.C., Acting Senior Commissioner at Tanga, started to run the District Office with entirely African staff. I was made head clerk. The work was rather difficult in the beginning because most of the clerks were new to the work. It was due to the efforts of Messrs. P. E. Mitchell and F. W. C. Morgans that the whole scheme became a success. In the beginning we always had to work from 7 a.m. to 7 p.m. without an interval for midday meal. We were bent to make the scheme a success. We were the first Africans in the whole of East Africa including Kenya, Uganda and Zanzibar to be trusted with such a responsible work. The morale of the African clerks was exceptionally good and every clerk was scrupulously honest. Our office collected £40,000 per annum, and the whole of the accounting for this money was done by a few African clerks, who had in addition to attend to administrative and clerical work. It has been proved that Africans can do the work if they are only patiently controlled.

We built our own Club building. It was the centre of much progress socially and in sports. Several distinguished officers visited our Club and gave donations. One gave us a football ground which the Club had to clear and put in order. The Club started the football game in Tanga and now there are several African football teams. It was the intention of the Club to start a library in the Club building, but owing to lack of funds this scheme was impracticable. The late Bishop F. Weston was invited to the Club and was very pleased to see something at last had been done which he never thought he would see, and that was Christians and Mohammedans, Africans and Arabs joining together as members of the association, and all being very friendly. Religion is the matter for the heart and must come first, but it does not prevent members of one religious community from combining with members of another religious community. I firmly believe that Africans will never progress well unless they realize the necessity for unity. A great deal of our progress rests with us. We cannot move if we do not wish to move together.

In 1928 I was appointed as a member of the Provincial Committee on African Education. In 1929 I was appointed a member of the Advisory Committee on African Education for the Territory. I have much advocated education for girls. In Africa, where the great majority of the Africans are uneducated, the education for girls is very important indeed and will help considerably the progress of the boys' education. The mother is the guide of her children. If she is educated there will be very few children who will not go to school and the hygiene at home will be thoroughly observed. Childbirth and child welfare will be better understood at home. African homes will be improved. We lack at present the co-operation of African women in social affairs and education. Their influence is very great and precious, but it has not been used, for lack of female education.

In church, I was appointed churchwarden from 1917. Our church was too small for the congregation and we decided to extend it. African Christians contributed fairly well towards the fund in proportion to their income, and our church has now been enlarged. The condition of Christians in Tanga is different to that of up-country Christians. We have a floating population and conditions are somewhat difficult, but on the whole we are progressing. The population of Tanga town is about 7,000 natives of mixed tribes. For most of them Tanga is not their home; they have migrated from the hinterland to Tanga in search of work, and return to their homes up country as soon as they have made some money; some of them come to Tanga periodically for work and return to their homes during the cultivation and planting season. Tanga, being a town, offers the Christians many temptations which they are not likely to meet with in their own tribal homes.

Early in 1931 I was appointed as a witness from Tanganyika to the Joint Parliamentary Committee on East Africa. The story of my visit to England forms the next part of this autobiography.

## Part II

## My Visit to England

Since 1924 there had been a rumour in East Africa about the proposed federation of the East African Territories, *i.e.* Kenya Colony, Uganda Protectorate and Tanganyika Territory.

The Ormsby-Gore Commission was sent out in 1924. It toured through the East African Territories and eventually made its report on the matter. The Hilton-Young Commission was sent out to East Africa in 1927 on the same question and made its report, as the result of which the Joint Committee on Closer Union of the East African Territories was appointed in England, composed of members of the Houses of Lords and Commons, to make further inquiry into the matter. The Joint Committee required witnesses to be sent to England to give evidence before the Committee on the subject, and for the first time in the history of the British Empire, and East Africa in particular, three Africans were required from each of the three territories of East Africa, *i.e.* Kenya, Uganda and Tanganyika Territory, to go to England to give evidence to the Honourable Committee, on behalf of ten million natives inhabiting these territories.

The following were selected to represent Tanganyika: Chief Makwaya, K.M., of Shinyanga, Mwami Lwamgira, K.M., of Bukoba, Mr. H. M. T. Kayamba of Tanga (the writer).

The Tanganyika African delegates left Dar-es-Salaam by S.S. *Francisco Crispi* on 30th March, 1931, together with P. E. Mitchell, Esq., M.C., Secretary for Native

Affairs, and O. Guise-Williams, Esq., District Officer. Chief Makwaya was accompanied by his son-in-law, Makoni.

Two of us were Christians and two Mohammedans. Christians have no difficulty in sailing by European steamers and to European countries, as they can eat any food cooked for European tables. But there was a small point to clear regarding the food of our Mohammedan colleagues. Chief Makwaya and Makoni are staunch Mohammedans and were very particular about food. Mr. Mitchell arranged with the District Commissioner at Mombasa for Chief Makwaya to consult with Sir Ali bin Salim, K.B.E., C.M.G., of Mombasa in order to remove the scruple from his mind about food.

On 31st March we arrived at Mombasa; the first thing we did was to drive by taxi to the District Commissioner to see Sir Ali bin Salim. The District Commissioner took us to Sir Ali bin Salim, who kindly invited us into his office. After the matter had been explained to him, he told Chief Makwaya that Mohammedans are not forbidden by their religion to eat food cooked by Christians or meat of animals killed by Christians or Jews, because Christians have the Gospel (Injili) and Jews have the Deuteronomy (Torati). Both these books come from God. He had been to England himself for one year and during that period ate the same food which Europeans ate. The only meat which a Mohammedan is forbidden to eat is pork, and he strongly warned Chief Makwaya that they should not touch it. In confirmation of what he had said he was willing to come on board S.S. *Francisco Crispi* to lunch with us. We were very pleased to invite him to lunch. At 12 noon he arrived on board and had lunch with us. At 4 p.m. he kindly sent his car to take us round Mombasa Island, and we enjoyed the trip very much. Sir Ali bin

Salim is famous for his hospitality and charity to all races in Kenya Colony.

Kenya Native delegates embarked on board the steamer on 1st April. Arab delegates also embarked on the same day. Our steamer left Mombasa at 12.30 p.m. for Kismayu. We left Kismayu at 2.30 the same day and arrived at Mogdishu at 7.30 a.m. on 3rd April—Good Friday. We landed at Mogdishu and strolled round the town. The Roman Catholic Cathedral there is a fine building. The native village is rather poor and filthy, especially the market place. There is no shed for the market, and natives have to sell their goods on a sandy place. Some of them stick dirty pieces of clothes on pieces of wood as shelters for themselves and their commodities. The Governor's palace is a fine building. The Sultan or Sheik of Somalis has his residence here.

We left Mogdishu at 5 p.m. on 4th April for Hafun. On board there were always cinema shows in the evenings and music. We were very well treated on board. On the 6th we arrived at Hafun.

On the 9th we arrived at Massawa. It is a fine port belonging to the Italian Eritrea. There is a fine pier, and our steamer was berthed alongside it. An Italian man-of-war was at the harbour. The natives of this town are mixed—Arabs, Abyssinians, Danakil, etc. There are nice buildings of stone for Europeans and natives. This is a sign of the wealthiness of the natives of this town. Chief Makwaya made friends with one wealthy Egyptian who invited him to his house and made him a nice dinner, and gave him a present of a beautiful fez. He offered to pay his expenses to Mecca on pilgrimage, but the Chief was unable to accept his kind offer. When Chief Makwaya told me this, I was doubtful if the man was genuine and was not one of the slave dealers enticing the Chief to go to

Mecca and on the way dispose of him to Arabian slave dealers on the Persian Gulf.

At daybreak on the 14th we arrived at Suez and at 9 a.m. entered the canal. Here we were shown the Sinai Mountains, where Prophet Moses received the tablets containing the ten Commandments.

Ismalia is a fine town. I saw the monument erected to commemorate the defence of the canal during the Great War. On the eastern side of the canal palm groves and cultivated land can be seen. It is said that this country belongs to the Biblical land of Goshen where Patriarch Jacob and his children settled. Here also traces of the ancient canal of the Pharaohs have been discovered. We were shown the supposed track of the Israelites crossing through the Bitter Lakes. El Kantara (the bridge) in the olden days was an important place of caravans between Egypt, Palestine and Syria. It is related that probably Abraham and his sons spent a few days at El Kantara on their way to Egypt. We arrived at Port Said at 12 midnight. Port Said is a fine port. On this day it was decorated with electric lights in honour of the Egyptian Prime Minister, Sidky Pasha, who visited Port Said on the same day.

This is the western gateway of the canal. At the entrance of the harbour there is the statue of Ferdinand de Lesseps, the builder of the canal. Some of us landed and saw very little of the town, as it was night time. This was the last port of Africa on our journey and we were now sailing through the Mediterranean Sea. Up to this port we enjoyed a fine voyage except for the heat in the Red Sea.

The sea after leaving Port Said was rough. Two or three of our colleagues were seasick and unable to touch food.

On the 18th we sighted the island of Stromboli which has a volcanic mountain. We could see the smoke issuing from the peak of the volcano. The town is built on the sides of the hill, which looks like a man sitting on the furnace. All of us were amazed to see the inhabitants of this volcanic island living around the volcano with ease and happiness and without any fear of the possible eruption. We were told that vine trees are grown on the island and the soil is very fertile, which may be the inducement to the inhabitants to hazard their living on the volcano.

On the 11th at 3.30 p.m. we arrived at Naples. It is a big town and a nice harbour. We could see the volcanic mountain Vesuvius. We were first shown the Cathedral, which is said to have been formerly the temple of Minerva, the Roman Goddess. We saw many fine statues in the public gardens. The buildings are of fine stones and beautiful in appearance. There is a big glass house and in the night it is illuminated with electric lights of multi-colours. This town is very beautiful and clean. The harbour is surrounded with a breakwater. There are electric tramways; horse-carts are still used for carrying passengers and are very cheap. This was the first big town of its size we had seen since we left East Africa.

At 6 a.m. on the 20th we arrived at Livorno. It is a small harbour, which has a canal going into the town. Two submarines, one Italian dreadnought, four British destroyers and about four Italian cruisers were lying in the harbour. A seaplane was flying over the harbour, and a ship was on construction. We did not land to see the town as time was too short.

At 3.30 p.m. the same day we arrived at Genoa. There were many ships in the harbour. I counted nearly two hundred ships at various docks. This is an old Italian port and its merchants are famous. It was the birthplace of Christopher Columbus, the old explorer who discovered Mexico. The Customs House is beautiful. Here we saw many Alpine soldiers having come down for a holiday. Several launches were carrying them for a picnic. On seeing them, Chief Makwaya was greatly astonished and remarked: 'At home they ask for men when they are themselves men'! He meant in Africa they ask for working men to serve them but here they are workers themselves. This sudden exclamation caused me to laugh, and turning to my right I beheld a European from East Africa, who understood Swahili; he also heard Chief Makwaya's remarks, and laughed. Apparently the chief had in his mind a picture of a few Europeans in Tanganyika employing African labourers and never doing any handiwork themselves; when he now contrasted it with what he saw at the pier he was amazed. The crowd at the pier was evidently enjoying itself. They had band and music of all sorts and were playing and singing to their hearts' desire.

Here we had to show our passports. It was the end of our sea voyage between Africa and Europe except for the English Channel. We landed and were motored to the hotel Astoria, where we were not allowed to go out. Tanganyika delegates were lodged in one room and Kenya in the other. The hotel is grand and very nice. We could reach our rooms by the lift.

The next morning we left by train at 9.15 for Paris. All the way we found nice farms and excellent roads. The peasant buildings are small and some of them are very poor. It is within the means of the Africans to build such cottages provided they are properly trained to build them themselves. Some of the roads are narrower than our roads in Africa, and some villages have paths similar to the usual African paths. The size of some of these farms is in most cases the same as that of African farms. Probably the only difference lies in the method of cultivation, which is highly superior to the African's, and therefore the quantity of crops is comparatively greater in Europe than in Africa, for the same size of a farm. I much admired the terrace cultivation on the Alps mountains; the ground in many cases is stony, but this defect does not preclude the Italian farmers from making a good use of every bit of land. I was thinking of the natives of the western part of the island of Zanzibar in Chwaka area. That part of the island is very stony and the natives have to use wooden hoes in cultivation and planting of their crops. If these people had come to Italy and seen the Alpine peasants they could no doubt improve their method of cultivation on stony land. Farms are dotted about on stony patches on the Alps and snow is flowing right up to the foot of these big mountains. The reproach that Africans are scratching the land to grow a few crops is here disproved. Peasantry cultivation in Europe did not appear to me to be dissimilar to that of the African, so far as the sizes of the farms are concerned. The construction of farm houses is different, but some of the peasant buildings in Europe are not up to the mark that one expected. So there are weak points everywhere in comparison to the degree of civilization. Undoubtedly the farms throughout those parts of Italy and France we passed are excellent in cultivation and planting and are beautiful to look at.

Modane being the frontier of France and Italy, we had to show our passports to the French authorities prior to our entering the French country. The next morning we arrived at the southern station of Paris. It was very cold that morning, and streams of people were pouring into Paris from the towns outside Paris to work. We disembarked and had our breakfast at the station restaurant. We then motored through broad streets of Paris to the northern station. The superb buildings lined on each side of the streets were most imposing and pleasant to the eye.

It was a great pity that we could not see much of this famous city.

At 8.25 a.m. our train steamed off the Paris station. The farms of France are very beautiful and are scattered all along the railway line to Boulogne. Pretty farm cottages are built here and there. Fat cows and fowls are to be seen in these farms. The sizes of farms are about the same as in Italy and Africa, the difference as in Italy is in the way they are kept. We all thought it would be a valuable lesson to Africans to come to these countries and see how farms are kept, and acquire an object lesson. One can learn much more by seeing the actual work done than by reading from books.

The English Channel was calm that day, so we had a fine sailing to Folkestone where we arrived at 1.25 p.m. The Folkestone harbour appears to be rather exposed to rough weather during storms. Mr. Mitchell told us that we would find England to be a very clean country and this was perfectly true. We landed and showed our passports to the authorities. Mr. Mitchell through his great kindness arranged for us to travel first class from Folkestone to London. We had our lunch on the train. The English train travels very fast without shaking, and we enjoyed it very much. On the way we saw nice English farms, some of them with best poultry and livestock. Hops, apples, cherries and peaches are grown in these farms. Some of the farms are not big and are similar in size to those of France and Italy, but the agriculture, as in France and Italy, is superior. The soil is fertile and watery. Hedges form boundaries of farms and partitions of farms and pasture-land. Farms are kept thoroughly clean everywhere.

At Victoria Station several gentlemen were present to meet us, also ladies were there. Newspaper men were present. Of those present I knew Mr. and Mrs. McGregor

Ross, Mr. and Mrs. Buckley, Mr. Surridge, Archdeacon Owen, Rev. Canon Leakey and Dr. Leakey. We were introduced to Mr. Harris, Secretary of the Anti-Slavery and Aborigines Protection Society, and other ladies and gentlemen. Mr. and Mrs. Fazan were also present.

One thing struck me most at the first appearance, it was brick buildings. In the parts of England where I had been I saw they used bricks more than stones. On inquiry I was told the brick buildings are cheaper, and in that part of England there are not many stones to be found. It is true, on our way from Folkestone to London we did not see many stones, but we saw much chalk at places. What caused me much surprise was, all my informants of England never mentioned to me that bricks were much used there for building purposes, although they are not so much used in Africa. One gentleman told me he did not like brick buildings. In the vicinity of the railway stations in London the buildings are black on account of smoke. This I expected to see because I had read and heard about it. I think it is more in France than in London. The passages in French trains and lavatories are sooty. Third-class carriages in France are no better than third-class carriages of the Tanganyika Railways. Some of the delegates thought the buildings in African towns were cleaner in appearance than some of the buildings in European towns owing to smoke. In London buildings are too close together and compact. African huts are built separately with open spaces between them. The compactness of buildings in English towns and European towns is probably due to less building spaces available in those towns, which is not the case in Africa, except in few cases of coastal Arab towns like Zanzibar.

To return to my narration of our reception at the Victoria Station. We were very well received and we soon saw that we had many friends or at least people who were sympathetic with our cause. Mr. McGregor Ross I knew in Kenya when I was a boy of fifteen years of age. I served in his department as a tracer in the Drawing Department and afterwards as a store clerk.

We cleared our kit from the luggage room and got ready to start to our new home in London. We were very sorry to part with Mr. Mitchell, who was kind to us all and rendered us every assistance in his power during our whole journey to London. About 5 p.m. we left Victoria Station for Hitherwood, Sydenham Hill. We stayed at the International Hostel. It was very cold at the time and we had to make the best of the new climate. At first it was very trying indeed. I was provided with six blankets yet I felt as if I had no blanket on me. Fortunately we soon got used to the climate and felt quite at home.

Mr. Fazan showed us our rooms. Each one was allotted a separate bedroom, except Chief Makwaya and Makoni shared one room and Headman Mutua and Mr. Ezekiel Apindi shared another. My room was No. 16, this number I had to mark on my clothes and napkins, etc. A big hall was provided for our exclusive use as a sitting-room and dining-room. The building is three-storeyed and very comfortable. There were three Indians staying in the hostel and several Europeans of various nationalities. The other visitors told us that at times Africans from America and other parts of Africa stay at the hostel. We liked the place because the company was friendly and obliging.

Mr. Fazan explained to us the arrangements that had been prepared for us to see various places. The only difficulty was that before leaving Africa we were promised to be paid 21/- per diem for our food plus free accommodation. On this account the Kenya delegates thought the money would suffice for all their expenses. On the way and when we got to England we were informed that the whole matter of our allowance had been altered. The allowance was to be retained by the Government and all our expenses would be defrayed by the Government. As we were unprepared for this it spelt difficulty to some of the delegates who had not made provision for the financial emergency. The situation was explained to Mr. Fazan, who kindly took up the matter with the Colonial Office, and it was arranged to pay us an allowance of 8/- per diem for out-of-pocket expenses and 2/- for theatres and cinemas. The latter amount was kept by Mr. Fazan. As I did not attend any cinema or theatre during the stay at Sydenham this allowance was not expended by me.

It was arranged that we should be accompanied with officers whilst going out as we were strangers and did not know London streets. The London streets are so many and so intricate that it is very difficult for a stranger to find his way to any place. A stranger can get to a place by the aid of a cabman, who can take one to any place if he is told the address. I was informed that no cabman can get a driving licence unless he knows most places in London. It would be easy for any one to lose his way in London, and it would take him a long time to learn. A guide-book can be procured showing all London streets, but even this is of little help, as the streets are so many and intricate like a cobweb. A reverend gentleman who is living in the centre of London told me that he did not know streets of some parts of London.

It was questioned several times by the members of the Committee if Swahili was a suitable lingua franca for East Africans. The Baganda delegate was against the introduction of Swahili language in their country. However, here at Sydenham, Swahili proved its usefulness. First we were six different tribes staying at Hitherwood—Sukuma, Ziba, Kilindi, Kikuyu, Kamba and Kavirondo. If it were not for Swahili it would have been impossible for some of us to understand each other except those who understood English, and these were not all. When Uganda delegates arrived we had three more different tribes added to our number—Baganda, Banyoro and Basoga. While travelling by the Italian boat and passing through Italy and France we had to speak with Italians and French by gestures as we did not understand their language. I remember after passing Modane a French soldier sat with us in our carriage and was anxious to talk with us; we did not understand French, but thanks to his knowledge of German he could talk with Mwami Lwamgira who understands German. After that a charming French gentleman entered our carriage and we travelled with him up to Lyons; with the greatest difficulty we could understand each other a little by gestures, but it was tiresome to draw any meaning from them so we had to drop it and sleep. At Hitherwood Swahili made us great friends and we were happy together there through its knowledge.

There is a ping-pong game at Hitherwood and some of us tried to learn it. We were quite at home there, in the evenings we arranged our seats around the fire and enjoyed our evening conversation discussing what we had seen during the day and what we expected to see the following morning.

Sydenham being situated on a hill was rather colder than the central London. So no sooner had we taken our bath and changed our dresses than we dashed to the sitting-room to warm ourselves by the fire. We usually had our breakfast at this time. At 8 a.m. we were at the station waiting for our London train. The way to the station from

Hitherwood is steep and slippery during the rainy season. Near the station at the top on the side of the road we met two men with a harmonium. One of them was playing the harmonium and the other was collecting pennies in his cap given as charity or in exchange for the music which the passers-by were not enjoying. Apparently these men were poor, begging by means of music. In Zanzibar and Mombasa, Arab beggars go about playing cymbals and singing and visit every door begging. I remember when I was in Zanzibar, one of these professional beggars was said to possess about 500/- but was still begging. To him it was a profession and not due to poverty. At Mombasa it was said some of these beggars were very rich and owned shops which were managed by members of their family. At Sydenham we soon got used to these two people and not once or twice we dropped a few pennies into the cap of the collector, until we found it was a daily business.

At the station the train came very fast. It was an electric train and stopped only for a minute. Every one of us had to dash into a carriage near at hand and in about ten minutes we arrived at Victoria Station. Passengers in the train are invariably polite and kind. Railway fares are higher in England than in Africa.

At Victoria station we were shown lavatories and these cost a penny to use. The door of each lavatory has a slot into which a user drops a penny, and sesame! door opens. We have no such system in Africa and I wondered what happened to those who had no penny to drop in. Near the lavatories outside there is a man with his brush ready to clean any boot or shoe that is produced to him on payment of one penny. This is another proof of cleanliness which we lack in Africa.

It was raining heavily on that day so it was not possible for us to see the change of guard, moreover His Majesty was sick at Windsor and we were told there would be no band on that day. So we hurried to the Colonial Office. On the way, for the first time, we saw what a heavy traffic the London streets carry. Thousands and thousands of motor vehicles of all sorts were passing to and fro. Horse carts are also still used in London and other parts of England for carrying loads. Pedestrians walk in thousands on sidewalks.

It is impossible to walk slowly in London as we walk in Africa. We soon found we had to run most of the way or walk very fast. This in itself was a bit of an exerting experience to us. Those Africans who think that England is a place of leisure and pleasure would be surprised to see people hustling and bustling in the London streets. Children, young and old all walk very fast in London. People in England are more active than in Africa and look younger and with more vigour. Mr. Fazan took us from place to place through underground railways, and here again we saw for the first time the moving staircase. Some of the delegates were afraid to step on the moving staircase and did not know whether to walk down or stand still while the staircase was moving, and when they got to the bottom they did not know whether they should jump off the staircase or walk out, either seemed to them dangerous, as they are a puzzling problem to a newcomer. The underground trains run very fast and stop at stations for only about a second. One day we caught a wrong train owing to its swiftness; it hardly gives one time to make inquiries about its destination. All these things and many others were a new experience to us.

The Colonial Office and other Government offices are situated near the Cenotaph in big buildings. At the Cenotaph there were always new wreaths placed. The Trafalgar Square is another junction of streets where innumerable numbers of people pass to and fro. The house of the Prime Minister is opposite the Colonial Office; it is not a big building. Many Prime Ministers have lived in this house. The Buckingham Palace is a majestic and imposing building. The fountains in front of it are very beautiful indeed. I especially liked to see the stone lions with the fountain water passing through their mouths. The whole place is attractive. Every one of us gazed upon the palace with awe and veneration. There was always a large crowd of people coming to see the Buckingham Palace, the change of guards and the movements of guards on duty. I wondered for how long those spectators have been pouring to view this majestic building and for how long will they continue doing it! To an African such a scene is most attractive and appeals more to his veneration and estimation than to other people. He is by nature an adorer.

For the first time we had our lunch at the 'Lyons'. The place is grand and nice. We were taken up by the lift, and were placed at a nice and clean table. The Lyons Restaurant is always full and thousands and thousands of people have their meals here at one time. There are several storeys to this building. Band was playing and we were enjoying the best meal to the tune of the band. We were served by maid servants who were quick and dexterous at their duties.

That morning we had been at some shops to buy overcoats and some clothes. We first went to the Army and Navy Stores, which is a large shop building. It has a department for every kind of article or group of articles, and we were taken by the lift to various sections of this shop. We also visited Messrs. Austin Reed's shop to buy suits of clothes. Whilst shopping at Austin Reed's a newspaper journalist came and saw Chief Koinange and Mr. Ezekiel Apindi selecting their overcoats. He asked them some questions and then went and made a funny report about us in the issue of that day. To our disgust we read the news that evening, most of which was incorrect. Most of the delegates were very sorry to see this, and it was arranged not to speak to newspaper journalists again.

At 2 p.m. we visited St. Thomas's Hospital. It is a beautiful range of buildings on the Albert Embankment, facing the Houses of Parliament. We were taken to one section where we saw an apparatus for causing fever in order to diagnose certain diseases; some delegates had it tried on them and they felt fever instantly. In the children's ward, sick children looked very cheerful and healthy. Two picture plates on two sides of the room were presented to the hospital by Emperor Menelik and King Ras Tafari of Abyssinia. Miss Florence Nightingale who founded in June 1860 a school for nurse-training to this hospital came. Now nursing is fully recognized as an integral part of modern medical and surgical treatment. We fully appreciated the most valuable work that was done to humanity in that great hospital. The gentlemen who took us round were very kind to us. The principal doctor in bidding us farewell said he was very pleased to have had such intelligent visitors to show them the hospital. Chief Makwaya on our behalf thanked him and the other gentlemen who were so kind to show us everything of interest. The hospital was a real lesson to us as we had never seen such a big hospital before. The outpatients have a special department for their treatment. It would be many years before we could get anything like a quarter of such a hospital in Africa, especially in the case of African patients. African money spent on such an institution would be worthy of the cause and expenditure. We need more medical services in Africa and proper hospitals with up-to-date appliances for African patients. A beginning has been made and we anticipate the full realization of the worthy object. The system in England is for such hospitals to be maintained by charitable funds. In Africa this would not be possible for generations, as the vast majority of the African people do not understand the benefit of the European medical treatment. They still think that their medicines are good or at least as useful as Europeans'. It is therefore necessary that hospitals should be provided by the Government from the African taxation.

On the morning of the 24th we went to the Mint. The officers of the department kindly met us and took us round. We were shown various processes of coining. Everything here is done methodically and with faultless accuracy within human ability. The Director of the Mint was very pleased to see us and told us that our East African shillings were coined in his department. He said very little silver was used in coining them and asked us to make representation to our Governments to have them recoined and more silver added to them. He said the Nigerians have better coins because their Government paid more for them. We were sorry we could not make such representation to our Governments as suggested by him, although after hearing his advice we would have been very pleased to carry out his advice and thereby obtain better coinage if possible, but the fact that we do not deal in such matters in our countries was explained to him. We bade him good-bye and thanked him for the great kindness shown to us by the officers of his department and himself.

We then went straight to the London Tower, but as we were late by a few minutes, the Governor of the Tower was unable to receive us and show us round himself that day. So it was arranged for his officers to take us round. We were shown the most important historical places in the Tower and ancient armaments, all of which were of much interest to us. What terrified us most was the block and the axe which were used in the olden days for beheading noble traitors, etc. In those days poor people were hanged and nobles were beheaded for treason at the will of the King. The armaments started from bows and arrows, the most primitive weapons of the people of the world, and then axes and the first primitive guns. In those days the Europeans were using the same kind of weapons as the majority of the African people of our days. The sight of these weapons instantly brought to our mind the common origin of humanity. We appreciated the progress made by the European nations from bows and arrows to big guns, aircraft and submarines; all these deadly weapons of today have had their humble origin. When one leaves the Tower and goes straight to Portsmouth and Woolwich, he sees what a vast progress has been made in the art of armaments by the English nation. It would be impossible otherwise to understand the change or even to believe it.

The next item was to see crowns, sceptres, swords, etc. of His Majesty the King and crowns of Her Majesty the Queen and H.R.H. the Prince of Wales. The great and famous diamond 'Koh-i-noor' is also there, and various medals and brilliant crosses. The whole place is resplendent with the lustre and brilliancy of these priceless jewels. Several visitors were there to see them.

We were shown the place where two young princes were thrown to the ground from the Tower by order of the King in the olden days. The story is horrible and very sad to hear. We thanked the officers and walked to the Lyons for lunch.

At 2 p.m. we went to the Tower Pier and embarked on board S.S. *St. Katharine*, a fine steamer. Before we reached the Tower Bridge, the bridge was raised mechanically and we passed through under it.

It was through the great kindness of the Port of London Authority that we were invited to see these great docks; and the gentlemen who took us round by this steamer were very kind to us.

At 4.15 p.m. we had tea in the fine saloon on board. Our head host then delivered a nice address to us, in which he said he hoped that our country would send more goods to the London Port to the prosperity of both countries. He explained to us what a big port London is and that it handles a very large volume of cargo. This we saw ourselves with our own eyes and could not compare it with anything we had seen before. Chief Makwaya replied to him on our behalf and thanked him most highly for the very great kindness they had done to us and the most wonderful view we had had of the greatest port in the world.

It really gave us the true idea of the greatness of London and the huge bulk of cargo it handled. Before us was one length of port the end of which we could not see. We saw docks everywhere.

This was one of the most magnificent scenes we saw and we were much pleased with it. We thanked the authorities very highly for their unspeakable kindness to us.

On the 25th April we travelled by two cabs to Wembley to see the Cup Final Football Match.

The Wembley Stadium is a big building like a Roman Amphitheatre. On the way we found many cars, charabancs, etc., proceeding to Wembley. We were informed that some of these people had arrived the day before especially to see the match, and had travelled very long distances for the purpose. Some of them wore ribbons of the team to which they belonged. On our arrival at Wembley we found the car-parking place was full of cars, etc., and I thought it would be very difficult for us to find our cars again at the end of the match; so I looked round for some mark that would enable me to tell where our cars were parked. Multitudes of people were pouring into the Stadium, and we had to keep very close together in order not to lose sight of each other. Our seats were on the third row from the bottom. The first box was for Their Majesties, who did not come that day owing to His Majesty's illness. The second box was for the principal members of the Match or Association Football and distinguished personages; the third was ours. So we had a very fine view of the football ground before us. Our seats were said to be very expensive. We were very well received by a gentleman belonging to the Association, who afterwards invited us to tea. He was a distinguished person. In the second box before us there sat H.R.H. the Duke of Gloucester, who afterwards presented the cup, the Prime Minister, Mr. Ramsay MacDonald, Mr. Baldwin and other high personages. The match was between Birmingham and West Bromwich Albion teams. Bands of H.M. Irish Guards and H.M. Welsh Guards were playing. First there was Community Singing. The reader will realize what a huge singing it was when he is informed that ninety-five thousand people were present at the Stadium and all these people had to sing at one time. The following songs were sung:

1. Daisy Bell
2. John Brown's body
3. Loch Lomond
4. Pack up your troubles
5. Love's old sweet song
6. Cock Robin

7. John Peel
8. Poor old Joe
9. The British Grenadiers (Whistle)
10. Annie Laurie
11. The man that broke the Bank at Monte Carlo
12. Abide with me.

The last is a church hymn. An African reader will be interested to know that in England in almost every ceremony the Church has a place and religion comes first. In Africa it is difficult to understand this and what religion is to people in England.

The players were marched to the ground with both bands playing in front of them. The day was not fine. It was very cold and was drizzling. So the football ground was very slippery. But the game was very fine and so interesting that we hardly felt the cold and its bite. Faces of spectators around the stadium could not be recognized. We could only see black spots which represented the heads. How wonderful it was, ninety-five thousand people crowding together without a single person creating a disturbance! This would have been impossible in Africa. Such a crowd had never been seen by us all our lives, and the reader can imagine what was in our minds when we saw it. The population present was equal to that of the whole of the Tanga District, the place where I am living. The contesting teams got one goal each, and spectators were anxious to know as to who would win. When each goal was scored the crowd was excited, some with joy and some apparently with disgust and some were throwing their caps up. As I am an ex-football player, I could not understand why I impulsively wished the Birmingham team to win. At last the Birmingham team was beaten by two goals to one and I was sorry. Chief Koinange as well as every delegate was interested in the game. The West Bromwich

Albion team was marched with band to H.R.H. the Duke of Gloucester, and to the rejoicing of all present triumphantly received the glorious cup, and each player shook hands with the Prince. The Birmingham team came next to shake hands with the Prince and the game ended.

Few players were hurt and doctors were ready to attend to them. Of the spectators only one person collapsed and was carried by the ambulance. In about ten minutes all seats were vacated without any disturbance or quarrel. Our kind host took us downstairs to have tea. There were many people taking their tea in the room which was completely full up. After tea we left to find our cars. The marvellous thing was that the whole play had been reported by the newspapers and circulated just as we left the Stadium. The whole thing was done in a twinkle of an eye like a magic. It would be inpossible to explain this to Africans because they would not believe it. There is nothing to compare it with in Africa, hence the incredulity natural in the African mind. My colleagues could not understand how it was done when they bought the paper containing the news at the Victoria Station after we had left the Stadium the same evening ten minutes after the match. If the story had been related to us without seeing the paper, no doubt we would not have believed it. While the play was going on, there were aeroplanes hovering above the football ground reporting on the game. These aeroplanes could stop still in the air without moving about.

Outside the Stadium not one of us could tell where our cabs were standing. Motor vehicles were so congested that we entirely lost the situation of our cars. It soon flashed into my mind that I had a mark showing the direction in which our cars were situated, I looked for the mark and found it and looking opposite the mark I saw our driver beckoning to us. We gladly got into our cars and drove to the Victoria Station, but the speed of our cars as well as of all other cars was very slow owing to the density of cars. It would have been quicker to walk on foot than driving in a car.

The kindness we received from the gentleman of the Association is unspeakable and Chief Koinange thanked him much on our behalf.

On Sunday 26th April at 11 a.m. we attended the morning service at St. Stephen's, Sydenham Hill. We could easily detect that in church there were more women than men. I saw this in all churches I attended in England and also in Naples at the two churches we entered. On my inquiries I received confirmation of my experience. Some think owing to much work and other reasons fewer men go to church than women. Others think that it is because there are more women than men in England—women exceed men in England by two million women. Others thought it was due to men taking a true interest in church that those few who attended churches did so with more real interest and belief than those who did before out of custom. Materialism may have something to do with it. In Africa it is the reverse: more men go to church than women. Africans are naturally religious. It is true, the old England was more religious than the present, but religion still holds a very high place in England. We saw many churches wherever we went, I should reckon a church after every five minutes, but I was told some of these churches are empty, due partly I think to their great numbers. Some people told me that the lack of true interest in the parish work accounted partly for this. Where much interest is taken the church is full. In some places the working classes have thought they were not wanted in church to mix up with high-class people.

Baganda, Banyoro and Basoga delegates arrived that

evening with Mr. Bruton, District Commissioner of Uganda from Africa.

Preparations were made to meet the Secretary of State for the Colonies the next day.

At 8 a.m., 27th April, we were all ready to start for London. Each one of us put on his best dress, which some of the papers in London called 'immaculate.' The Uganda delegates wore their robes. At 10 a.m. sharp we arrived at the Colonial Office and at 10.30 we were presented before the Secretary of State for the Colonies, Lord Passfield, in the State Room of the Colonial Office. The delegates of each country were lined up together and our Native Commissioners stood on one side to the right. Messrs. Maxwell of Kenya, Mitchell of Tanganyika and Bruton of Uganda. Mr. Fazan who acted as an interpreter stood on the left. Together with the Secretary of State for the Colonies were Dr. Drummond Shiels, Under-Secretary of State, and Mr. Bottomley of the Colonial Office—there were also other gentlemen present whose names I do not know. Each one of us shook hands with the Secretary of State in the order of seniority.

Lord Passfield then read the following speech:

'Chiefs and Counsellors,

I am very glad to welcome you today in this room which is, as it were, the centre of the administration of the great Colonial Empire of the King. Here it is that for many years have worked the Secretaries of State for the Colonies—the statesmen, that is, who have been entrusted with the seals of the Colonial Department (you see them there before you) by the Great Queen Victoria, by her illustrious son King Edward VII and by her illustrious grandson King George V, who rules us today.

'This is an historic occasion. Never before have representatives of the native population in East Africa been gathered together in this room. Khama, the famous Chief of the Bamangwato, has been received here; only last year Tshekedi, his son, was received here; and other native Chiefs from various parts of Africa have been received here. But it is the first time that there has been occasion for a Secretary of State to receive here natives of Kenya and Tanganyika and Uganda, and so it gives me special pleasure to extend to you, the representatives of more than ten million Africans, a warm greeting on your arrival in London after your long journey from East Africa.

'The immediate purpose of your coming here is to give evidence, on behalf of the peoples whom you represent, before the Committee, composed of members of the House of Lords and House of Commons, which is considering the question of linking together more closely the administration of Kenya, Uganda and Tanganyika. It is very fitting that when important and far-reaching changes in the political administration of your countries are under consideration you should have the opportunity to state the views of the African people resident in those countries. I do not yet know what you may have to tell the Committee. But I would say this to you : When you speak, speak fearlessly and say the things which are in your hearts. Your Officers here, who will be with you when the Committee wishes to hear you, will guide you to speak, and upon all these matters I say to you again that you must tell the Committee exactly what you and the native peoples of East Africa are thinking. Your selection for this important task means for you a great honour. But you cannot have great honour without great responsibility also. If the life blood of a body fails, the body dies. So, if you fail to fulfil the trust which your selection imposes upon you, the honour of that selection becomes as dust. . . .

'I could speak to you at length on many things, both here and in East Africa, but this is not the time or place to do so; and I will make an end of speaking by repeating my words of welcome and by asking you on your return to take to all the native peoples of East Africa a message of greeting and well-wishing from myself and all those who, under His Majesty the King, are specially entrusted with the care of the interests of East Africa.

'I have spoken.'

Headman James Mutua read the reply of Chief Koinange on behalf of the Kenya delegates. The following is the English translation of his reply:

'We rejoice at our arrival here and give thanks to the Government of His Majesty the King for having required our presence. We are grateful for the manner in which we have been received, and for the opportunity which has been granted to us of presenting ourselves before you, and we know that it is as though we should see His Majesty the King. For you have been appointed to this high position by His Majesty, and we, who are of small account, cannot expect such honour as to present our salutation to him in person. We know the unceasing care which he displays in the protection of his subjects, and he has made you his right hand that you may direct the courses of the countries of his Empire in which we live.

'We pray God to grant His Majesty health and great prosperity.'

Chief Serwano Kulubya replied in English on behalf of the Uganda delegates:

'My Lord,

'On behalf of the Uganda delegates and that of myself, I humbly beg to express first and foremost our unswerving loyalty to His Majesty King George, also our untold appreciation of the kind welcome which has been extended to us on our arrival in this country, and also for this reception.

'Above all, My Lord, we would wish to state how the Native Governments we represent received with the greatest appreciation your kind invitation to send to this country their delegates to give evidence in this burning question of the proposed Closer Union for the East African Dependencies. This invitation will always remain in our minds as a token to prove to us the British Fairplay and Justice. . . .'

Sultan Makwaya read in Kiswahili the reply of the Tanganyika delegates. The following is its English translation:

'We, who are the representatives of the natives of Tanganyika Territory, give you our sincere thanks for having invited us to this interview, and for having called us to England to give evidence on behalf of our brothers in Tanganyika. For this is the first time that natives from East Africa have been summoned to the councils of those honourable houses, the House of Lords and the House of Commons, to speak on their own behalf. Neither ourselves nor our brothers nor our sons will ever forget the goodness of the British Government in this matter and it will be remembered for ever as long as the history of the African people endures. . . .

'May Almighty God bless His Majesty and his Empire, and may God's blessing attend every endeavour which you undertake.

'We are your humble servants.'

All these speeches were interpreted by Mr. Fazan into Swahili and English.

After the delivery of the speeches the Secretary of State for the Colonies bade us 'Good-bye' in Kiswahili—'Kwaherini'—and we shook hands with him again and left the State Room in the same order.

It was a very solemn reception and everything was done with the highest dignity and respect. I had never been to such an impressive ceremony. The room is grand and stately and inculcated in our minds the highest respect for the British Government.

As Mr. Fazan told us on the day of our arrival, the British Government had decided to accord us the respect of the ten million Africans whom we represented, and we highly appreciated this honour on behalf of our brothers. It must be admitted that we were treated with the greatest respect and honour, so much so that we felt that we had been as if by a miracle transported to another world. It is really impossible for any of us to say how we thank the British Government and all those who participated in making our visit in England an enjoyable one. We therefore commend to Almighty God to bless them all for all they did for us and grant everlasting prosperity to the British reign of Justice and Fairplay.

To compare what we have seen in England and how we were treated is well-nigh impossible. We made many friends and found the truth for ourselves that we have friends in all political parties: Conservatives, Labour and Liberals, and all sections of the communities in England and the church. We had an opportunity to see things for ourselves which we could not otherwise have understood. When I arrived in Africa I told all those I saw: 'It is impossible for me to relate exactly what we have seen and how we have been treated because you would not believe me, as there is nothing to compare it with in Africa; but if you have money, take a trip to England and see things for yourselves.' Some replied: 'We know these people are very good in their own country.' Some people thought we were so treated because we represented ten million Africans and it was even suggested to us that the respect we received was not meant for us but the ten million Africans we represented. That is true. But I was blessed with the opportunity of gauging things for myself after my colleagues had left and when I was no more representing ten million Africans, and I ascertained that the treatment of good Africans in England is above reproach. The atmosphere in England is such as to make a wide opening for an African who wishes to improve himself thoroughly in every branch of knowledge, provided he possesses sufficient funds for his travelling and maintenance expenses while in England.

It is a fact that coloured people are not admitted in some hotels, etc., in London, but I was given a confirmed reason for it. I am glad to say I did not experience it and I was lucky for having been well treated wherever I went. Padre Dyson told me one day on my return from Blackheath that the attendant of a certain restaurant where we usually had our meals asked him during my absence where I had been and thought I was a welcome customer to their restaurant. Good and respectable Africans are welcome in most places. Probably the crux of the whole matter is, it is difficult to differentiate between Africans, but the atmosphere may change in future. Outside London there is not much of this; Africans are welcome everywhere according to the information I received. London has a cosmopolitan population, and no doubt people with racial prejudices from other countries are there in great numbers and this may account for infiltration of the system of racialism there. However it is consoling for the Africans to know that there are some places where they can be received and these places are more comfortable for them than those others where their presence is not tolerated. I would advise Africans to stay at places where they are required and not to thrust their presence where they are not required. It is happier for them to be in congenial places. In trains, omnibuses, etc., there is no colour prejudice. On the whole one can safely say that English people in England are very respectful and kind. To me this seems to be the reason why they rule one-third of the world today—they deserve it and are worthy of it. Several Europeans who are not English, and Africans, agreed with me on this. The character of the majority of the English people in England is excellent and incomparable.

In the afternoon at 3 p.m. we visited the Friends' Society's House where we had been invited to tea. We found many European and African friends awaiting for us, and we were very well received.

The Society has always been rich in the zeal of its members for social reform, and Friends were in the forefront of the long campaign against slavery. In the meetings of the Society women equally with men may address the Friends. They have their Mission at Pemba. After we had been shown round we were taken to tea in a big hall and were introduced to several friends. Here I met Rev. Dyson, priest in charge of the English church at Tanga. It was a very happy gathering. Mr. Roden Buxton addressed us and in his speech assured us that we have many friends in England and that all those who were present were friends of the Africans. His father did much work towards the abolition of slavery in Africa and elsewhere and is buried in the Westminster Abbey in honour of his noble work. Mrs. McGregor Ross also addressed us and said she was sorry to see we did not bring our wives with us to England and hoped the next time we went to England we would take them with us in order that they might gain the experience which we were gaining during the trip. Rev. Andrews from South Africa gave us a message from our brothers in South Africa who were very glad to hear that we had gone to England to speak for our people. It was simply by a coincidence that we met in England.

Chief Serwano Kulubya replied to the speeches in few words and I spoke on behalf of Chief Makwaya and Tanganyika delegates. Several persons present came and told me afterwards that I had spoken well about co-operation between Europeans and Africans. It really came out of my heart. The meeting then ended and we left with the most sincere feelings in our hearts of the great and most wonderful kindness of those present. The impression made on my mind was that they felt more for us than we did for our own selves, and they are true and real friends.

Experience that an African gains in forty years in Africa is not equal to one month's experience in England.

At 10.30 a.m. Tuesday, 28th April, Kenya delegates appeared before the Joint Committee on Closer Union of East African Territories, to give evidence. Uganda and Tanganyika natives were present to listen to the evidence. Several Europeans were present and the King's Robing Room was full of spectators.

Dr. Leakey interpreted for Chief Koinange and Headman Mutua; the latter understands English but he thought it safer for him to speak in his African tongue, although he did not speak in vernacular. Having a thorough command of the Kikuyu language, he spoke in Kikuyu, a language which Dr. Leakey speaks and understands like a Kikuyu.

The Ven. Archdeacon Owen interpreted for Mr. Ezekiel Apindi, who also understands English. The Committee sat in the King's Robing Room in the House of Lords.

As is well known, this was the first time East Africans gave evidence before the honourable members of the Houses of Lords and Commons. Many people thought that the delegates would be nervous and afraid to speak.

One African before our leaving Africa ventured to write in the *African Standard* that when the delegates reached the Houses of Parliament they would be so frightened and trembling that they would be unable to utter even a word. He therefore suggested that all delegates should meet at Mombasa and be put on speech-making test prior to their selection to proceed to England as fit representatives. Happily for all, this was unnecessary and was not done, and the reverse took place in the King's Robing Room, for the delegates could speak more than they do in their own country and with ease and without fear or fright. The delegates were in preparation from Africa for the important work before them. Some of us thought that the sightseeing should have been postponed until the evidence had been given. But I am glad to say the sightseeing programme did not make any difference to our preparation. The African delegates did their duty without fear.

Chief Koinange who does not understand English at all spoke with vigour and tact. He is a straightforward and steadfast Christian and I am compelled to admit that he is one of the best African chiefs. He was anxious to do his duty and help his people and I saw him at times so worried about it that he thought he was not doing enough for his people. One English gentleman from Africa told me one day that Chief Koinange has got brain. One of the Arab delegates told me he never thought the Kenya delegates would be able to speak what they spoke, and quoted an African proverb: 'Those you think would not do the job are the very ones who would do it well, and those you think would do it are the ones who would fail.' The London papers also admired the way the delegates gave their evidence, and mentioned that they were not frightened by the big buildings of the Houses of Parliament.

It is true the duty before the delegates was heavy, but

undoubtedly they knew what it meant to them and what they and their people wanted. It was evident that the English public did not know what was actually happening in East Africa and what the African point of view on such matters was.

Up till now the African has not been given a chance or an opportunity to speak for himself or to air his feelings. Many people think the African is so childish that he cannot even open his mouth and say whether he is well or not. To some of us it seems that even a child can speak and parents are always anxious to hear his voice and his requests. Those gentlemen who wisely planned to get Africans to England to speak before the Joint Committee have done the most noble service to the African community. The African cannot claim as yet that he can champion his cause as efficiently as the best Europeans, but he can justly claim the privilege for an opportunity for his voice to be heard and his views to be sought where matters concern his vital interests. Nobody knows the African's requirements better than himself. His mode of living, his customs and habits are peculiar to himself and require a thorough study. In order to understand an African as he actually is, it needs one to live like him, with him, and be intimate with him, which is very difficult. The Africans have a proverb which says: 'No one feels the bite of a bug on a bedstead except he who lies on it.' To seek the opinion of the Africans on matters concerning them is to render them the best service. The African may be suffering through misunderstanding and there is no way of removing the misunderstanding except by consulting him in every way.

We were all very pleased to find that we were lucky indeed to have as a chairman the Noble Lord Stanley of Alderley. His Lordship was very just and sympathetic. He allowed the African delegates every opportunity to speak out what they had in their minds and those of people whom they represented. In him the true British justice is symbolized. His Lordship's attitude to the African delegates gave them more courage in the delivery of their evidence. The honourable members of Committee were also kind and reasonable in putting their questions to the African delegates. We were surprised at first to find that fewer questions were put to the Kenya delegates than we expected would be the case. My curiosity impelled me to ask one of the members whether they thought the evidence given by the Kenya delegates was so unimportant or outside the range of the Committee's terms that they did not think it worth while to ask questions. Apparently this was not the case, and when we gave evidence we were so inundated with questions that we thought the onslaught was meant for us.

In the afternoon the Kenya delegates returned to the King's Robing Room to finish their evidence. Uganda and Tanganyika delegates were taken by Mr. Charleton to be shown the Houses of Parliament. We could not go into the House of Lords as the Noble Lords were sitting at the time. The Speaker proceeding to the House of Commons with the Chaplain and Sergeants-at-arms was very impressive indeed. We saw the historical Westminster Hall.

In the evening we were invited to tea by Lord Henry Cavendish Bentinck at his house. Lord Passfield, Lord Stanley of Alderley, Lord Olivier, Lord Lugard and other distinguished gentlemen were present. Lady Cavendish Bentinck was our hostess; and we were very well received. The party was excellent and we enjoyed it exceedingly. I sat next to Lord Stanley of Alderley, and his Lordship was kind to us and talked freely with us. He asked me how long the Tanganyika delegates would want to deliver their evidence. I told him that it would be difficult to say then, as we did not know the number of questions that would be put to us. I requested him to allow us sufficient time to give our evidence and not to rule out our evidence; otherwise it would be difficult for us to state our evidence clearly. He agreed and said it was for the same reason he had allowed the Kenya delegates to state much which was outside the terms of the Committee. He understood our difficulties quite well and was very sympathetic. Lady Cavendish Bentinck came and asked me to speak with her and we talked briefly on the question of women. I had the honour of being introduced to Lord Passfield and exchanged a few words with him. Nothing encouraged and inspirited us so much as this meeting with the noble lady and gentlemen of the highest society in England, and we owe them a great debt of gratitude for this. Every one of us had an opportunity of talking with them. The party broke up at about 6 p.m.

On the morning of 30th April we left by train to Croydon. In the Air Office there is a large portion for booking offices. From the top of the building we could see aeroplanes flying and the open aerodrome ground. There is an instrument for sighting airships when they come to the aerodrome.

In the sheds there were several airships belonging to the French, Germans, Hollands, Belgians, etc. The airship *City of Glasgow* which brought H.R.H. the Prince of Wales from France was in the shed.

At 3 p.m. the same day we arrived at the Zoological Gardens and were received by Mr. C. W. Hobley, ex-Provincial Commissioner of Kenya Colony. Here we had the most thrilling show we ever experienced before. The birds' house contains hundreds of species of parrots and other birds. Parrots are from Africa, America and Asia.

In the lion house, there are African lions and Asiatic tigers. They were very hungry at the time we went to see them, and were restless in their cages. There were hundreds of spectators present. The keepers came to give them meat ration, the lions were roaring furiously.

The sea-lions kept in water were very exciting. They dive and come out and make much noise. Bears are also in a pond.

Indian elephants are in their house. I made inquiry about 'Kiberege', the young elephant sent to the Zoo by Sir Horace Byatt from Tanganyika, but I was sorry to hear it was dead.

We saw many animals which we had never seen before, even some of these from our own country. The time was so short that we could not see them all. It requires two or three days to see everything in the Zoo. The garden of the Zoo is very big and beautiful. The visit was most interesting and we enjoyed it much. Hundreds of people were about the gardens to see the animals. Hills have been made for hill-monkeys and other animals. The habitation of every kind of animals has been made more or less similar to their original habitation except for those in cages. The animals nevertheless look happy and comfortable in their strange environment, except for lack of freedom. The lion house does not provide enough space for lions to roam about freely as they do in the African jungles, where they travel long distances at ease. It is human to feel how we would have liked to be in their places at the Zoo.

It is evident that people who visit the Zoo get better knowledge of these animals than people like ourselves who live near their natural habitation. Rarely do we have a chance to see them at ease in the African bush, and for such animals as lions no one would dare to go near them with a stick as in the Zoo. One has to arm oneself with a gun to approach a lion in Africa and even then one has one's life in one's hands, yet in the Zoo you can see them without any fear and at close quarters with a stick in the hand or nothing at all.

On 1st May, through the kindness of the War Office, we were invited to see the rehearsal of the Trooping of the Colour on the Horse Guards Parade and the Changing of the Guard by the Life Guards. It was a splendid show. We stood near the Statue at the Whitehall building. We were informed that it is not usual for many officers to take part in the rehearsal but on our account it was arranged especially for them to take part. A battalion of soldiers marched to the ground with band playing in front of them and their colour. The officers were standing in front of Whitehall and the Officer Commanding was riding a horse with the officer under him who received orders from him and gave them to the battalion. The striking display of drill was magnificent, and the marching soldiers were stamping their feet as if it were done by some machine. Every motion was manipulated as if it were done by one man. It was one of the most enjoyable sights I ever saw. The head-gear of the soldiers enhanced their dignity in appearance. The march past the Colour, and the Officer Commanding Troops taking the salute in place of His Majesty the King, was a marvel. The soldiers swivelled their heads at the order of 'Eyes right' facing the Colour of Officer Commanding Troops as they passed him with the perfection of machines. Our faces were attracted towards the soldiers as if it were by magic. The bands were playing beautiful tunes and the leader of the bandsmen twisting his stick dexterously. The Trooping of the Colour was a splendid ceremony carried out with rigid reverence. After the Commanding Officer had taken the salute, the soldiers marched away with pomp and to the strain of the Scottish flutes. We stood still gazing on the soldiers until they finally disappeared from our sight, our hearts beating with joy at a smart show of military splendour we had just seen.

We were then invited to the officers' quarters and were given some refreshments in accordance with the military custom. From the window above we could see the fine change of guards. The guards were dressed in glittering brass plates and their horses obeyed orders as if they were trained human beings. We were shown the horses, stables and the guards' quarters, and we saw their kit brought in by a horse cart. We thanked the officer who took us round very warmly for his great kindness to us. We then left and went to do some shopping and had our lunch at the Charing Cross Station Hotel.

At two o'clock we left by train to Woolwich Arsenal. From Woolwich town we were driven by car to the Arsenal. It is a big place with several workshops. We were kindly shown round and saw many things which I do not think it proper to mention in this book. We had tea at the headquarters of the Arsenal. The Director of the Arsenal and the officers were very kind to us. He showed us pictures of great generals and took tea with us.

In the evening we left by train to Sydenham Hill. To return to Whitehall again, I must relate what happened that day. When we got to Woolwich Arsenal we found one of the party was missing. He was Chief Koinange who was cut off from our party owing to his dilatoriness and was lost. I told Mr. Fazan I thought we had lost him near the Whitehall. Mr. Fazan phoned to the Colonial Office about it, and an officer of the Colonial Office went out in search of him and found him near the Whitehall. Chief

Koinange said he first did not recognize the officer and thought it was a newspaper journalist who wanted to obtain some information from him in order to write about him in the papers, as a journalist had done on our arrival. So he tried to evade him. But when he found that he was an officer from the Colonial Office he gladly followed him. He was always talking very highly of him to us. When he left England he presented him with his stick and said he would always regard him as his friend.

On the 2nd May, we travelled by train to Wye to see the Agricultural College there. Most of the Chiefs were anxious to see the college farm as they are most interested in farming.

We got to Wye at about 10 a.m. and were kindly received by the Vice-President. In the garden there are cherries and other fruit trees. Hand motor tractor is used for cultivation. The machine is very handy and labour-saving. One man can use it without the aid of another; the cost of this machine is £100. The second machine is more economical than the first and costs £35. Most of us thought we could afford to buy the latter. We asked for a catalogue of this machine and it was kindly given to us. The method of cultivation is very efficient and economical. The machines can do one or two acres a day.

We found tomatoes are grown in a hothouse. I was surprised to hear that tomatoes could not grow in England except in hothouses owing to cold. They flourish better in the hothouse than they do in some parts of hot countries in Africa. I remember I planted tomatoes in my garden in Africa. During the wet season they flourished nicely, but in the hot season they all died. In Nairobi and Nyeri, where the climate is cold, they do well. So before going to England I was under the impression that tomatoes did well in cold countries and I was amazed to hear that this was not the case, unless planted in hothouses.

In the Engineering Department there are various sorts of agricultural implements such as ploughs, mills, corn threshers, etc. Most of them are very economical in use and expenditure. It was evident that African agriculture could receive much improvement by the introduction of these implements.

The poultry was the most interesting part of what we saw. Here there are 6,000 fowls in the compound, which is partitioned and contains many cages for breeding fowls. The incubator is kept in a big room and is heated by means of a heating machine. Thousands of the best eggs are hatched here. They take twenty-one days to hatch. The chickens are kept in the 'brooder' until they are grown up. They are fed with wheat, etc., and lamps are kept in the brooder to keep them warm. The brooder is kept very clean and the delegates noticed it at once and admired it.

It was explained to us that only the best eggs are put in the incubator, small eggs are sold in the market. The best hens and cocks are kept in the farm for breeding. The other cockerels are sent to the feeding house, where they are fed with the best food for about five days and then subjected to artificial feeding for about ten days, after which they are sent to the market and fetch a handsome price. The artificial feeding was displayed to us. A tube was inserted through the beak of a cock right into the crop and the food was pressed into the crop through the tube. It requires a very expert handling, otherwise the cock would be killed. The feeder was so expert and quick that the feeding was done very quickly without causing any pain to the birds. Planters bring their birds here for crossing or competition for a cup. Only the best birds are kept here; African fowls cannot compete with them.

On the farms we were shown very big cows, well kept and fed and producing much milk. The cowshed is very clean and is disinfected. The milk utensils are cleaned with hot water and steam and are therefore rendered free from germs. Each cow stall has its board which gives the weight of the cow and the weight of milk it produces every day during the year. Each cow gives easily over 2 gallons of milk at a time or over 4 gallons of milk a day. The bulls are huge animals and look as if they were small elephants. They are well kept and fed. They fetch a very high price, some as much as £70 each. Horses are very big. There were four different breeds of the highest standard. They are used for work in the farm. There is a very fine pony.

Here we got a profitable lesson. All of us were interested in farming and we took much interest in everything we saw and had explained to us. We were very keen to gain some knowledge of farming in England in order to put it in practice in our own country. We could see many defects in our method of farming after seeing the method of cultivation in England. The crucial thing is the animal husbandry. In Africa our people pride themselves on quantity rather than quality of their cattle. Owing to great numbers of cattle kept by the pastoral tribes in Africa, the pasture is poor and consequently animals are weak. Pastoralists have to live a nomadic life, continually moving from place to place to find fresh pasturage and water. In the new camps they have to fight wild animals such as lions, which take a toll on their herds. If our pastoralists confined themselves to improving their breed of cattle by importing pedigree bulls and reducing the number of their cattle and improving pasturage and water supply, undoubtedly they would be richer than they are today. At the Smithfield Market the Director told us they could not use our cattle beef because it was not fat enough for the English market, and this is perfectly true from what we saw of the fat beef in the market. So much attention can be paid in improving the cattle industry to the benefit of all concerned and the country.

It is difficult to explain the difference between our beef and English beef unless one sees our markets and then goes to Smithfield to see the fat beef in that market; he would then realize the vast difference between the two. A trip to England of our cattle owners and dealers would be worth a thousand lessons given in Africa on cattle industry.

At present much cannot be expected from this line of business until our people are sufficiently progressive to understand the defects in their methods and what loss they mean to them and their cattle. But we hope that with the help of the Government much will be done in future to encourage Africans to take the necessary steps to improve their herds under the guidance of the Veterinary Department.

The English agriculture has much to teach to our primitive method of cultivation and planting. Through the use of the primitive method of cultivation much arable land is wasted by casual farming. An African usually has two or three farms which he uses interchangeably. When one piece is worn out and does not produce enough owing to the lack of manure, the African farmer moves to another piece and leaves the former fallow until after one or two years when it has regained its productive properties and is ready for use again. It comes as a surprise to an African to hear that one piece can be used for ever without losing its productivity; and this is the mystery of farming in use throughout Europe.

Ordinary manuring is one thing and scientific manuring is another. For a long time Africans practise the former, as the latter is too expensive for them at present. Here again the African requires the aid of agricultural experts to train him to make the best use of his land. We were shown round the other parts of the farm. On top of the hill we saw a large crown made on the ground by means of planted grass and cleared ground. It was explained to us that the crown was made when King Edward visited the farm.

We enjoyed the day very much and we were very well treated by the Staff of the College. Chiefs Koinange and Makwaya highly thanked the Vice-Principal and the Staff for the great kindness shown to us in showing us the various things in the farm and College which were of vital interest to us and our country. Africa is an agricultural country and requires to learn much about its mother-industry.

Mr. Ware and other gentlemen of the College saw us off at the station, and we left Wye with the happy memories of the day.

On 3rd May the Uganda delegates left in the morning for Manchester to see the cotton industry.

On Monday the 4th May we visited St. Paul's Cathedral. It is a very big and beautiful church. We walked up the whispering wall and could hear sounds on the wall whispered from the other part of the wall. It is 143 steps from the ground floor. Chief Makwaya did not go right up as he was afraid. The altars in the Cathedral are several and very beautiful. Several people were praying at the time. The brass and iron screen is magnificent. The Cathedral is a handsome building and is a perfect symbol of the Church of England.

At 11 a.m. we visited the Cattle Market at Smithfield. We were taken to the office of the Director, and he gave us a long instructive lecture on the cattle breeding and consignment of beef from South America, New Zealand, Australia, South Africa and Rhodesia. Here one sees the benefit of keeping good cattle and sheep. Every piece of meat we saw was full of fat. Carcasses showed that cattle of those countries from which the meat came are very big.

In the evening at 10 p.m. we went to the Foundling Hospital Site to see an open-air school for poor children. It was said as it had been arranged for us to see colleges and schools of rich people it was proper that we should also see this school as it gave us an outlook of another side of life, which some of us were most anxious to see in order to form a right idea of the conditions prevailing in England. It is a one-sided view and most imperfect to see only the best side of a country, when the most important side is that of the poor people who are in a majority in every country in the world. Big people sprout from the people who are poor.

Two ladies were very kind to take us round and explained everything to us thoroughly. We saw open-air classes of boys and girls from adjacent schools, whom we were told came every afternoon from the neighbouring schools to enjoy open-air classes on this site. Some of them were gardening. Boys and girls have separate pieces for gardening. In the nursery there were babies in cots and some were playing about. We were informed that some of these children could not obtain fresh air in their homes as they were too congested and stuffy. At the nursery they were very happy and everything is done to make them comfortable, but in the evening they are taken back by their mothers to their poor homes.

Nothing touched me more than the kindness shown to these poor little babies by the members of the staff of the institution. The babies were quite at home when we saw them, and it was evident that they were having a better time than at their homes in the night time.

Mr. Mitchell started giving his evidence to the Joint Committee on Closer Union this day.

On 5th May, 1931, at 10.30 a.m. Tanganyika delegates —Chief Makwaya, Mwami Lwamgira and myself—gave evidence to the Joint Committee on Closer Union in the King's Robing Room.

The room was full of spectators. Our joint memorandum had been delivered to the Committee on our arrival in England, therefore the Chairman asked us if we wanted to add anything more to the memorandum already submitted. Each one of us was asked separately. Chief Makwaya spoke first, then Mwami Lwamgira, and myself last. Mr. Mitchell interpreted for Chief Makwaya and Mwami Lwamgira because they do not understand English and I found I could not do both interpreting and giving my evidence to the Committee. I gave my evidence in English.

In the afternoon we were questioned by the members of the Committee. The questioning was not completed that day and we were requested to return the following day in the afternoon to reply to further questions. The next day at 3 p.m. we returned and were questioned up to 5 p.m.

We were glad that we had done our duty to the satisfaction of the Committee. It was a difficult task, for which we were prepared and knew what we and our brothers wanted. The African delegates after collecting the views of their brothers in Africa conveyed to the Committee in their evidence the actual feelings of their people and themselves without fear or demur. It is therefore to be hoped that this opportunity will be repeated in future whenever their interests are concerned.

I take this opportunity of thanking the Chairman and the honourable members of the Committee for the kind interest they took in hearing and questioning our evidence.

We were all pleased to see that H.E. Sir Donald Cameron, our late Governor, was present when we gave our evidence. He was so good and kind to us that he gave us his photograph in remembrance of his work among us in Tanganyika. Several officials from Tanganyika were present.

At 8 a.m. on Friday morning, 8th May, a charabanc took us on a long drive to Oxford. It is fifty miles from London. We had a nice view of the country on the way. We saw fine farms and one or two buildings thatched with grass or hay. It is very easy to mistake stacks of hay for grass huts and these are to be found everywhere. We were informed that there are some grass houses in some parts of England, and having actually seen them myself in pictures I was very anxious to see them in reality. In some parts of Kent these houses are to be seen. At Oxford we drove straight to the School of Forestry and were very kindly received by the authorities. Pictures of forests and places in our own country and several specimens of timber were shown to us.

We then went to see a club of graduates. Here we were pleased to meet Messrs. Harvey (Headmaster of Tanganyika) and Culwick (Asst. District Officer of Tanganyika); both gentlemen were studying anthropology. One gentleman was shown to us who was preparing for his first tour to Tanganyika as a cadet in the Administration.

We were shown the Christ Church College. The Christ Church Cathedral is attached to this College. The Cathedral is beautiful. Mr. Fazan, D.C., Kenya, was educated in this College. Mr. Morrison, a tutor of this College, visited Tanganyika, Kenya and Uganda. Most of Oxford Colleges are very old, but the architecture is handsome. The façade of some of the buildings has been renovated. The new work is hardly discernible from the old. River Thames is winding its way near the Colleges. Barges and the rowing boats for the Colleges are on the river, and some graduates were rowing their boats when we were there to see them and we were introduced to their captain. The boats are not made at Oxford, they buy them from London. At Eton College they have a special workshop for making them.

They have a big cricket ground. The gardens are very beautiful and varieties of nice flowers are in these gardens. Swans are in ponds and in the river.

We saw the world-renowned High Street of Oxford. Traffic on Oxford streets runs very fast, more than in London, and I found it more dangerous for the pedestrians walking on Oxford streets than on London's.

Miss Margery Perham kindly invited us to tea at the Rhodes College building. Professor Einstein was lecturing on that day in the Rhodes College. The tea party was excellent and we had the opportunity of meeting Oxford Professors of several Colleges. The Principal Professor of the University College was present and also Miss B. E. Gwyer, the Principal of St. Hugh's College. We had a delightful afternoon party. Miss Perham was so kind as to request us to see her College, St. Hugh's. It is a modern building and well kept. Here one finds the difference in beauty and cleanliness of the two types of Colleges, that of men and that of women. Our photo was taken in the garden of the College.

We saw an Indian lady graduate in this College. Miss Perham is ex-tutor of St. Hugh's College and has won a

Rhodes Travelling Fellowship. She visited Tanganyika, Kenya and Uganda, and is much interested in Africa and its people. She is conducting researches in Africa and we hope her work will be of great value and benefit for the African advancement.

We thanked extremely all those who helped to make our visit to Oxford an enjoyable one.

At Oxford we saw several Indian students. We were very glad to hear that a Buganda student at Oxford was making a splendid progress. He is studying Law and has passed his matriculation examination. The Professor of the University College spoke well of him. In his College there is a West African student and they are both very friendly. I was told that the secret of making acquaintance at Oxford is for the African student to take much interest in sports, this makes him popular and wins for him many friends. The cost of education at Oxford varies from £250 to £400 per annum inclusive of boarding and lodging.

The African students I met informed me that the great difficulty for African students from East Africa is the fact that the present standards in the African schools are too low to enable one to enter the English Universities straight away. An East African student is forced to spend from three to four years to qualify for an entrance into the University. He has to pass rudimentary and matriculation examinations, which he should have passed in the African schools. Thus he is compelled by lack of proper education in Africa to spend unnecessary money and waste of time in England in order to qualify for University education. Such being the case we hope something will be done in Africa to remedy this defect in the education of the Africans, which at the present time leads one nowhere.

A reverend gentleman told me one day that the African

delegates asked for more literary education as if it were a remedy for all their ills. Evidently this seems true. Nevertheless the Africans think that without literary education their present rate of progress will be very slow indeed and unnecessarily slow. The civilized education in England has done a great deal to uplift the English people not only in knowledge but also in good behaviour and polished manners. The high polished manners that a visitor notices on his first arrival in England are the result of this perfect education and discipline.

It is also impossible for any branch of education whether agricultural or industrial to be thoroughly mastered unless one possesses a good groundwork of a sound education. In these days of scientific evolution, it is impossible to apply science even to a rudimentary agriculture unless the scholar possesses literary education. A carpenter, a blacksmith, a farmer, a cook, etc., have all got to study books in order to improve their work. Most of the best classical books are in English and other European languages. It is therefore essential that literary education should be the base of the proper education conducted everywhere in the world in these days, and it is more so in Africa where there are no books for scholastic use in the vernacular, except a few story books. The African vernacular for some time will have to depend on foreign European languages for scientific and classical books. It has not much that can explain scientific terms and ideas which are most important in giving scientific education. Those who think that literary education is unsuitable for Africans ignore the fact of its importance and indispensability to any sort of education, and therefore deny the Africans the very means of progress.

Africans today, as is said, are thirsty of education and are determined to acquire it at any cost. So there is a danger that in their ignorance of what is proper education they may pick up anything that comes in their way whether good or bad. It is therefore proper and essential that the education provided for them in Africa should be of such a standard that would satisfy their real needs, so that those who elect to advance their education in foreign countries should have a good groundwork of a sound knowledge which would enable them to select only the best education provided by excellent institutions of foreign countries.

I remember when I was in England a lady asked me if a chief who did not understand English in England found himself happy, as he could not converse with anyone. The Chief himself told me he did not enjoy the talk as other delegates who understood English and was very sorry indeed for this. He said if he were young he would have at once joined school and then come to England to acquire better education. This shows the importance of literary education. We had to explain everything to these Chiefs who did not understand English and it was a pity to see them, they could not join even in a simple talk in English, and this was felt more by them, and it was their look of dejection which touched me deeply.

In London I saw a West African lady from Sierra Leone studying law at the London University. She came to Hitherwood one day and we had a long discussion with her in regard to law work for African women. She thought she would be able to practise for African women in Africa. Except in West Africa, where civilization is far ahead of East Africa, I contended that Africa was not ready for this yet and that we had to work to improve our native administration in accordance with the pace of progress. She said the educated African men and women had to instil the civilized legal innovation into the primitive African code of law, as it was done by one African lawyer in a native state in West Africa. The contention was rather heated and no one could convince the other of the fundamental principles for the improvement of the African code of law, although it was agreed that education is the base of all improvement.

There is a Buganda student studying economics in the London University. He has wasted over four years in an attempt to pass a matriculation examination and has unfortunately been still unsuccessful. There are several Africans studying in the London University and other Colleges, but they mostly come from West Africa.

On the 9th May we drove in a charabanc to Windsor Castle to salute Their Majesties the King and the Queen. We left Hitherwood a bit late and the charabanc driver had to drive us very fast to get us at Windsor Castle in time. We were to be at Windsor at 9 a.m. He drove us very fast indeed and got us there at the proper time, for which we gave him a present. Our charabanc entered the outer quadrangle. We were shown Guards' rooms and were then taken to the inner quadrangle to await Their Majesties leaving the Castle palace. We took our places along the road in the inner quadrangle. Two gentlemen of the Household showed us the place we stood. We took off our hats and were ready to bow down at the appearance of Their Majesties. We soon saw very handsome cars being driven into the Castle and these were for Their Majesties and their suite.

In a moment we saw Their Majesties entering the first car and driven towards us. No sooner the car approached us than all of us at one motion reverently bowed down. His Majesty took off his hat in acknowledgment of our salutation and Her Majesty was smiling. The car drove so slowly and very near us that we could see Their Majesties quite clearly. We were so much impressed by Their Majesties' acknowledgement of our salutation that we felt this was the climax of all the honour conferred on us during our whole visit to England. Our salutation was actuated by the real feeling of awe and reverence. We realized how Their Majesties are loved by all their subjects during our stay in England, and for us the most humble subjects of the Empire to have an opportunity of seeing Their Majesties was surpassing all our joys and expectations. It revealed to us the affection that Their Majesties have even for their humblest subjects.

It has been related to me by certain East Africans that during the reign of his grandmother Queen Victoria, His Majesty served in the East African Squadron on the suppression of slavery on the East Coast of Africa; it is therefore evident that African people are not new to His Majesty, and that His Majesty has personally served to effect their salvation from slavery. I am therefore confident that His Majesty is interested in our welfare.

We were very sorry to hear at the time we arrived in England that His Majesty was sick, and it was a great joy to us to hear that His Majesty was better when we went to salute him at Windsor Castle. We heard afterwards that His Majesty was very pleased with the arrangement that was made for us to salute him and the way the salutation was done.

After the salutation ceremony we were taken to St. George's Chapel and Eton College.

On Tuesday, 12th May, the Uganda delegates gave their evidence to the Joint Committee on Closer Union. They all gave their evidence in English. They delivered their evidence in an able manner and without fear. The

Kenya and Tanganyika delegates were there to listen to their evidence. There were many spectators in the room.

In the afternoon the Tanganyika delegates were shown the Westminster Abbey. We saw the graves of the Unknown Warrior, Dr. David Livingstone and Mr. Gladstone. The tomb of Queens Elizabeth and Mary were also shown to us and graves of other Kings and Queens and distinguished people.

In the evening the Tanganyika delegates saw the Secretary of State for the Colonies at the Colonial Office, Mr. Mitchell was with us. We spoke with him on matters which had no connection with Closer Union. We much appreciated the way we were allowed to state any matter that we had to say and everything we said was noted. Dr. Drummond Shiels and other officers of the Colonial Office were present at the interview.

This day I was asked at the Colonial Office if I would agree to give a speech to the Labour Parliamentary Group at the House of Commons on the 18th May, and I agreed.

At this time arrangement had been made by the Secretary (Canon E. F. Spanton) of the Universities Mission to Central Africa in London with the Colonial Office for my further stay in England after my colleagues had left for Africa, in order to be present at the Anniversary of the U.M.C.A. held in London on the 19th May. Mr. Mitchell recommended me to be granted the extension. It was further arranged that I should return by French boat on the 29th with Archdeacon Elliot of Zanzibar.

Mwami Lwamgira, through the kindness and goodness of Mr. Mitchell, was granted an extension equivalent to mine. Mr. Mitchell requested the Roman Catholic authorities in London to look after him during his further stay in England, and they kindly agreed. Mwami Lwamgira afterwards returned with me by the same boat to Africa.

In the morning of the 13th May we travelled by a charabanc to the Royal Air Force, Farnborough.

We were motored to see an aeroplane firing a machine gun. A target was placed in front of the aeroplane and the propeller was turning round at a high velocity while the machine gun was firing at the target. Several shots hit the mark. The wonderful thing was the firing through spaces of the propeller while it was turning round so fast without hitting the propeller itself.

There was a wireless box in the middle of the ground and an operator was talking to the aeroplane flying far away. Chief Serwano and myself were asked to speak to the aeroplane and we sent messages to the pilot to come down and fly on our right and left sides respectively, which he did. This was marvellous. Everything we saw here was most interesting, and it proved to us how far human genius can do in inventions. Several planes were flying above us. The officers were very kind to us and we enjoyed the trip immensely. The photographs that were taken of us were presented to us at the same time.

At 4 p.m. we arrived at the office of the Church Missionary Society and there was a large gathering of missionaries. We were received by the Rev. Hooper, Secretary of the Church Missionary Society for the East African Section.

The Chairman of the Mission addressed us, and after him Rev. Ash. We were much interested to hear the Chairman, who is one of the old Committee members who sent first missionaries to Uganda, and Rev. Ash, one of the first missionaries sent to Uganda when the country was independently ruled by King Mutesa. Chief Serwano Kulubya ably replied to the addresses and made one of the best speeches I heard him making in London while with us.

That evening we were all busy packing ready to leave Hitherwood the next morning. All delegates were returning to Africa except Mwami Lwamgira and myself. As most of us had come from different countries we were very sorry to part after having stayed friendly together at Hitherwood for about twenty-three days. On the 14th May after breakfast our photo was taken together with the staff of the hostel. We presented Mrs. Mellor, wife of the manager of the hostel, with a silver plate on which our names are engraved.

We left Sydenham at 9 a.m. by train to Victoria Station where we met many friends who had come to bid us goodbye. We were presented with silver spoons on which it is written 'Domine Dirige Nos'—'O Lord, direct us'. Messrs. Parkinson and Eastwood of the Colonial Office were present. The boat train left at 11 a.m.

Rev. O. Dyson took me to the Central Mission House, Wood Street, near Westminster, where I was to stay, and after depositing my loads in my room I went with him to St. Matthew's, Westminster, to see Rev. Father Cornibeer, Vicar of St. Matthew's. This is the church where the late Bishop Weston first worked as a curate before coming to Africa. Father Cornibeer showed me the beautiful memorial built in memory of the late Bishop Weston and presented me with its photograph. He told me that I could come at any time to the vicarage to have meals and spend my time in his sitting-room.

In the afternoon I travelled with Rev. Dyson by train to Brighton to see the mother of the late Bishop Weston. I was glad to find her in good health. She is very old but looked strong. She is eighty-eight years of age. Her granddaughter is looking after her. As the late Bishop Weston was my chaplain at Kilimani and teacher at St. Andrew's College, Kiungani, Zanzibar, from 1902 to 1905, I was very pleased to have had the opportunity of seeing his mother. The late Bishop was so dear to East Africans who knew him. Before I left Africa I went to Magila to see his new grave in the Magila Church and the 'Tabernacle' built in his memory. Several Africans contributed to a fund to build a memorial to him whom they truly loved.

Brighton is a nice place on the coast. It has a fine pier and summer holiday-makers flock on its shores to enjoy the English summer.

We were late for our train so we had to travel by another train in a Pullman carriage. At 8 p.m. we went to see St. Joan d'Arc play at the Theatre Royal, Haymarket. It was a beautiful play, which ended at 1 a.m. London in the night time is shining with coloured electric lights and looks brilliant and magnificent.

On the 15th May I visited Bloxham School via Banbury accompanied with Rev. O. Dyson. The Bloxham School is a place where my father was educated from 1882 to 1885, when he was in England. The school has all the time kept in touch with him by sending him the School magazine. Before my leaving Africa my father asked me particularly that if time permitted I should try my best to visit his old school, and gave me a letter to the Principal. He was uncertain if his Headmaster Mr. Wilson was still living.

We travelled by train which left the Victoria Station at 1.30 p.m. and detrained at Banbury at about 2.30 p.m. Banbury is famous for its cakes, but I was unfortunate for not having tasted one.

The Principal took us to see Mr. Wilson, the old principal and the teacher of my father. I was surprised to hear Mr. Wilson call me 'Kayamba' the very moment I appeared before him. So I could not help asking him how did he know me. He replied that he saw my father's face in mine. My father was under him when young for three years. I had a photo of my father with all the boys of Bloxham at that time and I showed it to Mr. Armitage. To my further surprise Mr. Wilson produced to me a full record of my father kept by him from the time he joined the school to the time he left Mombasa in 1920—and I added the time he has been in Tanganyika since then. It struck me as strange to see the old principal, who is eighty years of age, taking so much interest in an African for forty-six years after his leaving the school. He had many similar cards in his hand, apparently the records of old Bloxhamists. An elderly gentleman was with him and he told me afterwards that he was in the school at the same time with my father. He was a distinguished gentleman.

Mr. Armitage had arranged that I should address all the schoolboys in the school and they were all ready then, so we walked to the school. There were 150 boys in the school. The Principal first introduced me to these boys. I spoke to them in English for about twenty-five minutes. After that the Principal told me they would like to hear me speak in my language. I spoke to them in Kiswahili for about twenty minutes, Rev. Dyson translating my words to them. At the end of the speech the boys cheered me for nearly five minutes. Rev. Dyson said it was a great ovation. It appeared to me that the boys were much interested in what I had spoken to them and to hear an African language spoken which probably none of them had heard before.

We were then invited to tea by the prefects. One of them showed me round. They were all very cheerful and kind to me in a way I have hardly seen before. The tea party was grand and there was plenty to eat, more than both of us could even dare to tackle. The reception was one of the best I ever had and I enjoyed it very much.

The head prefect was excellent and I must admit that I highly admire the high qualities of these smart well-behaved English boys. They were kind and sincere to me and evidently very much interested to hear about Africa. My father and myself were afterwards enrolled as Friends of the Bloxhamists.

On the 18th May at 3 p.m. I went with Rev. Dyson to the House of Commons and sat in the Distinguished Visitors' Gallery listening to the debates. Many questions were asked and answered. There was a long discussion about Russia, started by Sir Austen Chamberlain. It was a very interesting subject discussed.

We left at 6 p.m. At 7.10 p.m. we were met by Mr. Whiteley in the Central Lobby, House of Commons; Sheikh Mbarak bin Ali Hinawy was present, and we were all taken to dinner in the House of Commons. Mr. Wellock was also with us. After dinner we went to the Parliamentary Rooms. Mr. Lansbury was in the chair and invited me to sit on his right-hand side. Lord Snell and Lord Noel-Buxton were present, also Miss Bondfield, Minister of Labour, Messrs. Wellock, Whiteley, Roden Buxton and others. There were thirty-two gentlemen and one lady present altogether. After I was introduced by the Chairman I delivered my speech in English on the conditions of Tanganyika Territory before and after the war. The Chairman thanked me for the speech and spoke kind words about it, for which I was very grateful. Sheikh Mbarak bin Ali Hinawy also made a short and interesting speech. Lord Noel-Buxton then took the chair when Mr. Lansbury left on business. It was a very busy day in the House of Commons and Mr. Whiteley told me afterwards that those who had attended were there because they were greatly interested to hear what I had to say.

I requested them to ask me any questions that they

wished to put to me. Some questions were asked to which I replied. Lord Noel-Buxton then addressed those present on what I had particularly said. His Lordship mentioned that the progress that had been made in the administration of the Tanganyika Territory was especially due to the work of Sir Donald Cameron, one of the most courageous Governors of the British Empire. The whole proceeding was very successful and interesting. I much appreciated the honour conferred on me of being the first East African to have been invited to speak to Members of Parliament in the House of Commons, and I shall for ever remember it.

Tuesday, 19th May, was the much expected Anniversary of the Universities Mission to Central Africa.

It commenced with the corporate Communion in St. Matthew's, Westminster, at 8.30 a.m.; the celebrant was Bishop Gore. The sermon was preached by a blind priest. It was astonishing to see how fast he was reading his notes by touch of his fingers on paper. He could read more quickly with his fingers than others can read with their eyes. He was born blind, and he explained to us the misery that blind people suffer through their loss of sight. The sermon was very impressive and it touched my heart deeply, especially the feeling that blind people are most unhappy in their life. I could realize this the more when the words came from one who really felt it.

The first meeting was held at the Church House, Westminster. Chairman was Rev. D. T. H. Archer-Houblon of Oxford. There were about nine hundred people present in the Church House and to me it was the first time to address such a large gathering. I was allowed ten minutes for my speech.

I met many friends, old missionaries and relations of

distinguished missionaries. It is difficult to express how one feels when he meets those who knew him when young.

The evening meeting started at 8 p.m. in Queen's Hall. There were about 2,500 persons present, and the hall was packed full. I could see people everywhere round the hall. It is true, I had never seen such a sight before except at Wembley. It was a gathering of Christians who had come from long distances to attend a meeting in order to hear the account of the missionary work amongst Africans. It was this feeling which impressed me more than anything else. Here I came face to face with ladies and gentlemen who have taken much interest, some of them all their lives, in the Church work in Africa. Africans do not know or have had no experience of the number of Europeans who are interested in the spreading of the Gospel in Africa, except very few, who had, as myself, the luck of visiting England. So it makes one wonder what these Africans would have said if they had the privilege of meeting these ardent English Christians assembling together to hear the news of the people they never met. One lady told me one day, 'I am glad there are Africans through whom we people in England can serve God.' What an opportunity these people think they have to serve God through doing good work amongst us! The mere presence of 2,500 English missionaries in Africa meeting together to hear about the work of Christ in Africa would have been sufficient to convert thousands of Christians. These people would have met in a real Christian spirit, which the African is anxious to see in reality. I was told that a gentleman was asking when I would speak in order that he might come to hear me. Probably many others were anxious to hear an African Christian speaking. This in itself proved the spirit with which those who came to the meeting were inspired. They were animated with a desire to hear from the mouth of an African the result of their work in Africa, and this I was prepared to tell them in a few words. It would have taken me days to relate to them everything.

The *Church Times* described the evening meeting as follows: 'The U.M.C.A. proved that it had outgrown the limits of the Central Hall by filling the Queen's Hall, which is considerably larger, in the evening. The frail but resolute figure of Bishop Gore, President of the Mission and Chairman of the meeting, side by side with Mr. Martin Kayamba, an African of splendid physique, presented an engaging contrast, and seemed to personify the venerable wisdom which the European can offer to the African, and the strength and youth which the African can give in return, "in just exchange one for the other given".

### Africa Calling

'Mr. Martin Kayamba was undisguisedly delighted at the warmth of the welcome accorded to him when he rose to speak. "I will address you," he began in excellent English, "not as my lord, ladies and gentlemen, but as my father, my mother, my brothers and my sisters." He stoutly refuted the charges made against "our English missionaries". "We people in East Africa owe all our education, our religion, which is the true religion of Jesus Christ, to the English missionaries. They have done much for us in our country, and as an example you see me here today," he added modestly. He pointed out that the influence of the missionaries could be seen in the personnel of the delegation, of which he was a member. Out of the ten men who had come to England to represent ten million Africans, nine were Christians. "There is nothing that can save the African but the Christian religion," he said, "and I am glad to see here a larger assembly than I have ever seen in my life—except at Wembley—of men and women interested in the work of our mission in Africa. . . . There are sufficient here, I should think, to convert to Christianity about a million African men and women a day. We Africans, you know, are backward people, are the most backward race in the world. We are helpless. We cannot stand alone in the present world. We want your help. I appeal to you on behalf of my brothers and sisters of Africa. We want to co-operate with you, to be friendly with you. We have our African priests, but they cannot do without you. God is working in Africa through them and through you." '

The meeting ended at 9.45 p.m. Several omnibuses carried people to far places from the meeting and London looked very bright with its multi-colours of lights. I walked to the Central Mission House to sleep dreaming of the happy events of that day.

On the 21st May I attended the Advisory Committee Meeting on Tropical Education at the Colonial Office. Chief Lwamgira was there. Lord Lugard, Sir Robert Hamilton (ex-Chief Justice of Kenya Colony), Major Hans Vischer, Rev. Fraser (the Principal of Achimoto College) and other gentlemen and two ladies were present, Sir John Shuckburgh was in the chair. It was a nice meeting and Mwami Lwamgira and myself were asked for our views on female education in Africa.

Female education in Africa is much needed. The education of men without that of females is defective. It means progress of men in work and outside their homes, but not in their homes. Such education is superficial. The true education should start from home. Instructions in hygiene can only be practised by educated women in homes. Men can do very little in this respect and can do nothing at all if their wives are uneducated. The homes remain as they were a century ago with very little difference if any. Education of children is also retarded by the conservatism of mothers. If mothers take no interest in the education of their children through lack of education, it is difficult for fathers to do much in the education of their children, especially their daughters. It has been known of some African mothers refusing their children to go to school and, if fathers insisted, mothers instructed their children to run away to their far relations. Mothers have been a great hindrance to the education of their daughters. So the real progress of the Africans lies in the hands of African mothers. Education should start from home and not from school.

It was interesting for me to see that many important Englishmen were interested in matters concerning the welfare of the Africans. I was favoured to see here and there the evidence of the true interest taken to do some good to help us. Apparently here and there was a lack of knowledge of the true facts of African affairs, and it is a pity that these interested people do not spend sufficient time in Africa to study things thoroughly well.

Rev. G. N. Bacon, Curate of St. John's Church, Aylesbury, was so kind as to invite me to his parish Aylesbury. On the 22nd, Friday, I left by coach for Aylesbury. The fare by coach was about 4s. return, which was about half of the train's fare for the same trip, but the latter travelled faster than the former.

Aylesbury is one of the oldest towns in England. The whole country is spread over with nice farms. I was informed that people of Aylesbury are not in many cases wealthy and very few of them have servants. In the evening Rev. Bacon had arranged for a meeting and I was requested to speak to the audience. Evidently every one of them present was much interested in mission work of Accra Mission and U.M.C.A.

One of the ladies was very old indeed, nevertheless, she was so anxious to hear me that she attended the meeting. After the meeting I thought it was a Christian duty to push her bath chair to her home and this I did with much zeal and zest.

That evening I had seen an old lady of ninety years of age. She knew Miss Thackeray, my godmother, and probably saw my mother when she was in England. The old lady can still speak, hear and see. She moves about in her house, and attends to her housework. In Africa it would be difficult to see such old people still capable of attending to their housework and even move about. She would probably be put in the sun to warm herself during the day and have everything done for her. This is the difference between communal and individualistic systems. I was, however, pleased to see wherever I went many old people very active and strong, hopping on omnibuses and agile in movements. People seem to live longer in Europe than in Africa and I saw more old people in England than in Africa.

There was a choir practice in church that evening, but we were late for it, when we reached the vestry choir were coming out. I saw several small boys. Some of them were too young to have started work, but when I asked them what they were doing I was amazed to hear that they were working as office boys, etc. It is not surprising to imagine that these small boys gradually supersede the old men in their jobs and consequently swell the number of unemployed. Some of these boys told me they were anxious to come to Africa one day.

As I have already said, Aylesbury is an old town, I soon found out on inquiry that it still keeps some of the old customs. The churchwardens who took me half-way with Rev. Bacon explained to me that the town fair is still held weekly in the midst of the town on open ground as in the old, and farmers from various places come with their produce and livestock for sale in the open market. The sale of agricultural produce in open markets is still in vogue in Africa according to the old African custom. At Aylesbury the old lanes like those of Zanzibar still exist. To my great surprise one of the churchwardens told me that it is not very long ago that thieves were hanged in Aylesbury according to the old law which was slightly different to that of Africa. According to the old African law thieves were sentenced to cutting off of their hands and it was lawful to kill them when caught red-handed. The Digo had a saying—'A thief is like a pig that raids one's farm and when found pays with his body.'

On the 23rd May I returned to Wood Street and left with Canon Spanton the same day at 3.30 p.m. for Herne Bay. Herne Bay is like Brighton situated on the south coast of England.

An African in England is struck with the sight of glass windows in buildings without iron bars and asks at once whether there are no thieves in this country. To this question Canon Spanton told me that the breaking of glass windows takes place incidentally but not often. This is proved by the fact that glass windows are used everywhere. I think in England thieves go in for valuables rather than trifles as is the case in African towns, villages excepted.

The town of Herne Bay is spotlessly clean and a visitor can see at once that it is intended for attracting visitors.

On the 25th May Canon Spanton took me to Canterbury. Canterbury is an old town and the seat of the Archbishop of Canterbury. There are many ancient buildings. We visited the Cathedral, which is one of the finest buildings in England. Several altars and many memorials of Kings and Archbishops are in the Cathedral. Archbishop Thomas à Becket was killed in the Cathedral at the feet of the altar of St. Benedict. I was shown the place he was killed. One lady from America said she wanted to see the place Archbishop Thomas à Becket was killed, as she was particularly asked by her people not to leave England without seeing it. Canon Spanton showed her the place. Other visitors were discussing and one said she did not believe what she saw. She said it was sufficient for one to do good acts on the inspiration of one's conscience regardless of religion. This was bare scepticism. Conscience without religion is like food without salt, and is apt to be perverse. It requires a guiding force and the best force is religion.

I left Herne Bay by the afternoon train with the happiest recollections of my stay there.

At Victoria Station Rev. H. Allen was waiting for me to take me to his home at Blackheath. That day there were sports and games of all sorts and Blackheath was merry and gay. It was wonderful that a few minutes after my arrival there an English boy came and wanted to make friends with me. We had a nice talk together and he explained to me about the games that were going on at Blackheath that day. He was a charming youth and I was much interested in all he said to me. He appeared to be very smart.

Owing to the short time at my disposal I could not see cinemas and theatres as often as I wished. I once visited the Victoria theatre near Victoria Station and saw a talkie there. This is a new theatre and is magnificent inside, the films and singing were excellent. Theatres and cinemas are an expensive item, although they are very interesting to see.

In London one has to do a great deal in a short time. The time is always precious there. On my inquiry as to why people moved very fast in London I was told that they had to do much and the time was not sufficient. I realized this when I was there. I soon found that punctuality accounted for much haste. It is necessary in England to be punctual at every engagement and the failure to do so is a grave social offence. Punctuality is next to holiness in the proverb there. Punctuality is not an African virtue and Africans are often great sinners in this respect. Through education and discipline the habit of punctuality is gaining ground in the African mind. When this habit is strictly observed there is a necessity for quick movements in order to keep to time.

It seems that I have been fortunate to see mostly the best places and hardly the bad ones. If I am correct I am glad it has been so. It is for the good of our country that we should have seen the best part of the English life for our instruction.

Notwithstanding, a visitor can say that morals in England are very high and the discipline is exemplary. I have read very often about unemployment in England to be on the ascendency. In those places I visited it was not noticeable for the simple fact that the community as a whole seemed to me clean and cheerful and did not expose a sign of poverty. It was only here and there I saw a blind beggar or some one of the sort, but generally it was impossible to tell that there was a feeling of distress or poverty. A high personage shared my views that one heard a lot about unemployment when in Africa, but when he was in London he could not see it. People are moving in trains and cars and are filling cinema and theatre halls and do not show a sign of penury or need of money. Probably the shortage of money is felt by those who are unable to enjoy themselves as much as others by going to cinemas and theatres, although they are not in need of food and clothing, which is the real proof of want to a visitor. No doubt much money is spent in travelling and cinemas, etc., and very little on the real necessities of life. This I proved myself, I soon found after leaving Sydenham that it cost me more on my daily travelling than on my food expenses; and would have cost me much more if I had frequented cinemas and theatres too often. A gentleman told me that he was spending much of his time on going to cinemas and theatres whilst in England, it soon struck me that he was spending heavily on these items. Luxury and pleasures drain off the pockets of many in a big city like London. The community appeared to me to be thrifty, but there is much travelling done either for work or holiday-making, and cinema-going is a fashion. Theatres do not seem to be as full as cinema halls. It may be a mistaken idea, but this is what I gathered during my short stay in England.

Unemployment is much relieved by the dole system. The most important problem which struck me was that of female workers. Every morning we travelled from and to Sydenham our train was full of lady-workers. I was told that owing to women taking places of men in business, it has been partly the cause of unemployment in England. Some said men having got used to receiving doles are not inclined to work again; there is work for some of them, but they are so inured to the dole system that they would rather be without work and draw this free allowance. If this system had been applied to Africans it would surely have encouraged an idle life, and spelt deterioration of energy to work. In England it is absolutely essential and its defect is outweighed by its benefit to millions of people who are relieved of penury. It is to be regretted that the time we spent in England was so short that we could not gain much experience of things in that country. What we saw has been of a very great value to us in life. The experience assiduously gained in one month in England is worth forty years in Africa. We who went to England thought differently of it before our visit and when we got there we found all our preconceived ideas were illusioned. We have returned with the best impressions of the country and affection of the people.

I was told in England by friends that when I returned to Africa and related my experience of England to my fellow Africans they would not believe me and would call me a liar. Apparently this is true because there is nothing in Africa that can be compared with the real marvellous conditions of progress appertaining to that country. To the African anything that he cannot believe or form an idea of is false and untrue. Happily for us Africans we are making gradual improvement in this respect and through experience, as that gained by us in England, this habit will, it is hoped, be eventually cast away. Our curiosity would have been enhanced, had it not been that we had seen in Africa so often such things as men-of-war, motor cars, aeroplanes, seaplanes, electricity and several other new inventions. It was this experience that made our sightseeing in England easy of understanding.

What was most striking to our view and insight was the people themselves, their behaviour, kindness, peacefulness, discipline and goodness to visitors.

The Police in England are of an exceptional quality. They are thoroughly disciplined and are friends of the people. They are always ready to help people who are law-abiding and strangers. They appeared to be very kind to us and helped us to cross London streets by stopping traffic. I pay a high tribute to their excellence in duty and civility. I noticed that they could always tell a stranger and help him.

Mwami Lwamgira left London by the 9 a.m. train as he travelled second class. I left by the 10.51 a.m. train, travelling first class from London to Marseilles through the kindness of Archdeacon Elliot.

Marseilles is full of Africans. I saw more Africans there than anywhere else in Europe. The system of controlling traffic in Marseilles is different to that in England. I did not see policemen controlling traffic.

We arrived at Dar-es-Salaam on the 18th June at 6.30 a.m. Mr. Brett, P.C., Dar-es-Salaam, and Mr. Kitching, Ag. Secretary for Native Affairs, kindly met us at the landing stage. President, Vice-President and members of the African Association also met us there. At 12 noon Mwami Lwamgira and myself visited the Secretariat and I saw the Chief Secretary, Mr. Jardine. He asked me of what I had seen in England and I briefly explained to him of my experience of that country.

On the 19th at 9.30 a.m. we were asked by His Excellency Sir G. Stuart Symes, K.C.M.G., to see him at the Government House. His Excellency was interested to know of our experience in England and we explained to him briefly of what we had seen and the impression made on our minds. His Excellency explained to us of the cause of progress made in England. It is the result of many years of civilization and discipline. We were much delighted to hear his explanations which were perfectly true, and he told us of what he thought would be good for our country. We courteously thanked him for the interview and bade him good-bye.

I left Dar-es-Salaam at 4 p.m. by the Holland steamer for Tanga. On my arrival at Tanga I went to see the Provincial Commissioner and related to him about England. I have ever since been asked many questions by various people of what I saw in England and the impression made on me. In order to relate the events of my trip and experience gained in England I have written a Swahili book about the whole trip which has been printed. I have had inquiries from places as far as Nyasa and I think my Swahili book will be of interest to my African brothers and sisters.

What we have seen can only be learnt and digested by slow progress and energy. We did not go to England to enjoy ourselves, but to perform a specific duty for our people, which we have done. In addition to it, we were given an opportunity of seeing many interesting and profitable things for the benefit of our country and ourselves.

Before I left Africa I was rather anxious about the climate and food in England, whether it would suit my constitution; fortunately both were very good for my health, and it is a great pleasure to me to testify that I never had such a better time for some time before. The climate was astonishingly suitable to my health and I daily found myself buoyant in spite of the heavy engagements I had to perform. The most important thing in England is to keep oneself warm and not to expose oneself to cold. As we had enough warm clothes this danger was averted.

The staff at Hitherwood were excellent and we are extremely thankful to Mr. and Mrs. Meller and the staff under them for the good services to us whilst at Hitherwood. They were very kind and obliging to us all. With the same spirit of kindness I was treated at the Mission Central House by the Housekeeper, Miss Inkpen and those under her. This made my stay in England a very pleasant one and I felt quite at home except for my family and people. I thank Rev. Dyson who spent most of his time in accompanying me to several places in London and out. His company was most friendly and good and I enjoyed it very much. Archdeacon Elliot was very kind to me and his last words to me, when I thanked him for his help and kindness, were: 'I am sorry I have not had the opportunity to do more for you.' I shall never forget these words of kindness.

Of all the good things we saw in England and Europe, there is one thing which struck me as strange, it is the system of tipping. Wherever one is served, either in a restaurant, hotel or driven in a cab, it is a custom to tip a server or driver. In some places it is considered as an act of appreciation of one's services to the served. I was particularly instructed that the non-observance of the custom renders one to be considered as a vulgar. So wherever one was served he had to pay sixpence over and above the usual value for service rendered. This is equivalent to the system of giving 'Bakhshish' in Africa, except in the latter country the system is dying off, and in some places is punishable. I was surprised to see this system in use in England and Europe; it seems to be rather expensive.

Since my arrival in Africa and during the time of writing this book, it has happened that Mr. Rennie Smith, M.P., has visited my house at Ndumi and I was very glad to see him. Rev. R. Allen with his family also visited my house. It is very sad indeed to note the death of Lord Stanley of Alderley which has happened within a short time of our leaving England. His name will never be forgotten by the African delegates. There has also been the change of Government from Labour to National and it is expected every day that there will soon be a General Election. How far all these changes will affect the Joint Committee on

Closer Union of the East African Territories and its report we Africans do not know. We hope the labours of the Joint Committee and the evidence of the African delegates will not be in vain. The world depression of trade and the financial crisis in Europe has also had its repercussion in Africa, and things seem to have changed so suddenly as the occurrence of the war of 1914 that it is uncertain to tell how all this deplorable state of affairs will come to pass; still we hold a hope that Almighty God will clear the dreadful horizon and bring us back to better times again to the happiness of all humanity.

# IX

# The Story of Gilbert Coka of the Zulu Tribe of Natal, South Africa

*written by himself*

This is a short story of a Black South African. Although he lives in a wealthy, civilized, Christian land, he enjoys none of its amenities. He stands in the way of a White South Africa, White Prestige, European Supremacy, Western Civilization and other projects which are inimical to his interest. Denied opportunity of development as an individual, discriminated against as a race, exploited as a worker, a black South African leads a precarious existence in his native land. His services as a worker in developing the country and his desire to increase its prosperity to all sections are both ignored. Insecurity, starvation, poverty, ignorance, unemployment and injustices are his portion.

But to return to my story. My parents lived in a grass room on the banks of the Mfolozi, one of the historic rivers of Natal, the birthplace of Chaka, the great Zulu military leader and the founder of the Zulu nation, and Dinizulu, the last of its rulers. Both my father and mother hailed from the district of Vryheid, where they had converted a great number of people to the Methodist Church. They were of warrior stock. Father fought in the last battle between the Boers and Zulus at 'Mtashana', in 1901.

During those disturbed times many Boer farmers had fenced huge tracts of land and afterwards claimed them. The Zulu War, and annexation of Zululand, occurred closely and disorganized the life of the natives. Before they knew what had taken place they found themselves homeless. Their only tenure in their fatherland was at the mercy of their landlords who soon evicted them and confiscated their stock as they pleased. My father returned from the wars to find that his home at Hlobane had fallen under a farmer who demanded his labour and that of his mother, brothers and sisters. The region abounds in many historical scenes, such as Hlobane, Kanbule, Intombe and other famous battlefields. The people were comprised of the remnants of tribes scattered by Chaka during his career of conquest. These last 'Old Zulus' refused to live like slaves in their own country. Some left for other districts or Crown lands. Others made arrangements to share crops with their landlords, but my father could not get such conditions and therefore sent his family to the Mahlabatini reserve. When he married he decided to live near a town so that he would be able to work and educate his children.

He made an agreement with a farmer twelve miles from the town of Vryheid. For a time they lived in a rondavel or round house, and then they built a rectangular hut by weaving grass round upright poles. I was their youngest child, born in January 1910, eight years after their marriage. When I was two years old, our landlord demanded the services of Lawrence, my elder brother, who was already attending the Wesleyan Day School, in Vryheid. My father objected, left the farm, our home, and decided to move into town. We stayed in a two-roomed zinc house at the back of a bakery shop.

My childhood companions were white children. We played and frolicked together unconscious of the difference in our colour until we parted to our different schools. My parents were too pious and had little time for earthly affairs. Apart from religion, their chief topic of conversation was the recapitulation of the 'glorious days of the Zulu people'. These early lessons influenced me to revere my race, be proud of it and forget our superimposed and artificial inferiority.

I used to send dinner to father at the shop, where I saw many people. I learnt to know the prices of many goods. I usually gave sweets to scholars on their way home. My father was an active steward in the Church and was also interested in African National Congress affairs. He usually attended the late King Solomon and became one of the first Committee members of the Zulu National Fund (Inkata ka Zulu), a Society for the upliftment of Zulus. He was a great reader of the Zulu-English weekly, *Ilanga lase Natal*. Churchmen, men interested in Zulu national affairs and the Congress, came to our home and talked till late at night. I listened to their speeches and admired their ideas. I soon learnt to read the Bible and Hymn Book. I read it from beginning to end before I attended school.

At school, allocated into a beginners' class, I got promotion for my fluency at reading. That was the beginning of a long series of triumphs. I was a leader of my classes in every test until the end of my primary school days. Teachers, scholars and our neighbours usually told me that I was a prodigy. I exerted myself to become distinguished at football and singing as well. In the first, despite my tender youth, I soon attained my object. In the last, I succeeded after long failures. All the same, my weight was beyond my years. I was a monitor in my early teens. And many of my fellow scholars were in their early twenties. I was very popular with both teachers and my fellow pupils.

The Town Council hired stand-sites in Bester Spruit, four miles from town. People were notified that they would have to live in a location. My father wanted to rear a few cattle. A limited number was allowed to every stand-renter. We left town in 1920. Everything outside town looked strange. Apart from school associations, I had had no intimate acquaintance with other children. I soon learnt to live with them as the location grew. We played football every afternoon. Sometimes we went to swim. In the evenings were held singing competition groups. From the start I could not fully get into the life of children. I was more interested in important subjects like religion and politics. Whenever there was a chance, I quietly remained at home and listened to my elderlies' conversations. At times I discussed many important subjects with father.

Eunice, my sister, was at the Indaleni Girls' High School, Richmond, Natal, and I had to go to the cheapest Intermediate school at Dundee. The prospect of leaving home filled me with joy. I imagined that it would be a pleasant excursion. I was soon undeceived. No sooner had we alighted at Dundee and entered the Swedish Mission Boarding School, than I found what school life meant.

We woke up early, held meals at regular hours and worked long in the gardens and other sanitary work. Our dormitory was an unceilinged cement building. We slept on wooden boards and had for our chief menu unsugared porridge. We were compelled to attend prayer meetings every morning and evening and services every Sunday.

Maintaining my lead at lessons, I exuded the exuberance of my energies in defying some minor school regulations. I was ringleader in fruit-stealing from the orchard, taking sugar from the mission kitchen and sending love messages to girls. All such tasks required dexterity. My companions were older than I was. In order to ensure my equality, I showed my ability to do all the things they did. I was ever ready for competition with others.

During the Easter holidays, my parents sent my train fare late. When I saw other scholars glad of the prospects of spending their vacations at their homes, I became homesick. I walked sixty miles, mostly by night. I had had no experience of travelling. I walked close to the railway line instead of along the main road.

'Where do you come from, Gilbert?' Eunice asked, when dusty, fatigued and famished, I tottered in at the door. After a long sleep and bath, I told them how I had walked away from households for fear of injury, how I had slept in the veld and how I had lived on drinking fermented porridge from railway workers. They applauded my courage but warned me against such dangerous journeys. I told them how I disliked the boarding school and that in the next session I would live with one of my teachers.

Life with my teacher was fairly pleasant. I kept his room clean, cooked for him and also did some slight washing. I found no difficulty with my lessons. In my spare time I read newspapers and books. *Hereward the Wake*, by Charles Kingsley, *Up from Slavery*, *From Log Cabin to White House*, and others influenced me. My broodings were mostly of my future eminence. Teachers and many people with whom I came into contact spoke highly of me. I had a fixed idea that I would be a Great Man. I perused the biographies of famous men with avidity. I spent every odd sixpence in buying books from second-hand dealers.

I had little time for frivolity. After showing my aptitude in mischief, I withdrew to myself and weaved the most fantastic dreams of future grandeur. At that time I came across an old copy of *The Negro World*. After reading it, my ambition was fired, I decided I would be instrumental in uplifting Africans to a position they formerly occupied in the world during the heyday of Egypt, Ethiopia, Timbuctoo and Prester John. I unconsciously became politically minded.

At thirteen I was ready to enter college. When I left the Intermediate school, my ideas were crystallizing. I had made my mark. I had maintained my position as the leading and most promising boy and my ambition was growing with leaps and bounds. My heart beat high with hope at my mind-picture of college life and education. I would be one of the few Vryheid children who had advanced so high.

If my mother was not fond of cattle could I have gone to college? If I was not thrown on my own resources, could I have made any attempt to better my education?

Hitherto the cost of education had been insignificant in comparison to the expenses incurred in obtaining college education. Our parents saw nothing wrong in paying school fees, sixpence a month for beginners and a shilling every month for higher class pupils, and also buying books. Thus the poorest-paid section had to pay for every educational item for their children in contrast with highly paid Europeans whose children got free education. Moreover, there was no need for them to leave their homes in order to enter into higher classes.

Owing to their low wages many fathers were unable to give their sons and daughters higher education. Father called me to his side and with tear-stained eyes, for he had given my brother and sister the best education he could afford, told me to be patient and wait for another year in order to enable him to become financially able to educate me. I resigned my hopes for a time. My mother wanted me to look after cattle. I had no objection, but I resented mother's remarks that it was good luck that my school career had ended and I would thus be able to herd cattle. I carried books to the fields. I meditated over my future distinction.

During Easter vacations again, some students returned. To see my former schoolmates in school colours roused in me a determination to obtain similar achievements. Without divulging my plans to anyone, I decided to approach our Superintendent and ask him if he would shoulder the responsibility of my education. He decidedly refused. His refusal reminded me of Booker Washington. I decided to emulate him. I walked to our District Inspector in Dundee.

He was astonished to hear my fervent pleas for assistance. His companion, Mr. Fortescue Kumalo, supervisor of schools, applauded my sentiments. We concluded the matter satisfactorily to all. I was to obey Mr. D.'s orders. He gave me train fare and, in all ways, I looked upon him as my patron. Eager to see what would be done, I did not stay long at home. I returned to Dundee within a couple of months. My journey was my first close contact with teachers in conference. My discovery of their light-heartedness taught me many things. I found out that they did not care for the deliberations of the conference. Many missed an instructive address by a professor of anthropology. Likewise were many absent when vital issues were decided. They usually left several important items for the Executive Committee. Many delegates hailed from the country districts, wanted to see town life and thus turned a meeting into a pleasure hunt. Lady teachers paid more attention to their toilet than to the proceedings of the annual conference of the Natal Native Teachers Union. The Union is a body formed for the protection of their interests. It has shown no signs of so doing but is distinguished only for convening conferences.

My connection with teachers was for a time ended. I left the Swedish Mission where we had boarded to see Mr. D. in his house. I carried strong impressions of certain particular individuals and teachers as a whole. My reply to all inquiries as to why I was not at college was couched in bombastic language. 'When financial embarrassments are no longer in my way, I shall retrieve the lost time in herculean endeavours to increase my intellectual distinction.' All had laughed. But most had predicted a wonderful future for me.

I was rather taken aback when Irvine, my new fellow worker, Mr. D.'s house-servant, regarded me coolly. I was used to constant admiration. To have any person speak sneeringly at me, was a strange experience. But, as a beggar, I could not choose. All his jeers would not deter me. I had decided to be an African Washington and so would put up with slight inconveniences until the return of my patron.

I woke up every morning to light the stove, work in the garden, wash dishes and do all sorts of odd jobs in the house. For a week after his return, my patron found no time but gave instructions that I was to be made useful. Mrs. D. and her two daughters were also back. And I found my first lessons as a servant to Europeans. I got into the knack of domestic service. As I washed and wiped dishes my fertile imagination weaved scenes of Booker Washington in parallel circumstances. My resolution did not shake. I would be distinguished. Every spare moment I had was spent in studying, reading all the textbooks of the Junior Certificate syllabus, reading history and other interesting books from my patron's library and asking many questions for information.

The only thing that disturbed my mind was that nothing was said of my schooling. I had enough delicacy not to pursue the subject. All the same I was getting ill at ease, when, one Saturday afternoon, Mr. D. called me into his library. 'You see, Gilbert, education without character is useless. I believe that you are eager to secure it. I am glad that hitherto I have had cause for complaint neither in your behaviour nor work. I am setting you to a difficult task. You will leave on Tuesday to teach a school in the country districts of Umsinga. Your college education depends upon what success you make of that.' He lit his pipe and dismissed me without a word.

The following day, after Church services, Mr. Fortescue Kumalo, now my fast friend, called me to his house. He detailed to me the importance of the task. 'Mr. D. is very interested in your future. He has not forgotten your courage in walking such a long distance, your eager determination to secure higher education, your hard work and patience in his house and your undoubted abilities. Now he wants to see if you are a balanced young man.' Those words thrilled me. I swore that no obstacle would stand in my way of becoming one of the best teachers. We discussed every point and parted as usual on the best of terms. His home was like a second home to me. His wife was as kind as my own sister and I was perfectly at home with them. He gave me a suit and pair of shoes. Mr. D. paid me five pounds, half of which I promptly sent home and with the rest prepared for my 'Great Adventure'.

I was perched on milk cans with a book in my hand. To me it appeared delightful that I should travel by an ox waggon. I had never done it before and would learn something new. Moreover, it brought resemblance between me and my prototype nearer. Three women sat beside me.

We were all bound for Pomeroy in Umsinga near the Tugela river. In that early morning hour my heart throbbed with hope and intense anticipation.

The driver cracked his whip and the waggon moved. Slowly we passed town and were fairly driving into the country. Familiar scenery disappeared. We passed through hills and dales. My fellow travellers pointed out the many farms in the plains and fertile vales we passed. African tenants usually occupied sterile parts; cattle were seen in abundance. When I asked to whom they belonged I was told that their owners were landlords. Africans were not allowed to rear more than seven head of cattle. I wondered why such things should be.

The weather became inclement. At noon the oxen were outspanned. We got off the waggon. We made some fire and cooked porridge. After our frugal meal the waggon was inspanned and we proceeded in spite of the heavy showers. The road was muddy. We could make slight progress. We slept on sacks under the waggon. In the morning it was difficult to inspan early because many oxen had wandered far. When they were all back, we continued with our journey. Now and again I peeped out to see the strange countryside. At noon of the following day, after passing through woods, hills and streams, we saw the buildings of Pomeroy.

Anything like a town was welcome. I was pining for it, for all the way we had passed through farms. Most of the native houses were beehive-shaped huts with low entrances. Not that Pomeroy was much of a town. Half a dozen Indian shops, a Post Office, Court House and hotel for Europeans comprised its whole buildings. I paid my fare and got off.

Outside a shop stood a girl eagerly watching me. She was about fourteen years old, pretty looking and fairly intelligent. 'Good afternoon,' I greeted her. After her response, she entered the shop. I stood outside, undecided what to do. I had a box for my books, a travelling rug round my arms and my other goods in a big linen bag. After a while the girl came out. She so examined me that I asked her if she recognized me. She replied in the negative. Just then someone from the shop called 'Ottilia'. She re-entered to come out with a companion, who was at least ten years her senior. 'Good afternoon,' she said. We shook hands. 'I am Coka from Dundee who has come to teach at the Mumbe school.' 'Oh yes!' Her astonishment was evident. How could a fifteen-year-old boy go and teach? 'I am Miss Bhengane who used to be there until last week.' Within half an hour we were conversing like old friends. Ottilia took some of my kit. We walked out of the village. The footpath was long and zigzag. After four miles, we reached our destination, a mud building like those of the Vryheid location.

A beautiful middle-aged matron welcomed us. I later learnt that she was Ottilia's mother. She asked me about my mother and many interesting things. She gave me tea and soon after made me some delicious dinner of beans, sweet potatoes and meat. Her conversation was so pleasant that we had become good friends when Miss Bhengane left and her husband joined us. They were a nice couple, who in their religious fervour and other things reminded me of my parents. I had a comfortable sleep on a bed for the first time since I had left home. I began to hope that my 'wilderness' would be endurable.

The following morning dispelled my day-dreams. Ottilia and her young brother were my scholars and accompanied me. Out of deference they would not walk with me. I urged them not to be silly but they refused. Through thickets, over dongas, our stony path led us to the school.

I saw the school house half a mile away. It was a huge stone building whose windows, walls and roof were in a dilapidated state. On closer examination it appeared more like a stable than a place in which children would either be instructed or people worship. I had little time to examine it as my attention was absorbed in watching my new scholars play. I got into the house unobserved and flung myself on my knees to utter a short prayer. Nervously ringing the bell, I waited a few minutes and then went out to see my scholars in line.

The majority was composed of girls because boys were either looking after stock or engaged at work in the towns. Most were dressed in coarse cotton dresses. Many were as old as I was and some were older. Of my forty-eight pupils only eleven were boys. They all looked at me with amazement. I knew why, but put on a bold face.

'Attention. Stand at ease . . . right turn . . . left turn . . . arms across bend . . . arms fling . . . mark time . . . forward march.' Long before I concluded my first drill lesson, I had recovered my equanimity. When they marched in I asked them to sing a hymn and then I led prayers.

'I am here to help you. You must help me to make our school a success.' I concluded in my appeal for co-operation. I called the roll and shook every scholar by hand. My nervousness had given way to pleasant thrills. I took myself and everything seriously. I put some regulations of punctuality, cleanliness and orderliness. I caned a tall boy who made a noise and thus on my arrival showed that I would not be defied. I remarked upon unwashed feet and dirty dresses. With a sigh of satisfaction, I closed my first day.

In the afternoon, I reached my new home with the elder of the district. From the first meeting there was hostility between us. 'You ask from me how to conduct the school,' he said. 'Moreover, do not visit these people for they are secessionists from the Church' (meaning the Free Church). These advices made me resolve to see things for myself. For the present I kept quiet and wanted to know where I was to stay. 'You will occupy one of the huts with the boys.' I did not like the idea but had to submit. Thus, for the first time, I lived in a hut. It was no easy thing to crouch every moment I walked in or out. There was no bed. I spread grass mats and slept on them.

The following day, I commenced my disciplinary actions by using the cane. Without any training in school management, I merely used methods which our teachers had utilized. I was free with my cane. Latecomers, scholars who appeared shabby, those who made mistakes in lessons and all who wanted to disturb others were all severely punished. The elder took me to task for it and said that I would destroy the school because many children would leave. 'I was sent here to do my work and will do it in the best method without consulting you,' was my reply.

'He is too young,' was the universal comment of the parents at Mumbe when I greeted them after Church services on my first Sunday. Well they might thus exclaim, for I looked younger than my years and therefore appeared little more than a smart urchin. 'The young tree bends quicker,' was my humorous reply. I marvelled at their simplicity after talking with them. I decided to visit them in their own homes.

Every afternoon, I took my way to strange households. I was generally received with great hospitality. The people lived in a location under Chief Kula. They were almost cut off from civilization. Men and women ploughed the fields. There was little arable land, for the whole district was stony and thorny. Agricultural produce was insufficient to ensure their living. Most of the men went out to work in towns. There were hardly any young men at home. Girls did most of the work. All were shabbily attired in coarse cotton clothes. Poverty was written on all sides. Mealie-pap from ground maize was their staple food. They lived in huts and were addicted to their primitive modes of life. There was neither a clinic, hospital nor doctor in the vicinity. Living in ignorance, they found contact with the outside world through their working sons, brothers or husbands. Their food was of a coarse quality and insufficiently nourishing. Children died in hundreds. There were no highways. The district was overcrowded with people and overstocked.

The people retained many of their ancient traditions of which I knew little. One day I was invited by a few young men to accompany them to a 'Thanksgiving' ceremony. When we approached the kraal whither we were bound, we espied a white kerchief tied to a pole. One of us went to the elder of the household and sent his respects. We were then motioned to a hut where we found many maidens gathered. For a long time we sat without saying a word. The silence provoked the girls to hilarity, and merry peals of laughter followed. After a long time, our leader addressed them. 'We have come to thank you, White Lady, for having sympathized with us.' Merry peals of laughter again followed. Beer was brought and we left. On the way I asked what it was all about. 'We had gone to thank one of the girls for falling in love with this young man.' It was then that I remembered how he had been so silent and solemn while I also recollected a girl, his sweetheart, who had behaved in a similar manner in spite of all provocations to mirth.

Another evening I attended a strange ceremony. A girl was being admitted into the ranks of maidens and would thus be eligible for becoming someone's sweetheart. She could not fall in love before getting the consent of others of her age and older ones. So now I accompanied some girl friends to the house. Young men were not allowed to see her as she sat surrounded by elderly women who instructed her about intersexual intercourse and her decorum with men and counselled her as to how best to secure her virginity on which depended her marriage and Lobola (bride-price of cattle). We feasted and had a mixed dance. Half of it was the old Zulu dance of hand clapping, and the other was a Europeanized ragtime march, which blended so well that, although ignorant, I was pleased to watch it. The young candidate could not participate. She was subjected to severe advices and plain talks from her mentors. Such diversions amused me. They did more. They were the cause of my great popularity, for when the people saw a townboy, a teacher, and an educated young man so freely mingle with them and show such an interest in their lives they responded with love and sympathy. Women were specially my friends. They lamented the shortsightedness of those who had arranged my lodging with the silent man whom they accused of being a 'wizard'. Hearing that I was not used to mealie-pap, they endeavoured to lighten my fare by sending me sweet potatoes, some meat, beans and better food. This exasperated my guardian. We hardly agreed.

To relieve the otherwise unbearable monotony of reading and visiting people, I took week-end excursions to the Gordon Memorial Mission Station settlement, six miles away. I found that people lived a better life. Their houses were mud buildings. Meat was frequently on their tables. Most of their children were attending school. But in other respects they lived almost the same lives.

My companions were usually girls, for there were few young men. I was saved from flirtation by conscientious scruples as to the propriety of such conduct during my probation. Moreover, as most of them were but indifferently educated, I looked down upon them as country louts. However, I managed to win their abiding friendship. In other respects my conduct was irreproachable. Although I frequently used the cane, I was a great favourite with my scholars.

'I am pleased with you,' said Mr. D. and Mr. Kumalo after examining my school. I had only three failures. It was a great day for me to obtain an excellent bursary. Such words of praise inspired my ambition. I valued my success at its worth and saw that henceforth it would take a first-class catastrophe to debar me. I would close the school with such entertainments as we used to have in town schools.

Once again I learnt a new thing. Instead of the evening, the closing concert took place during the day. Herdboys, scuffling maidens from the fields, mothers and a few fathers all seated on stones composed a vast audience. The dumb-bell and reed-drills, recitations, dialogues and musical programme were of such variety as won the admiration of all. Tremendous applause followed every item. I left with colours flying and knew it. Now I will go further.

I had every reason to be proud of my achievements. On a small scale I had paralleled Booker Washington. I had been highly commended for all I had undertaken. As a scholar I had been unequalled, as a worker I had proved indefatigable, and as a teacher I had been superb. Now, through my own efforts, I had my way clear for college. I had recently gone to the Vryheid East station to book my seat for Amanzimtoti, the American Board Mission in Natal, whither I was bound in a week's time. It looked like a dream. My parents were glad of the distinction I was acquiring. My prospects were bright when I entrained with a few scholars to different colleges in Natal.

Tears had been dried, the last advices given, and the last handshakes over, when the whistle blew and the engine was in motion. I was excited, for besides my great hopes of college success this was my first long journey by train. At Glencoe Junction we changed and took the Durban-Johannesburg mail. In every town our numbers increased. Different hat-badges distinguished students of various colleges. We made many hearty friends in the way. We ate provisions in common. Girls usually carried more provisions than boys and we dined at their expense. At eleven in the night, we were separated from girls, although white students travel together. We rejoined one another in the morning. Most of us were sleepy, but the electric engine still annihilated time and space. We had passed Ladysmith, crossed the Tugela and were at Maritzburg before nine in the morning. At noon we reached Durban, the harbour-city of Natal, the largest town in the province and the third largest in the Union.

Amanzimtoti means sweet water. It is so called because one of Chaka's Impis passed that stream after having had no water for two days. 'This water is sweet,' said those doughty warriors as they quenched their thirst. However, their tramp had been succeeded by that of the gentle-moving, ever-smiling missionary. All those regions suddenly became mission reserves. The inhabitants were compelled to pay rent.

The settlement was extensive. On all sides from the station, we saw white houses and large cane-fields. Our highway was through thickets, scrubs and woods. We would have fared ill if we had carried our luggage. Fortunately two waggons were sent to meet us and so we had placed our boxes away and marched. Now that the exciting journey was ended, fears began to assail me. Most of my companions had been older than I was. Moreover, in my corner, I had always been an object of admiration. The behaviour of some of the boys as we neared the mission houses gave me cause for fear that I might be tormented.

'Newcomer! tails off!' they hissed. That was the signal of a smart thrashing. It was uncomfortable to have to run after such a long journey. It was either that or severe thrashings from unknown boys. What irritated me was that the others appeared to treat it like a joke. It was a crude one, all the same, when switches broke upon one's ears. It was with a sigh of relief that I espied and was shown the Chapel. A little further were brick buildings. 'That is the Normal School. . . . That is the Boys' High School,' said my informant, pointing out a smaller building under a mulberry tree. 'That house on the right is the schoolroom of agricultural students and theologists.' Further up was the boys' dormitory, known as the Jubilee Hall, built on an elevated eminence. 'At last!' we sighed.

We found the Boarding Master a conceited little man who allotted us to our different dormitories. I was sent to one with eight others but, when we appeared, some of the older comers hissed us away. Thoroughly frightened, because we were all newcomers, we refused to go. The Boarding Master came and heard our story. Instead of promising to punish our tormentors, he merely laughed and assigned us another one, upstairs. It was a change for the worse, as we soon found out when we went to bed.

But, before then, the Principal came in to say a few words. 'I welcome you, boys, particularly the new ones. I hope that you will learn valuable lessons in a Christian institution and in future become torches to light the whole of Africa. Do not drift, boys. Hold steadfastly to your purpose.' We felt a bit reassured. Hardly had he departed than the teachers also vanished. Belts were out in a moment and the older students were giving us a sound flogging. We were newcomers and did not know whither to escape. After a while the teachers entered and the belts disappeared. On our way upstairs the tale was repeated. We crouched into our beds like malefactors. Hardly had the lights been blown, when we heard footfalls. Blows showered upon us. We were afraid to scream. The older students with whom we shared the dormitory condoled with us and said that such was college custom, so that we had to submit with a hope of doing the same to newcomers in the following year.

The following morning we woke up at four and went to have a wash in a bathroom which was served by four showers. An hour later, the morning prayer-bell rang. Afterwards we went into classrooms. I was allocated to Form A, Junior Certificate. I resented that because I had an idea that I would be trained in the Normal School. However, I did not protest. After breakfast we went to chapel for divine services.

My first day at college had begun. There were no admiring glances such as those to which I had become accustomed. I was a nonentity, worse than a cipher, among three hundred students. Our first lesson was English Grammar and History. My teacher was astonished at the extent of my knowledge. Within a week I had been promoted to a higher form. That was one of my few college successes.

I could not assimilate myself to life among boys. They tormented me much. I retaliated by leading a recluse life. When my duties were finished I used to shut myself up in the library during all my spare time. I had outgrown my youthful ambition of leading classes. All I cared for was to store my head with useful knowledge. I spent little time in studying my lessons for I seldom encountered difficulties. I memorized enough Latin to pass every lesson. For the rest, I left things to the inspiration of the moment. I imagined it would bring me notoriety to pass examinations without hard study. Perhaps it did, but my methods were unacceptable to teachers. I would sleep in class and only awaken when called upon to answer a question. Physical Science interested me. I solved most Algebra problems. Geometry fascinated me. I adored Latin. In English and History I argued with my teachers. For these reasons I was no popular scholar. Few teachers took notice of me. Mr. Z. A. Matthews, B.A., LL.B., Ph.D., the African Headmaster, was one of them. Mr. Martin Luther Kumalo, now a merchant at Inanda, was another. The rest were as hostile as the boys. I rejoiced at that stage of affairs, for it justified my heroics. I went my way and they went theirs. I broke minor college regulations with impunity because I wanted to show boys and teachers that I was no mere bookworm but a creature of blood-impulses and feelings. I rejoiced to find myself the object of universal dislike, for I argued that genius was misunderstood.

We seldom mixed with girls except during Student Christian Association days. I became an active member of that body because everything with an air of seriousness attracted me. I was one of the Y.M.C.A. choristers. I occasionally ventured into the football field. Otherwise I made no ties except in stealing visits to girls whenever there was a chance. These had no evil motives. I wanted sympathy. I wanted to open my suffering heart to others. And women are proverbially suited for that task.

At the half-annual examination, I was third. That unique position roused my slumbering energies. I decided that I would show my fellow students what my capabilities were. I passed in First Class. The following session, I repeated my feat. All the same I had made no social success. I was as unpopular and as lonely as ever. I had now exhausted all the Natal educational resources. If I wanted to continue my education, I would have to enter into the Matriculation class at the South African Native University at Fort Hare.

My future course was decided by very slight causes. One of them was my homesickness. Instead of remaining at school after the closing I decided to return home, if not to work in Durban. I left school without reporting and took myself to the Amanzimtoti Hotel. I worked in a huge boarding establishment. The work was very heavy and irksome. We worked fourteen hours a day without a rest. At the end of the month I quarrelled with my employer over wages. I left and entrained for Vryheid. My parents had not expected me because the stipulation was that I was to partly work off my school fees. I decided to take another job and perhaps not to return to school. I went to the Northfield colliery. The Compound Manager was kind and offered me a job if I produced my passes. That was my first experience of the Pass laws. I had none and so missed my job. I returned on a Friday night. The following day occurred a series of events that finally decided my destiny. On July 2nd, 1927, Messrs. Allison W. Champion, D. L. Bopela, I. J. London and Sam Dunn, all of whom had earned reputations as native agitators, went to Vryheid to address a meeting under the aegis of the Industrial and Commercial Workers Union of Africa, better known as the I.C.U. (I see you).

'Watch the I.C.U.' was splashed in huge headlines over many posters. Newspapers devoted columns to its affairs.

The Union was growing in numbers and strength. It is said to have had an annual income of £15,000. The name of Kadalie, its general secretary, began to inspire me with admiration. I read the growth of the movement and watched its progress. Established in 1919 to advance and protect the interest of the black South African workers, it was becoming a formidable power in those days.

The reason for its phenomenal growth was not far to seek. The aftermath of the Great War had resulted in higher living costs. Black workers, unorganized and exploited, had at last started to organize themselves. Kadalie, an African from Nyasaland, who had a splendid platform presence and demagogic style of address, had preached a gospel of economic and political upliftment. A number of Europeans, for not altogether altruistic reasons, helped Kadalie to form the I.C.U. It began in Cape Town with a membership of 12 in 1919, and slowly penetrated to the other three provinces of the Union of South Africa. In 1925 the I.C.U. had become well organized. Branches were opened in Natal. Champion, the Zulu leader, was instrumental in the fight against many injustices to which blacks in Durban were subjected. He fought for and won the abolition of the obnoxious regulation of dipping every newcomer into Durban, a municipal regulation which was in every respect similar to that of dipping cattle. He won a lawsuit which judged *ultra vires* the municipal curfew bye-laws and got the abolition of payment for special passes. He also got landlords to give their tenants three-month notices instead of merely evicting them when they liked. By such and similar victories, he established the I.C.U.

Living under the most brutal oppression, hopeless ignorance, disease, poverty and starvation, Africans were ready to follow a lead to emancipation. When the I.C.U.

raised the clarion cry 'Awaken, O Africa, for the morning is at hand', they responded in their thousands. In April 1927, the annual conference held in Durban had approved of sending Kadalie to Europe to seek affiliation with the International Federation of Trades Unions. Champion remained Acting General Secretary. Added to his Durban successes, that appointment was the momentum that carried him high. He displayed superhuman activities in establishing branches. In May 1927, when he took over, the membership was said to be forty thousand; it was close to a hundred thousand when he handed over to Kadalie in November.

Circulars had been issued far and wide for a great public meeting in Vryheid. Many country people thought that the I.C.U. leaders were American Negroes who had come to deliver them from slavery. Distorted and exaggerated statements had brought about confused ideas about the whole movement. Others said that it would cause the Boers to disgorge their farms; others said it was the beginning of mobilizing to fight against whites; and still others said that the conditions of the workers would be improved if they joined the I.C.U. Many a man joined the I.C.U. and then as a gesture of defiance refused to go to work, stating that the I.C.U. would soon free him. Others passed through farm-lands and defied landlords to stop them. However, the coming of the I.C.U. leaders was a memorable event. It stirred the district for miles. Not since the news of King Dinizulu's death, had Vryheid seen such a huge multitude.

Old Zulu War veterans, ringed men from the farms (*i.e.* wearing the circle of wax on their heads, a mark of seniority), young men from farms, middle-aged men from the mines, workers from the town, were all marching, column upon column, towards the venue of assembly near the cemetery at the west end of Vryheid. There was a considerable number of horsemen. In fact I began to think that there would be a fight, for I had seen over seven thousand people go to the meeting.

'Zulu of Malandela, we want to know what bone of contention there is between us and the British Government. Didn't Queen Victoria promise King Cetywayo that his people would be free as long as the sun rose and set? Why is it that today men, women and children are all sjamboked to go and work for the farmers without pay? From whom did these Dutch buy those farms? From whom did they conquer them?' In those striking words one of the leaders, standing on a motor car, opened the meeting. His rich bass voice reached the farthest end. The singing of the African National Anthem had been so lusty that the dead might have awakened. Tense expectation, triumph, approval and joy beamed in over seven thousand countenances. Their spirit was high and, had any white man interfered with their gathering, ugly incidents would have followed.

'The I.C.U. is the hen that will protect you. Unless you are united to break your chains, you will always be landless in your own fatherland. Why should you leave the bones of your ancestors and go to strange places? Unite, and be one, and you will be able to live in your country, free and happy. Join in your thousands.' The speech concluded amidst deafening cheers. Before the meeting closed at sunset, they pointed to Mr. Isaiah London: 'Here is one who will be your mouth and ears, O people of Vryheid, the famous Abaqulusi, who are never conquered.'

Thus was London installed as Branch Secretary. Everybody wanted to join. Champion had said a few words to me and asked me to issue membership cards to intending members. I was absorbed in my task and I wrote until my arm ached. We put off many and asked them to come the following day. Vast crowds surrounded us. London asked me to help him to get an office. On Monday we were settled opposite the Dutch Reformed Church. I soon became Assistant Branch Secretary, because I attended to the people's complaints and got their statements ready for London.

The people's grievances were no joke. Their landlords compelled them to work for the year round without any pay. Moreover, they demanded the services of all family members. They sjamboked and maltreated their tenants. Cases of burning and shooting were frequent. From the daily reports handed in I discovered that there was terrorism right under my nose. And those people flocked to the I.C.U. as to the ark which would convey them to safety. What made matters worse was that their tenure was insecure. They were liable to eviction from farms at any season and moment. They had no time to attend to the proper cultivation of their patches of unarable fields. They could not build decent houses. Their best cattle were always wheedled by their landlords. They were compelled to dip their cattle frequently, while their landlords seldom did so. Failing to do so, or being in arrears with their dipping fees, they were criminally prosecuted. I had to take statements of all those things. In my investigation, I used my old methods of affability in conversation and thus charmed all who spoke to me.

I became a great reader of the *Workers' Herald*, to which I occasionally contributed a few news items. I was fascinated by my work and my dreams of eminence were taking a definite shape. I was to be a great African leader. The prospect cheered me and made me endeavour to fit myself for the rôle by every available means. So absorbed was I that I missed six weeks of school. However, I returned in time to pass my Junior Certificate examination. After the examinations I left school finally to plunge myself in public life. I returned in time to be elected as one of the delegates to the famous Special Conference of the I.C.U. at Kimberley.

Cecil Rhodes was besieged in Kimberley during the Anglo-Boer War. This centre of the diamond-mining industry occupies a comfortable niche in the history of South Africa. The discovery of diamonds in 1867 changed the prospects of South Africa from those of a pastoral and agricultural country, to those of a beehive of commerce and industry. Cecil Rhodes made his fortunes and laid his Empire-building schemes within the diamond town. Thus the conference was held in a fitting spot. The historical gathering was worthy of the place.

For a couple of days delegates from all the Union came in dozens. Most of them were young and well dressed. Accommodation had already been arranged so there were no difficulties. Kadalie had recently returned from Europe and I was tingling with excitement to see him. His address was bold and eloquent. As the discussions continued, he said he would like to bring a private secretary from England. 'Kadalie, you went out black; have you returned white?' asked a buxom lady from Boksburg. This attack continued until the first serious disagreement with Champion on the question of buying land for those natives who were being evicted by their landlords. 'I do not think that the I.C.U. funds will be sufficient for this great work. We should have a special Farm Purchase Fund,' Champion said in making his motion. 'Jews always want more money. The I.C.U. funds are sufficient enough to buy a hundred farms,' Kadalie replied, and a brisk duel was carried on.

Outside the conference I saw some of the 'deliverers of Africa' at first hand. It was an appalling sight. . . . All these and the developing disagreements made me rub my eyes. However, I was only a boy and so quietly watched. I was convinced that unless a radical change was made, it would be the beginning of the end. After a week we returned home. The total result of the conference was that an amended constitution had been adopted! Such are things of momentous importance in African assemblies. The constitution plays a part out of proportion to its usefulness. People are wedded to it. Whenever there is a programme laid down, they want to see a constitution. They have a fetish for it. And so our conference was a success in that we got another constitution!

The adaptation of the constitution was no remedy for the evils I found on my return. The Boer farmers had organized an eviction campaign. Throughout the countryside families were evicted in hundreds. Naturally they went to the I.C.U. offices where they had been promised freedom. Farmers refused to have tenants who were members of the I.C.U. They spied them out, felling their huts to the ground, burning out others, and throwing them on to the roads, confiscating their stock if they did not leave quickly enough. If farms were to be bought, that was the time when the sufferings of the people were becoming acute. Instead, secretaries enjoyed joy-rides in cars, lived fast and ran up and down the countryside.

Contributions were dropping. People everywhere clamoured for Kadalie. We hoped that his mere arrival would stem the downward trend. For two months we wrote him to come. Then burst that counter-offensive of the Natal farmers—the Greytown episode. None knows the perpetrator of the abominable crime of desecrating European graves at Greytown. But the farmers fastened the blame on to the I.C.U. They alleged that one of the former secretaries had done the evil deed. That was cause enough to make them adopt vigorous measures of intimidation. They attacked and raided the I.C.U. offices at Krantzkop, Weenen and Greytown. They even marched to Maritzburg. We trembled that they might visit us.

It was now a question of endurance. If the Africans would stand united for another twelve months, the fate of the landowners would be compromised, for their livelihoods and prosperity were dependent upon semi-villeinage labour for which they hardly paid a farthing. Africans were ready to do anything in order to throw off the chains of servitude and slavery. Everything rested with the higher officials. A general strike, passive, or even active resistance, demonstrations, or any militant move would, at that time, have changed the history of the Union. The masses were ready to follow the lead even to death. The news of the outrages had hardened their determination to strive to the last. Everything depended upon the leaders; and they gave no lead.

Instead a conference was summoned to meet at Bloemfontein. I enjoyed my first visit to the central town of the Union, the judicial capital of South Africa, and an important railway centre. When we alighted at the station, we found many people with I.C.U. badges. They conducted us to the taxis and we took our way to the Native Township or, as it is better known, the location.

We found the evidence of our popularity everywhere. Crowds of people followed us. In the 'model location' we found nothing model at all. Highways were sandy and muddy. Many houses were in a dilapidated condition. Crowds of ill-clad and underfed children met us from all sides. Nor were their parents in a better plight. Many of them hailed from the country districts from whence they had gone into town in order to escape from the rigours of landlord rule. Bloemfontein is not so industrially developed as Durban and Johannesburg are. The wages paid to African workers in the few secondary industries and domestic service in Bloemfontein are usually so low that they cannot make ends meet, even if they have to sublet some rooms in their houses and their wives and children have to supplement family incomes by going to work. Whatever improvements had been possible were brought about as a direct result of the 1924 insurrectionary upheavals, really location rent-strikes, in which the I.C.U. played a prominent part. However, we were much struck by this central city of the Union, more so as its Bishop was one of those who fearlessly championed the cause of the African. It was gratifying to find that he would address a few words to our gathering.

No sooner had all the delegates arrived than we saw that there was a storm. I had noticed it in the Head Office in Johannesburg, when the Acting Organizing Secretary and other high officials had spoken contemptuously about the former Acting General Secretary. On the day scheduled for the opening, we were disappointed because the African National Congress, in session also, occupied the hall. The next day, a compromise for the alternate use of the hall was agreed.

The Mayor of Bloemfontein opened our deliberations. After him spoke the Bishop, making a strong plea for moderation. After the roll-call of delegates, the President gave his Presidential report. It was long and interesting. It showed that the I.C.U. was flourishing, but lacked balance. In spite of the sums of money at its disposal, its influence and following, there had been nothing tangible done for South African workers. The report of the General Secretary did not materially differ. All discussions were overshadowed by an announcement that the National Council had decided to suspend Comrade Champion pending the investigation of his financial control of I.C.U. funds in Durban.

'This question should be properly investigated before the National Council takes a decision, otherwise it will have tragic results,' I said, but some of the senior officials shouted me down. I thought that Zulu delegates, at least those from Natal, would not be content to let the matter lie there. To my surprise many did. But a few bold ones stood like a rock and demanded a proper investigation into the whole affair. It was useless, for the end had been a foregone conclusion. Thus was Champion unfairly and unconstitutionally suspended.

'If I am a Jonah in the ship of the I.C.U.,' said Champion, 'let me be thrown out; but, if I am not, then I say Kadalie has committed a great fault. I was refused a hearing and——' The rest of the sentence was inarticulate, for he came from a sick bed. He had been sick since he left Natal, and it was only the threats that he was afraid because of his alleged misdeeds that compelled him to go and face his accuser. We all felt as if a great shade had befallen us. Whatever the merits and demerits of the case were, the manner he was suspended was wrong and led to dramatic results.

One other interesting thing was the question of the raided I.C.U. offices. Some of the secretaries who had escaped totally refused to go back. We were promised that the services of a trained Trades Union adviser from England would soon be possible because Kadalie had made all arrangements. After a few days' confabulation we dispersed.

For a time there was a lull. Then clouds began to gather. First Kadalie addressed a meeting in Pretoria. In the course of his speech, he said, 'The land belongs neither to King George nor Moshesh [the founder of the Basuto nation], but to the Lord, and the fulness thereof. Unless the South African Government concedes to our demands, we shall raise an army of labourers of which I will be Field Marshal . . .' For that he was neatly snapped under the Native Administration Act. He was accused of using words intended to promote hostility between blacks and whites. He won the case on appeal owing to a legal technicality.

Then came the Durban storm. It was heavier and more dangerous.

Champion had passed on to his home in Inanda. Delegates from Durban had reported the steam-rolling tendencies of his accusers. Then began a burble. A special meeting of the Natal Branch Secretaries and delegates was convened, but did not come off. We were, however, there with a few others. In the African Workers' Club a crowd of over two thousand was impatiently awaiting Kadalie who was due to go and give an explanation to the members of the Durban Branch. Comrade J. H. London, brother to my former colleague, was in the chair. Hour after hour we waited and yet Kadalie was nowhere to be seen. Tempers were running high, when London and a few others decided to go and fetch him from Maritzburg. Leaving at dead of night by car, they returned with him at 2.45 a.m.

'It is not for me to say anything in this connection. Like you I am awaiting the Commission of Inquiry.' Those remarks were enough. A volley of questions was fired at him. The Acting Organizing Secretary who accompanied him crouched away. Then pent-up feelings broke loose. 'We are gentlemen, Kadalie, and cannot be treated like boys by a Nyasalander like you,' said London.

I cannot tell who gave the signal, but Kadalie received one of the severest thrashings of his life. He managed to force his way out and ran away to a café. Later in the morning he got another dose of corporal punishment. That was enough and decided him to make for safety in flight.

It should, however, in fairness to Kadalie, be mentioned that the Commission of Inquiry, which was set up by the National Council of the I.C.U., was one which arose out of two incidents. The first was the severe strictures on the management of I.C.U. funds made by the judge when he dismissed an action for damages by Champion against a Basuto resident in Durban named Lenono. It was alleged that Lenono had, in a pamphlet dealing with I.C.U. Natal section affairs, libelled Champion. The other was the report of the Johannesburg firm of auditors and accountants which revealed a serious state of affairs relative to the general conduct of I.C.U. business. It was not possible to bring the real culprit to book, because of the general disintegration of the I.C.U. which followed the libel action and auditors' report, and because it was necessary to institute civil proceedings before criminal action could be attempted.

After that things happened fast. There were loud talks of Natal breaking from the Union. My sympathies were on that side but I feared that such a step would lead to disintegration. Being young and inexperienced, I resolved to keep a discreet neutrality. For that purpose I stayed a short time in Durban, watched processions and endless meetings, and when I saw that secession was only a question of time, I returned to Vryheid.

I found a copy of the Clean Administration Manifesto, signed by three leading officials, in which Kadalie was subjected to great criticism. The document was a scurrilous attack, personal, abusive, in many parts unfounded, and calculated to shake the people's confidence in Kadalie. The storm which had been brewing broke out on 31st May. On that day, the I.C.U. Yase (of) Natal was formed and Comrade Champion was asked to become its General Secretary. Enemies of the I.C.U. made use of that and of the Clean Administration Manifesto. I resolved to go to Johannesburg to help to save unity. I realized that once we divided we could not stand another month. The plain question before us was: would we divide or not? There was no possibility of a middle way.

Meanwhile the rank and file was getting out of hand. Many members ceased to pay their monthly dues. The wild promises about buying farms had given them eager expectations, and now that they were being ejected in hundreds from their farms under circumstances of revolting cruelty, they looked to their 'Saviours' for a lead. Instead, they found hopeless division. Disillusionment turned them against us. Some brought their membership cards and demanded their monies back. The splits in the higher ranks cut the ground under our feet. We had no answer for the rank and file. We could only hope that they would be patient and everything would come right.

Night after night, during the whole of June, our Committee met and came to no decision about joining the Natal I.C.U. They feared to convene a public meeting because the members were losing interest in the whole movement and were only challenging the fulfilment of promises. My desire to go to Johannesburg was no mad plan. I was weighing the question of either remaining in my branch and trying to restore the lost situation, or of going to our Headquarters and seeing what could be done from there. Moreover, I was excessively self-confident and doubted not that I could be of greater utility. There also came another question. 'A prophet hath no honour in his country.' That decided me, for Vryheid was my home and I feared that I would not get that distinction which it was my constant objective to attain. In the beginning of July, I crossed the Rubicon.

'Have you got a pass?' the ticket clerk asked me at the station. 'No,' was my answer. 'Then you cannot go to Johannesburg.' That unsettled my plans for a day. My father went to the Pass Office and got me a travelling pass. Before we got it they asked if I had paid my tax. So I had to pay it before receiving the precious documents. Now, armed with a tax receipt and travelling pass, I went to fetch my ticket. I got it and then entrained for Johannesburg.

My journey was delightful, and I saw many places, but met no noteworthy incident. I alighted on the following afternoon and went to the I.C.U. Head Office in the semi-slum district of Ferreirastown, Johannesburg.

'Good evening, comrade; so you are from Natal?' inquired the Assistant Branch Secretary of Johannesburg, when we first met, outside the I.C.U. Tea Room. He led me inside and, when I had divested myself of my luggage, he ordered some meals. The tea room was neat and tidy. Fine pictures of distinguished black men, like Marcus Garvey and others, decorated the wall. In an adjoining chamber was a library, which had been generously stocked by British workers' unions, and sympathetic British people such as A. Creech Jones and Miss Winifred Holtby.

My friend came along and told me many things. 'I tell you, comrade, the whole thing is finished. We have received no pay for over three months; lawyers confiscate our furniture, the *Workers' Herald* has ceased publication. . . .' 'And the rank and file?' I ventured to ask when

I recovered from the bitter shock at hearing of the downfall of our mighty organization, which I had devoutly hoped would bring about the emancipation of Africa. 'There one is at the moment uncertain what developments will take place.' 'Do they still attend meetings?' 'Not as much as they did. We all await the arrival of Comrade Ballinger [The Trade Union and Co-operative Adviser from Scotland] to put things straight.' After a while he took me to the Branch Office, on the opposite street. Many officials lived there and I was soon among old friends and introduced to others.

My fears grew as I heard their description of the situation. They all pointed out how monies had been squandered as much by maladministration as the habit of engaging lawyers for trifles. The salaries of officials had been extravagantly high. In short, money had been freely spent without bringing any benefit to the Union, or the workers who were consequently becoming indifferent. Two of us slept on papers spread over tables. In this guise we started our work in the Golden City. In a few days I had enough information to understand the seriousness of the crisis. Attachment orders became a usual phenomenon.

I looked round the locality. It was one of the most repulsive slums of Johannesburg, known as Malay Camp. The lives and conditions of people at Malay Camp were a direct indictment of the capitalist regime which crushes humanity on the wheels of industrialism, fosters a destructive competition for work, exploits the workers and leaves them ignorant, underfed and under-nourished. People lived in dilapidated buildings, fitter for pigs than for human habitation. Many had been reduced by unemployment to that deplorable condition of being illicit liquor-vendors and bootleggers, prostitutes and thieves, gamblers and illicit drug and liquor-sellers. Africans, Indians, Coloureds, Syrians and Poor Whites congregated in that part of the city, paid exorbitant rents and, being unable to educate their children, bred a type of wild, violent criminal, and generally lived amidst insecurity, squalor, crime, disease and poverty. Stabbings were everyday occurrences. It was a common sight to find women reel in the last stages of intoxication to fight against men in the same conditions. Houses were small, ill ventilated and full of vermin. Liquor smelled all round. The police frequently made raids and humanity was seen at its worst.

The I.C.U. Head Office showed all signs of anarchism and laxity. While the leaders of the workers were thus occupied, the Urban Areas Act was being enforced and Africans were daily segregated to the sterile, unhealthy and badly administered locations. The Municipality of Johannesburg was building houses for letting to Africans at high rentals. The high rentals are in large measure due to a policy of 'white labour' in the erection of native houses. The Western Native Township was fenced and Africans could make neither ingress nor egress without police supervision. The Pass laws were intensified. One could not leave one suburb for another without a pass. The curfew regulations hung like a millstone round the neck of every African. Their section-slums and locations were subjected to frequent police-raids which were conducted at all hours of the day and night, and displayed great severity, overturnings of utensils, indiscriminate sjamboking, and abusive language. At work, they suffered worse, because they were debarred from legally forming Trades Unions and thus could not collectively bargain for their labour. No matter how bad conditions were, no African could go on strike, for that was a criminal offence.

They accepted whatever wages and conditions the masters imposed. Those wages were insufficient for a decent living. The African worker paid half for rent, and the rest melted away for wood, coal, candles, food. He had nothing for clothing or educating his children. His wife had to supplement the family income. In many cases children went to work too.

Other workers had come from the country in order to earn enough money to pay their poll taxes and dipping fees. They took worse conditions and lower wages. They usually lived in compounds divorced from all social life. Meetings were prohibited. These men were herded and guarded day and night. They were encouraged to perform tribal 'war dances'. In consequence tribal fights often broke out in the compounds.

Many wives and girls, failing to get jobs, resorted to illicit liquor-traffic. They concocted many intoxicants. Some were poisonous. Snakes were dug out of one of them. Other liquor-brewers washed themselves in it before serving it, so as to attract many customers according to herbalist instructions. Big crowds of men visited liquor-dens after hours. They were prohibited from getting liquor elsewhere. They drank hurriedly in order to avoid the police. The liquor-seller and her assistants had to humour them in order to retain their patronage. Love-ties were formed. Friction followed after a clash because the liquor-seller was obliged to have as many sweethearts as she could.

Meanwhile, family ties are loosened. Children grow up in the streets without any discipline. Subjected to no control, they beg for pennies, steal, lie, swear, smoke dagga, become pickpockets, card-sharpers, drunkards and all kinds of criminals.

We conducted meetings at the Workers' Hall. The rank and file showed its hostility to some of the officials by rough-handling them. Comrade Champion had explained the position in Natal at a meeting in Johannesburg. The National Council (the governing body of the I.C.U.) had been adjourned until after the arrival of Comrade Ballinger. No one had any workable plan. All wallowed in darkness.

'You are doing in fifty years what the European worker has done in two hundred years.' Comrade Ballinger continued to elaborate his explanations of the African's place in South African economics and how to improve it by Trades Union and Co-operative Organization. The workers listened attentively to his first speech in the Workers' Hall on 18th July, 1928.

Optimism returned. Ballinger became a mystery man. The Communists, Trades Unionists, Joint Councils and the Government wanted to discover his intentions. 'Forgive and forget' was his opening remark to the members of the National Council. He attempted a compromise with Comrade Champion on the question of Branch financial autonomy. Negotiations broke down.

Urgent debts were discharged. Workers were organized sectionally. The *Workers' Herald* was revived. Active propaganda became the order of the day. Randfontein location was my first hostile gathering. We went out to hold a meeting during the National Council Session in order to raise funds and resuscitate the dying Union.

'What have you done with our monies?' was the frequently-asked question at our meeting. We succeeded in raising some money, for which we were highly commended at Headquarters. Going through the I.C.U. files I learnt the key to many riddles. I discovered how an opportunity for raising the working class to fight for better conditions had been missed by a policy of opportunism. There was no lead given except an appeal for funds. That done, all would be well.

The rank and file asked pertinent questions. They asked what had become of abolition of the Pass laws, the agitation for which they had paid a special levy; better working conditions for which they contributed every month. Disillusionment had followed. We were, however, successful in restoring some of the lost confidence in the I.C.U. I was appointed Assistant District Secretary for the East Rand.

Ballinger accompanied a deputation of I.C.U. leaders on behalf of the postal workers to interview the Minister of Posts and Telegraphs. The news caused a Cabinet crisis, which resulted in a political sensation and a reconstructed Cabinet. The incident was one of the last signs of I.C.U. activity. The resuscitation plans had not succeeded according to expectation. The rank and file was adamant in its indifference, although a considerable number of workers prepared to activize themselves. The secession movement in Natal damped enthusiasm.

'You have to do your best in reviving Maritzburg' were my final orders before leaving for my new sphere of work. Anything to get away from Germiston was welcome. Not that I hated my work. I was in fact deeply engrossed in it. Each upward surge I took for a prognostication of brighter prospects for the future. With a heart beating high with hope, proud of my puny achievement and the favourable opinions I still received from all with whom I came into contact, I entrained in an optimistic mood as to how I would conduct reorganization in Natal and check the tide of the secession movement. The Branch Secretary of Dundee told me a doleful tale. All efforts at reconciliation with the Yase Natal had fallen to ashes. The Branch Secretary had escaped death at the hands of irate agricultural workers who had been expelled from the farms on account of having identified themselves with the I.C.U. 'They wanted their money. I tried to explain and they said we were in league with the Dutch farmers. . . .' 'Anyway, how is your Branch?' 'It is dying.' We discussed its dying pangs until the meeting on the following afternoon. The audience received our appeals favourably and I left with the best hope that things were not as they had been painted. The stage was set for an active revival when the news of the resignation of Kadalie, the General Secretary, came as a thunderbolt. He immediately formed another organization, which became known as the Independent I.C.U. He toured the country complaining that the I.C.U. had been captured by a white man. In actual fact he objected to the financial control of the organization being placed in the hands of a treasurer and two trustees, and did not like the counsel of Mr. Ballinger, the Adviser.

Everybody was thrown into confusion. The banner of unity was long maintained in Maritzburg against dangerous odds. Ballinger had occasion to admire the determination and courage shown. But all was in vain. The mighty I.C.U. was no more.

The Yase Natal made some progress. When everything was in confusion, the workers of Durban prepared to struggle against senseless restrictions. They had already, as fruits of their solidarity, overthrown some abuses such as that of policemen who arrested every African in the early morning hours. The immediate point at issue was that harbour-workers were prohibited from fermenting their porridge to drink, in order that they should drink municipal beer at the Beer Hall. This liquor question is a peculiarity of Natal.

Municipal beer houses are established under municipalities to sell 'utshwala' (native beer), the African's original beverage made of fermented corn. The proceeds swell the Council coffers, while nothing is done for blacks. The workers resented this curtailment of their rights and retaliated by a boycott. They held a meeting in the I.C.U. office, where, as Secretary for the evening, I took among the notes the famous resolution to the effect that no African was to drink beer from a municipal beer house.

A railway policeman thought it fit to disobey. He got it in the neck. He left the hall faster than he entered. A crowd of workers were belabouring him with sticks. It was the beginning of the awful 'Bloody week' in Durban. Gangs of civilians perambulated the city in lorries, shooting. Blacks retaliated. Bullets whistled round. As we turned one street my friend dropped from a shot in the eye. Stones, bricks and bottles rained like hailstones. It was difficult to send him to a place of safety. The police charged with revolvers and batons.

One had to use every missile to fight his way. Life hung on a thread. The police, unable to quell the disturbance, looked to the mobile squadrons called from Pretoria, Maritzburg and other parts of the country for help. The women of Weenen and other parts of the country raided beer houses. The struggle collapsed after a week of heavy casualties, including death on both sides. A Government Commission of Inquiry was sent to investigate the causes of the riots.

On our return to Maritzburg, we found that most of the forward leaders were not prepared to hold a meeting for fear of the police. Our example gave them courage. But Maritzburg showed no signs of militancy.

I read Communistic literature. I studied industrialism, economics and revolutionary tactics with avidity. Having formerly been largely influenced by Garveyism, I was now able to discover some fallacies in the 'redemption of

Africa' methods. What was needed was first to give the masses knowledge and understanding of the way out of their oppression. It would be the work of years. They were so hopelessly ignorant, terrorized, disillusioned and standoffish that one was apt to be pessimistic about their future. Later I was expelled from the Communist Party for my 'reformist activities'. Now the first thing for a man to do is to get food, clothing and the necessities of life. I had been working for over eighteen months without a penny payment. Had I not discharged my duty to my race? It was high time I earned a living and supported my parents. I was in tatters. Sometimes I had no sleeping place. At others I had nothing to eat. The question decided, the problem was how to get a job.

'I am sorry we have no work.' . . . 'I am reducing the number of my boys.' . . . 'No work, Jim.' Such answers tend to become monotonous when one hears them every five minutes. It required great courage to get up early every morning, enter every shop and factory, and demurely ask for work—and get these answers. I was not particular what job it was, as long as I could earn money. Day after day I walked out to meet this same dismal tale. In my ignorance I thought myself to be the most miserable youth in the world. I soon discarded that when I met groups of men who had been looking for work for over a year. The great depression was beginning in full tide.

In my despair I tried to run a dancing house, but was soon compelled to close it on account of licence fees and other charges I could not meet. After three months of weary daily searches, my application to the Grey's Hospital as interpreter-clerk was accepted. Called for an interview, I read all I could about behaviour under such circumstances.

The hospital, at the eastern end of the town on the road to Durban, is situated under trees and near a stream. It consists of four blocks. One at the entrance, the Out-Patients', another to the right, European male and female wards; further down, the male and female wards for Africans; lower still, a European Children's ward. In addition there were a store-room, a laundry and administrative offices.

The Secretary's office was cosily furnished. My feet sank into the carpet as I stood before him. 'We pay three pounds a month, rations and uniform found.' 'Thanks, Sir.' 'You will go to Frank for other things.' The Frank referred to was to be my colleague. He soon taught me the essentials of my job. In white uniform I went to the Out-Patients' Department to interpret for the doctor.

'Don't speak English to me', said one of the sisters in Zulu, when I tried to do my work. I did not know that many Natal whites, who claim to know the African, do not want to have dealings with the sophisticated and English-speaking black man. They take it to be presumption and call him a spoilt Kaffir. However, I went on with my task. Among other duties, I was a telephone operator. The whites with whom we shared this job were paid eight times what we got. And yet none of them were culturally and educationally our superiors!

Life in the hospital was thrilling. Here came a miserable woman looking for her beloved one, a sickly old woman who wanted shelter, expectant mothers and ailing men and women—each with his and her tale of sorrows, which they imparted to anyone fond of listening. Some were stupid, and in interpreting for them it was hard to bear with their circumlocution. Ambulances brought dangerously wounded men—some stabbed and others injured in work and street accidents. People lost their distinction and became 'cases'.

Having completed the routine of clerical work, I was suddenly transferred to the wards as an orderly. A scheme was on foot to train first-class African orderlies, who would be required to pass the same academic and professional examinations as white nurses. I was thrilled at the prospect. A few days inside were enough to convince me how necessary such a step was. Patients felt like prisoners in the hospital. Forced to speak through interpreters, they could not easily make their wants easily known. White girls were averse to handling 'Kaffirs'.

Relief was seen all round when, after three months, a second African orderly came for training. There were three Dutch ones. We all had the same working hours. Our duties were alike. While a staff nurse was in charge of the Medical ward, I was in that of the Surgical. We changed places until I was the first African to go unsupervised, except by the night sister and staff nurse, on night duty. All those proofs of efficiency could not alter our wages. They were paid five times more than we got. White workers working side by side with black ones were inclined to put on superiority airs. Cordial unity between the two was almost impossible. They forgot their common economic interests in their racial antagonisms.

One found many tendencies among Africans. None ever thought of himself as a worker. He was a Zulu first and foremost. He worked so that he could buy cattle to pay Lobola for his wife. If he stayed in town, he wanted to educate his children so that they would get soft jobs. He was blind to the fact that there were no openings for them. He had no faith in his class and people. Individualism was giving him a petty-bourgeois outlook. This was largely reflected in the most advanced workers, who in other countries form the bulwarks of Communism, Socialism and Trades Unionism. Church positions and hand-to-mouth existence bounded their outlook. After the feverish excitements of the I.C.U. days, now fast setting, they turned towards churches, sports and beer drinks. They lost hope in any struggle for the betterment of their lot. Nothing was done to improve the lot of Africans in towns. Destitution, malnutrition, unemployment, degradation, crime, poverty and death claimed countless victims.

Sport was the great craze of the day. Every Saturday afternoon crowds flocked to the sports grounds to witness football matches. Indoor entertainments were confined to concerts. Ragtime comic songs provided the usual programmes. Dancing had already claimed adherents when the Town Council closed dance-halls. The native press echoed the sentiments of its subsidizers. It appealed for moderation and constitutionalism. The raw evils perpetrated upon the Africans as defenceless workers and as an oppressed nationality were not sufficiently exposed. It devoted huge space to sports and entertainments. The performances of our Bantu Concert Party under an official of the Native Affairs before a European audience on the City Hall steps was better news than the proposed branding of cattle at Bergville and Bulwer, although the latter almost led to bloodshed.

I was a lay-preacher in church and was meditating proceeding to Fort Hare for my theological studies. Was my duty to take the line of least resistance? No, I would fight until the abolition of African slavery. But how would I do it?

'*Ikwezi* is the paper that has the best news.' Such were my news-sales appeals as I sold copies of an English-vernacular weekly in the streets of Johannesburg. After that I had reported the proceedings of the Natal African Congress to the same paper which I was selling. A letter of my patron (the African lawyer, Dr. Seme) opened the gates of employment at Johannesburg, after my failure to get employment which would be congenial to me and also give me time to attend to public affairs.

I supervised all the Witwatersrand agents and also acted as Correspondent for the Transvaal. Although nearly 'genteel', the job was not so easy. Subscribers had fallen off; agents, often poor men themselves, had not resisted the temptation of keeping a few shillings and consequently sent no remittances to the Head Office in Eshowe, Zululand. It was adventuresome to go from town to town in the Reef canvassing for the support of a newspaper. I learnt that, all things equal, the contents of a journal are its decisive factor. Such was my first excursion into Journalism!

The Bantu Men's Social Centre was a club for African men where they could improve themselves culturally and entertain themselves with sport. The African intelligentsia had become wedded to the billiard tables. Most of the political renegades from national movements vied with one another for the favours of the authorities. A Bantu Sports Club to cater for healthy recreation had been established. Africans flocked thither in thousands. Those comprised some of the notable social welfare institutions which had opened under the aegis of the inter-racial co-operation movement in order to divert the energies of Africans into safe channels. Their success was unquestioned. The cream of African men of education was to be seen nowhere but in these institutions. And the depression was at its worst, while none cared to do anything for the masses.

'Special pass.' I turned towards the policeman who made that demand, while I was standing outside my room. I told him that I was staying in that yard and had only gone across the street for cigarettes. He handcuffed me to another man and we were all taken to the Central Charge Office, which we did not reach for another hour. Our arrest had been effected at 9.55 p.m. We entered the police station at 11.5. To our astonishment the constable charged us for having been out at 10.50 p.m. On trying to protest, I was silenced by a blow. On the following morning, we were taken into court under police escort.

The magistrate tried us in groups of six. When I explained the impossibility of obtaining a special pass while my masters were in Zululand, he gave me a caution and discharged me. I had not been long liberated when our journal ceased publication for a fortnight. I had no place in the new reorganization. I was once more thrown into the streets. And into those of Johannesburg, too! It was a great study.

White men stood in crowds at street corners. Their tattered garments and woebegone expressions indicated their hopeless plight. They were poor Whites, from the country, largely of Dutch origin, getting relief work by digging roads. 'Kaffir work', by which manual labour had been designated, had become a useless shibboleth. Droughts and other difficulties had reduced agriculture to bankruptcy. A great number of ruined farmers came into the Golden City. Trained for no special jobs, they competed with the unskilled Africans in all spheres of labour. They got soup kitchens, unemployment relief, free medical services and clothing. They were in many respects better off than the majority of African workers.

On being reduced to this army, my first desire was to write. I knew nothing of technique. I bombarded several newspapers with my manuscripts and got the usual rejection-slips. When the *Sunday Times* began to take some of my stuff, things slowly changed for the better. But no

African receives the usual journalistic rates. He is paid 'as a native'. The White Press was almost inaccessible to an African writer unless he happened to share anti-Africanism. It would rather publish third-rate stuff from white contributors than from Africans.

The failure of my journalistic efforts urged me to bustle for a job. It was the same old tale. There was nothing doing. I was a healthy young man, capable, fairly well educated, but I was black. The sentimental white employer would rather give an incompetent European a job than me. If he wanted 'anything' he preferred the 'unspoilt native from the Kraal' to the English-speaking nigger. Was it not time for me to look after my personal affairs and leave the public to themselves?

Once more my pen flew nimbly. Rejection-slips followed with the same rapidity. But my back was to the wall and I was resolved to die or triumph. One by one I made fast literary friends who were pleased to encourage my efforts. To be a free-lance journalist in South Africa is no joke, especially when one has woolly hair. He gets no access to newspaper files, public archives, museums and public libraries. The future will decide the wisdom and otherwise of my resolute determination. I am now trying to launch an independent journal to be known as the *African Liberator*. Its policy will be development and the launching of African industrial, political and co-operative movements.

And now that I am in my twenty-fifth year, many things have I seen and heard about the restrictions placed against the black man in his country. I have been to Johannesburg, where no black man dares to ride a tram or bus alongside with whites, although, if he is a servant and is accompanied by his master, he rides freely. It has been interesting to see the white South African prate of inherent superiority and then make all sorts of restrictions against the black man, denying him franchise rights, a decent standard of living, a decent opportunity to develop his talents, a sporting chance to educate his children, and say he does all this in order to defend 'White prestige'. I have seen him sack an African from work and then say he is lazy. I have seen him refuse to allow an African to buy land in his own fatherland; I have seen him refuse to pay him wages enough to keep body and soul together. I have heard him speak of liberty of all other nations while maintaining slavery. All these things have I seen and watched. The question has risen to my mind: 'If the European is so superior and the African so inferior, why fear him and restrict him so much?'

One thing is clear. The situation is developing abnormally. Unless some other means are adopted, the proverbial patience of the Africans will snap and then—revolution, stark, grim and terrible. History has a strange way of repeating itself. I am waiting and hope to see many things before I die. South Africa is a pleasant country for all that and things will not continue like this. Such a state is against history, science and common sense.

# X

# The Story of Kofoworola Aina Moore, of the Yoruba Tribe, Nigeria

*written by herself*

I am writing from London; it is January and a little snow has fallen. In October or November this year, I shall be going back to Nigeria. The difference between these two places seems rather to coincide with the conflicting thoughts in my mind. My departure from Europe fills me at the same time with joy and with regret, with eager expectations and with anxiety.

I am twenty-one years old and I have been away from Nigeria since I was ten years old. Considering that I have been in England for eleven years, I naturally feel there will be on my return advantages and disadvantages in my position. Opinions vary with regard to the status of the so-called 'educated African'. While some regard him as the greatest enemy of his country, from which he becomes detached, and for which he can only develop a sophisticated form of patriotism: others look upon him as the means of creating a link between two countries of such different culture, with both of which he is acquainted. It is in this light that I am thinking over my position.

I was born in Lagos, 21st May, 1913, being the second daughter of my parents. There was only the normal amount of customary rejoicings made at the birth of a female child; no extravagant display of wealth and honour usually lavished at the birth of the first female child of a family. My childhood was uneventful though it was a very happy and peaceful one. I was brought up against the background of essentially Western ideas, and from my earliest childhood my mind was formed in relation to Western culture and not to the background of untouched tribal life. My grandparents on both my mother's and father's sides were well educated. My great-grandfather was an ordained minister of the Church of England and my grandfather was at an English public school before he was likewise ordained for the ministry. The paternal branch of my mother's line originated from America. We are still in touch with these relations. Two of our cousins have visited Nigeria and my mother and elder sister have been in America in recent years. My father was educated at Monkton Combe School near Bath. Afterwards, he studied at the Middle Temple, London, and returned to Nigeria qualified as a barrister and solicitor. I can recall scenes in my childhood when my sisters and I used to listen with rapt attention to the accounts of his adventures in his student days in England. We were amused by his experiences in trying to drive a coach-and-four and fascinated by his riding in the Row. On his return to Nigeria my father set up a practice at Lagos. He was nominated by the Crown to the Legislative Council in 1915 and from that date he has continued his services to the Assembly. In 1934 he was elected First Member of the Lagos Division of the Legislative Council. My mother was educated at the C.M.S. Girls' School, then called 'the Seminary'. Later she proceeded to England for the general 'finishing' course available to 'young ladies' in those days. A friend who knew her told me she was a most accomplished young lady.

My parents did not set themselves to be blatantly Westernized, but naturally, due to their own education, they brought us up on Western lines. My sisters and I were made familiar early with everyday things of English life. We learnt, moreover, to converse in English with our parents: their method was to make us speak English the whole day every Sunday. Although in this way we learnt Yoruba and English contemporarily, I have no pleasant recollections as regards this practice. I look back with resentment to that particular Sunday when in rebellion against this rule, and insisting on asking for my favourite pudding in Yoruba, I had to go without it.

Changes were not as rapid in Lagos ten years ago as they are today; I have still vivid memories of settings with a strong tribal flavour. What excitement there used to be on the occasions of the demonstrations of Egun when the dead assumed mortal frames and moved about to bless some enterprise, or if Eyo, the 'Breathless God', appeared clad in bamboo-sticks in the streets of Lagos! Though these cults, which originally had great significance, had degenerated into mere masquerades, they were nevertheless very popular. The average European in Lagos does not, I think, realize to what extent we preserve vestiges of our old traditions, especially in such ceremonies as marriages, christenings and burials.

Soon after I was born my parents moved into a larger and more up-to-date house in a very central part of the town, and it was partly here and partly at my mother's farm, situated about sixteen miles out of Lagos, that I spent my childhood. Ours was a very large household, for although my parents had only three children then, many of my young cousins stayed with us, for, as we had more accommodation than we needed for ourselves, we were expected to entertain them. The result of this large family, as far as I was concerned personally, was that I very soon learnt the English alphabet and the spelling of a few simple English words from the other children who were all going to school. Furthermore, as I hated being alone after they had left for school and always clamoured to go with them, my parents decided to send me to school soon after my third birthday. I started going to the Church Missionary Society Girls' School in 1916 and continued there until I came to England in 1924 at the age of eleven.

There were two reasons for my coming to England at such an early age. The first was sufficiently vital. I was very delicate as a child, often suffering from malaria, and so my parents were advised to send me to a more temperate climate until I was stronger. The second reason was that the Principal of the C.M.S. Girls' School which I was then attending in Lagos, told my mother that although I was one of their most promising pupils, I could not sew, and my mother, feeling very much ashamed of me on seeing the grubby pillow-case I had submitted for our terminal examination in sewing, began to agitate for me to be sent somewhere where I could learn to use my hands as well as my head. These reasons, added to the fact that I had a severe illness in the latter part of 1923, hastened the completion of the arrangements to send me to England; and thus it was that, on 28th May, 1924, I landed at Plymouth with my mother and younger sister.

My sister and I stepped ashore clutching in our hands postcard views of Plymouth and London which our elder sister, who had come to England some years before us, had sent to us; so we were busier trying to identify the buildings on land with those depicted on the postcards than with getting first impressions. What struck me most on the journey from Plymouth to London was the advertisements and colourful posters: large attractive designs and clever drawings! I was fascinated by them and I loved them all. I remember, particularly, the 'Bisto Kids', woefully ignorant of what they heralded—meat pies.

The next morning, as I looked out of the window of our flat in Kensington, I was struck by the hundreds of chimney pots I saw. Rows and rows of them! I was used to seeing one to each house, but here there were hundreds. My sister and I proceeded to count the amount on the next roof; I counted ten and she counted twelve. The following months were spent in going round London's famous places of interest. My sister and I enjoyed these outings, but my mother was anxious about finding a school to which to send us.

We had little difficulty in getting into a school. This was remarkable considering the difficulty which African parents have to face nowadays in finding English schools of good standard where their children are accepted as pupils. In 1924, however, the majority of the large English public girl-schools were willing to accept us as pupils provided we passed their entrance examinations. My mother finally decided to send us to a private school in Reading for the particular reason that there were already in that school eight pupils from West Africa. There is a tendency among African parents to send their children to schools in England where there are no other African pupils, with the belief that in this way the children will assimilate English culture more readily and adapt themselves to their new environment more quickly. This seems reasonable enough, but, judging from the experience, it is my belief that individual cases need individual treatment. As this has always been a matter of controversy between African parents who send their children to England for further education, I feel I should express my convictions based on personal experiences. I have been grateful for my mother's choice, for I believe that only by a gradual process of introducing people into a foreign country and to foreign life can adjustment be achieved. There is less of a break and less harm done to their self-confidence and confidence in the world in general, so difficult to retain by children thus uprooted, than when they are abruptly transplanted into entirely foreign soil. In the first place we did not feel acutely that we were severed from West Africa; on the contrary, together we formed a strong connecting link with it. We constantly discussed African affairs; we read eagerly all articles on West Africa in every newspaper. We interchanged ideas on all subjects discussed; often, much to the amazement of some of our English friends, we disagreed violently on some of the points. In the second place, there was a keen spirit of competition among us, which urged each one of us to make her best effort. Reports were sent home periodically and we vied with each other to do our best, for we knew—at least those of us from Nigeria—that these reports would be circulated round our various families!

What seemed most important to my mother at the time was that the other West African girls would look after their young sisters and help them over the first rough passages of school life. In this, she was right. My sister and I were not only very well looked after, but, what was more appreciated by us then, we were also constantly ladened with sweets, an indulgence which our parents had regarded as an unnecessary luxury, but which, after a few months' stay in England, we cultivated assiduously.

On September 23rd, 1924, we started school. My first year passed uneventfully though happily enough. One strange thing that was noticed by the end of the year was that I had become very timid. This was due partly to the strain of adapting myself to a new background, and partly to the fact that I was placed in a form of a much higher standard than that in which I had been at the C.M.S. Girls' School. My new form was in the Middle School and I had been in what would correspond to the first form of the English Upper School at the Girls' School. During those first three terms at school I became nervous and easily moved to tears. Sometimes I did my homework and was too frightened to submit it; sometimes I left my sums unfinished. In the holidays my mother noticed that I disliked going out. On one occasion, I remember crying when I was asked to go out on an errand alone! My nervous reaction to England greatly disturbed my mother, who had always regarded me as a rather precocious child; she was, therefore, not a little uneasy when at the end of the year she had to return home, taking with her my sister.

Possibly I should have been found psychologically unfit to stay on in England had not an incident occurred which altered the course of my school life. The fact that I knew several Yoruba folk-lore stories fascinated my English school-friends. Several of them became very much interested in these stories. One night we dramatized the simplest of them, and it was a great success. I remember how enthusiastic my friends were and I cannot help feeling that these performances made them more sympathetic. I found myself gradually losing my timidity and having more confidence in myself. The next four years at school passed very rapidly. Each year seems to have been divided into months 'before' and 'after' exams., for school exams., music and elocution exams. succeeded one another in a very rapid sequence.

Every year, one or two African pupils left to return home, and other new arrivals took their places. In this way I was able to keep in close touch with Nigeria—most of the pupils were from Lagos—for letters were by this time serving merely as links of remembrance.

In my fifth year at school—a year when there were only three Africans at the school—the Headmistress died very suddenly during the summer holidays. As she had been our sole guardian, the days that followed were days of inexpressible gloom and anxiety. I was at this time preparing for my School Certificate, but I wanted rather to leave school than to sit for the exam. With great persuasion my parents urged me to take the exam., but arrangements were made for me to go on to Sheffield soon after to prepare for it, if necessary, again. I was convinced that I would not be successful and had already began to work on the new syllabus when news came of my success, which meant exemption from the London Matriculation.

Now came the choice of a career, a task which I found immensely difficult. Some of my English friends expressed their surprise at the difficulty I had in arriving at a decision; others seemed to have understood the situation when they advised me to choose a profession which would enable me to preserve the 'English atmosphere' in which I had lived for so long, and so make life a little easier for myself at home. My father wanted me to study Law because he is himself a barrister with a practice established over thirty years, and I would have been sure of a good beginning. Also, there would have been the prestige of being the second lady barrister in West Africa. Many African friends were in favour of the idea but I remained indifferent. Law as a profession had some attraction for me and I believed a fine legal sense is essential in dealing with any high branch of political life in West Africa. But I was overcome by my impatience. I felt there was a pressing need for the development of what an African friend of mine once called the 'sense of the modern world in all its intricacies', with which we are compelled by natural force of circumstances to come into contact. The most rapid way of attaining this aim, as I saw it, lay in education, and particularly in education as it could be translated by Africans who have had the opportunity to live in the Western world. I decided to take up teaching.

My father, not being entirely in favour of the idea, was willing to give his consent upon one condition, viz., that prior to my Teacher's Training I was to try for a degree at either Oxford or Cambridge. A vacancy was offered to me at St. Hugh's College, Oxford.

The most miserable days I have ever passed followed the receipt of the letter from St. Hugh's, for I did not want to go to the University. I felt at the time that I had been away from Nigeria far too long and the thought of staying away for another four years filled me with great anxiety. Oxford, I felt, would be remote from the life I would be living at home. I wanted to return home for the summer vacation before Oxford reopened, but this was impracticable. Instead, that summer final arrangements were made for my starting College, and in October that year I went to St. Hugh's as a commoner.

If I were asked to sum up my ideas and impressions about Oxford, they would be expressed in the wish that there could be, at least, two African girl scholars in Oxford each year. I would not say that my fears and dread of going to the University were without grounds; they have become modified, however, to the extent that I feel not a little ashamed of my attitude. I was reassured from the first when I discovered that my worst fears about Oxford were shared in the main by the other Colonial students. I refer here in the main to Indians, West Indians and Africans.

Oxford is no longer 'a city of dreaming spires', and no longer the secluded arbour of the privileged and the rich. With the incoming of the scholarship undergraduate, the Oxford outlook has widened and has become openly more liberal. No wonder Oxford is not silent when there is a hunger-march, or when there is a debate on unemployment in Parliament, but becomes throbbing with interest. Oxford is keenly alive to the question of the Colonies: India has recently been very much in the limelight; African questions are always at issue. In fact, though I have been disillusioned often by the Oxford Union, I find I retrace my steps there to hear debates on some problems of the Colonies. The education of Oxford is liberal in the old sense of the word. It does not train specialists for any trade or profession; its aim is to improve the mind and make it a good instrument for whatever work it may be put to. These then are the reasons for my expressed wish that there could be a number of African girls in Oxford.

College life has been an integral part of my training. I had never felt as out of place and as homesick in England as I felt in the first two weeks at Oxford. I seemed tossed in a sea of intellect with highly earnest students who were themselves occupied in trying to emerge from the surging whirl. But gradually I discovered we were all aground on dry land and that I was among a sympathetic crowd. I was particularly struck at first by the incessant thirst of the students for information, and I still retain a very refreshing opinion I formed on my first night at St. Hugh's that the Oxford student is never satisfied until he has searched out how a thing came into being, how it is functioning, and what is its future objective. The invitations I received to coffee-parties in my first two terms ranked higher than the number received by the other first-year students. The discussions at these parties invariably centred round Nigeria, particularly Nigeria from its political aspect, in the relationship between its people and the British Government. Sometimes the conversation was directed to me personally. On such occasions I have been horrified by the fact that I was regarded as an 'isolated case' in being the first African girl in Oxford. I remember the unpleasant experience I had in telling a white South African student, who was overstressing this remarkable case of isolation, that it was to the detriment of white South Africa that there were not more African girls prepared sufficiently well in their own country to be given opportunities to enter the University. Unfortunately, I was hostess at the tea-party she was attending and this mild remark had to suffice. The reactions of some of the students to my presence has been somewhat peculiar! Last year, this incident was related to me by a friend. A student—now a second-year reading English—and a person for whose intellect I have the most profound respect, suddenly sat up in bed at about one o'clock in the morning for she imagined she saw me enter her room. She then watched me walk over to her table, read her lecture notes, and walk out again! Yet so far I have not been certified as walking in my sleep by a doctor!

After my first year at College, it happened inevitably that my acquaintances increased and the number of my friends became more limited. I found myself within a group of six friends. This was a natural development and the ties with them have been perhaps the most beneficial and the happiest I have formed in College. Our group consists of characters so diametrically opposed, and of persons of such divergent views and varied interests, that our discussions admit controversial subjects and many-sided issues. The group includes students reading Greats, Modern Greats, History, Theology and English.

Our common ground is Music. We attend the subscription concerts given in the Sheldonian Theatre and the Town Hall in the winter terms; and also the musical concerts organized by different colleges. I had, of course, been familiar with English music from childhood, but my friends' understanding of my unappreciative attitude towards Bach and their interest in folk-songs of all nations helped to create a stronger bond of sympathy. Our taste in music is very varied. My next-door neighbour in College has often expressed her keen appreciation of the impromptu concerts of German and French, and sometimes Yoruba, songs given by us in my room some afternoons. I do not believe we are yet forgiven for the introduction of a gramophone record of a piece of orchestral music in imitation of an iron foundry, recently written by a young Russian composer.

The one side of College life that I think closely resembles life in Africa has been the 'communal borrowing'. St. Hugh's borrow *ad lib.* My bicycle—no thing of beauty, yet very dear to my heart—was borrowed in my third term. I wonder if the unknown borrower has been contemplating its return. The first cap I bought in Oxford is still on loan; likewise, I assume, are my sets of six tea knives and forks. Of the teaspoons, two heroic ones remain.

My activities outside College have been restricted by the limited amount of my spare time. I follow the Oxford tradition of having two hours in the afternoon—from two o'clock to four o'clock— free for exercise. Not being particularly good at winter games, I go to hockey and netball practices spasmodically, but usually afternoons are spent in walking. In summer, I play tennis and swim.

In my first term I joined the Africa Society and the English (Literary) Club. I have since then joined the

Labour Club. It is not that I think the principles of Socialism needed to be taught to Africans, but I believe a scientific study of them essential to mitigate the dangers of the individualistic and capitalistic attitude which contact with the Western world is introducing into Africa.

I have attended meetings of the Anthropological Society, of the Imperial Club, the Herbertson (Geographical) Society, and, more frequently, meetings of the Majlis, or Indian Students' Union. Attendances at these meetings have not only given me opportunities of hearing authoritative speakers on the matters affecting the different societies, but they have also led to many interesting acquaintances. I number among my friends in Oxford, Egyptian, American, Canadian, French, German, Swiss and Indian students.

I would have said that I understood English culture had not ineffectual remarks about our 'amazing cleverness' at being able to speak English and at being able to wear English clothes become exceedingly irritating. One fears at times that assimilation of superficialities can be mistaken for knowledge!

During my stay in England I have travelled extensively throughout the country; I have been in Wales, Scotland and Ireland. I have usually lived with families, so I have had opportunities to get a thorough knowledge of English homes. After leaving school I made my home with a family in Sheffield for nearly two years. From them, and from the many friends I made through them, I have learnt the life and thoughts of every type of society in England. I count this time in England among my happiest recollections. It has been really difficult to decide from my diary what impressed me most, and to select my choicest anecdote from this period. I remember how duly impressed I was when on the very first night of my arrival I found my friend occupied in giving notice to one of her maids! That eternal maid problem! I was first introduced to it then. It is one of the 'institutions' that have puzzled me most in England, perhaps because we have not anything quite like it at home, though I think that with the changing character of life and society in Africa it is bound to come. At present, our system is this. We undertake to educate and train girls in return for services. As there is no financial side to this arrangement, except in cases where the parents of the girls pay for their schooling, their position has no resemblance to that of the English maids. The girls, moreover, regard this training as a serious preparation to marriage, and are anxious not to have too many breaks and changes.

My friends in Sheffield were dears. They were warm-hearted and hospitable; genuine and open. What remark could have conveyed more welcome than that which was addressed to me one day when I went visiting: 'How very nice; it's only you!' The Yorkshire people appear to me to be a race within a race, having characteristics which distinguish them from the rest of the English and having in particular little in common with the Southerners. The Southerner strikes me as always claiming to be a little more than he really is; whereas the Yorkshireman is unpretentious and frank.

The first crime I committed in Sheffield was admitting without repentance that I did not know Yorkshire. 'Why, even Sheffield is beautiful,' I was told. 'You only have to go five miles out of the City and you'll see how beautiful it is!' So I was taken for drives over the Yorkshire moors and into the Peak District; shown rugged heathlands which were very unlike any kind of English scenery that I had seen before; and lonely villages, in wild desolate districts, very unlike those I had seen in Berkshire and which to the foreigner are more typical of English scenery.

I was taken to places of interest in Yorkshire and shown round in turn the larger steel factories in Sheffield itself. The friends I was staying with were keen gardeners and they taught me a great amount about English seeds and plants. They were always very anxious that I should miss no opportunity of learning as much as I could of English life. My range of occupation in my spare time was from gardening to helping to keep account-books of household expenses.

I have not found family ties as broken in England as most Africans believe they are. There is a reaction against the Victorian head-of-the-family attitude, but fundamentally I believe there still exists strong union between members of the family. I was pleased to be introduced to the various members of the large family of my friends. I gained for myself so many aunts and uncles and nieces in this way!

I was encouraged to visit art exhibitions and celebrity concerts of English performers, and through the discussions that followed I drew ideas about what constituted English life and thought.

From several other friends I have learnt various angles of English life. I would be doing an injury indeed were I to forget the Oxford undergraduate who only the other day explained to me very patiently and with characteristic English forbearance that what I had alluded to as 'football' was 'soccer' and that 'football' was the name applied to 'soccer' and 'rugby'.

Without being over-wary as to places I go, for fear of being refused admittance, I have not come across any acute form of colour-prejudice. But I have proved from my own experience and from the experiences of other Africans that this has been due partly to my sex and partly to the fact that, for an African, I am light-skinned. My brother, who is much darker-skinned than I am, can tell a very different tale. Last summer when he was looking for a flat in London, knowing how much African men in this country disliked any 'house-hunting', I volunteered to do the job for him. I went with an English friend round various addresses and we were able to select two possibilities out of the list of flats we had. I made no promises at either place, my task was to find 'somewhere suitable'. We had thought it best that my brother should make his own arrangements. On calling the next day at the house where the owner had been particularly anxious that I should take a flat, he was told that there was no flat vacant, and furthermore, that there had not been one vacant for the last six months! Apart from this incident, which serves to show differences of attitude presented at times to the African male and female, my brother says an account of his experiences resulting from colour-prejudices and racial antagonism would run into several volumes. For instance, after he had written to engage rooms at an hotel in London, he arrived there with his luggage to be told that the proprietor had concluded by the newcomer's surname that he was English; he did not accommodate 'coloured people'.

Another time, a man with whom he had been sitting in a railway carriage, for no apparent reason, since the destination marked on his suitcase was the same as my brother's, alighted at the first stop. My brother, who was leaning out to buy some cigarettes, saw him go down the platform and enter another carriage! Yet he manages to see the humorous side of such situations. I remember he said he returned to his seat to find the carriage less crammed, and in consequence the rest of the journey more comfortable. He has told me often, on his return from a tour of the City of an afternoon, that he felt he had deprived the Exchequer of pounds' worth of entertainment tax. First, there was that highly entertaining waiter whose attitude had been almost servile, because, as he revealed at the end, he had thought his customer to be Duke Ellington, the popular American negro band conductor! Then, there was the very obvious provincial-looking lady who had nearly pushed her companion down the escalator in her attempts to make her see 'that coloured man over there'. Lastly, there was the man whose undemonstrative business-like air had belied his somewhat childish curiosity. His wife had whispered to him, 'Black man! Black man!' and he was asking 'Where? Where?'

What is far more exasperating than the more acute form of colour-prejudice is being regarded as a 'curio' or some weird specimen of Nature's product, not as an ordinary human being; and that I have experienced. I recall being taken to tea to a lady who had never met any African before. After the first introduction she coolly told me, in a tone of relief, which however, failed to hide her disappointment, that I was not what she had expected. For the rest of the time I was with her she ejaculated 'How very interesting!' at the end of all the remarks I made; I believe she even said 'How very interesting!' when I was saying 'Goodbye'. An African friend and I once asked each other simultaneously how we could have survived in England without an abundant, and sometimes an exaggerated, sense of humour.

The strain is very great and, at times, good sense and all attempts to understand the other person's point of view fail miserably.

I have now passed my final examination and I go down from Oxford in June, after staying in England for eleven years.

I shall be going back to Africa shortly. I shall not be able to stay for another year, for the Teachers' Training. Arrangements have been made that I should take a short, concentrated course of training before I leave for Nigeria. My eleventh year in England will then have been completed. Has it been worth it, I have often been asked? The answer can only be given when I get back to Nigeria!

I feel my anxiety at returning home throbbing with tense excitement. I cannot take a pessimistic view of things though I visualize the difficulties my change of environment may involve. Although I feel that I shall be moving away from a solid background, and on to shifting sands, I am eager to get back home. I hold no theories on 'the African' and what he should be. I have sadly failed indeed to understand the phrase, which I have noticed is applied by the Europeans and never by an African himself.

I hoped, on my return home, to obtain work as a teacher at one of the village schools in the Yoruba country in Nigeria, but I have been told that this would not be possible in the immediate future. I must re-learn my own country and my best way is to start by joining the staff of one of the girls' schools in the towns! Yet, for all this, I am not despondent—it cannot take an African long to 'learn' Africa.

My problem, however, is not unique. Fundamentally, it is the problem of every African who comes to England for education and has stayed here any length of time. If the fact that I have been to Oxford makes an essential difference, I can only recall the words of an English student who told me that the value of the Oxford education for girls, as she sees it, is an attempt to create a means of 'leavening' the general educational outlook of the public. The value of the best education in England means much more than that in a country where the immediate problem centres round the intricate questions produced by a contact of the contrasting cultures and civilizations. The defects in my position will be avoided in the future, firstly, by a natural evolution. Schools in West Africa will be brought to such a standard that African girls will be prepared up to the standard of university entrance exams., and it will no longer be necessary for them to come at an early age to receive elementary education in England. Secondly, by the granting of scholarships for further education in England; in this way opportunities will be given to the best brains and the maximum results achieved.

To draw the threads of my thoughts together; I must look into the future. From whatever angle we view it the immediate problem in Africa today is the adaptation of modern life and thought in all their branches to the old conditions. The solution, as I see it through the medium of my experiences, lies in mutual criticism and mutual consideration between the Western world and the Africans, and I believe that people will have to become acquainted with one another upon an equal basis. I have enough courage to believe in the possibility of peaceful development among nations.

In conclusion, I state the views of Africans who have had similar opportunities and similar experiences to my own. The first quotation is from the letter of a friend who has been resident for the past year in England, and is perhaps the best authority from the African point of view on the attitude of the English public to African problems. He writes: 'As an African I am much relieved that the type of European philanthropic school of thought which becomes sentimental over the poor African competing with the Western world, is dying out; likewise, in the scientific world, the anthropologists and ethnologists who would fain keep Africa as the paradise of their rarest specimens, and the intrepid adventurer who would have the country as a permanent museum. We have a new school of European thinkers which views Africa on, shall I say, a world basis? They seem to have realized it fulfils some function in the world as an organic whole.'

The second is a quotation from the speech of a barrister, a Cambridge graduate, delivered at a recent debate in Lagos: 'This House considers the system of Indirect Rule of Government less efficient than a system of Direct Control in Nigeria.' I quote the speech, not for its political significance, but for the spirit in which it was delivered:

'It is by means of Indirect Rule that the Africans could probe, and probing into their own past, trace out their own literature and know something about themselves. The mover of the motion would have us adopt the past, the literature and everything that belongs to the Western world and forget we ever had any. England did not take Roman law, Roman literature and Roman institutions as her own; on the contrary, she developed everything from her traditional customs: why, then, should we Africans take everything European as our own? this is what the mover of the motion is asking this sensible audience to do!

'With the progress of mass education among the African people, Indirect Rule will become a boon in the system of British Administration of the African people, because by means of it, the Africans shall have been able to retain their identity, and evolve to the highest possible order of civilization, which the rest of the world may love to copy. The scrapping-up of the system of Indirect Rule will be a death-knell not only to African laws and customs, but also to the African's identity and existence.' These are the people worth while, the sort of people who believe in wearing African clothes when they return to Africa! And yet, in taking an African friend round Oxford last summer, we came to the famous view of the city from the roof of the Radcliffe Camera; there was also an English undergraduate with a party, to whom she was gesticulating and pointing out enthusiastically the buildings of some of the Colleges. My friend turned to me and said that, if she stayed in Oxford for ten years, she could never wax as enthusiastic because to her Oxford was essentially English. I was silent, for only her timely remark prevented me from acting as the other undergraduate, with whom I was in sympathy and whose feelings I understood!

# Index

# Index

# Index

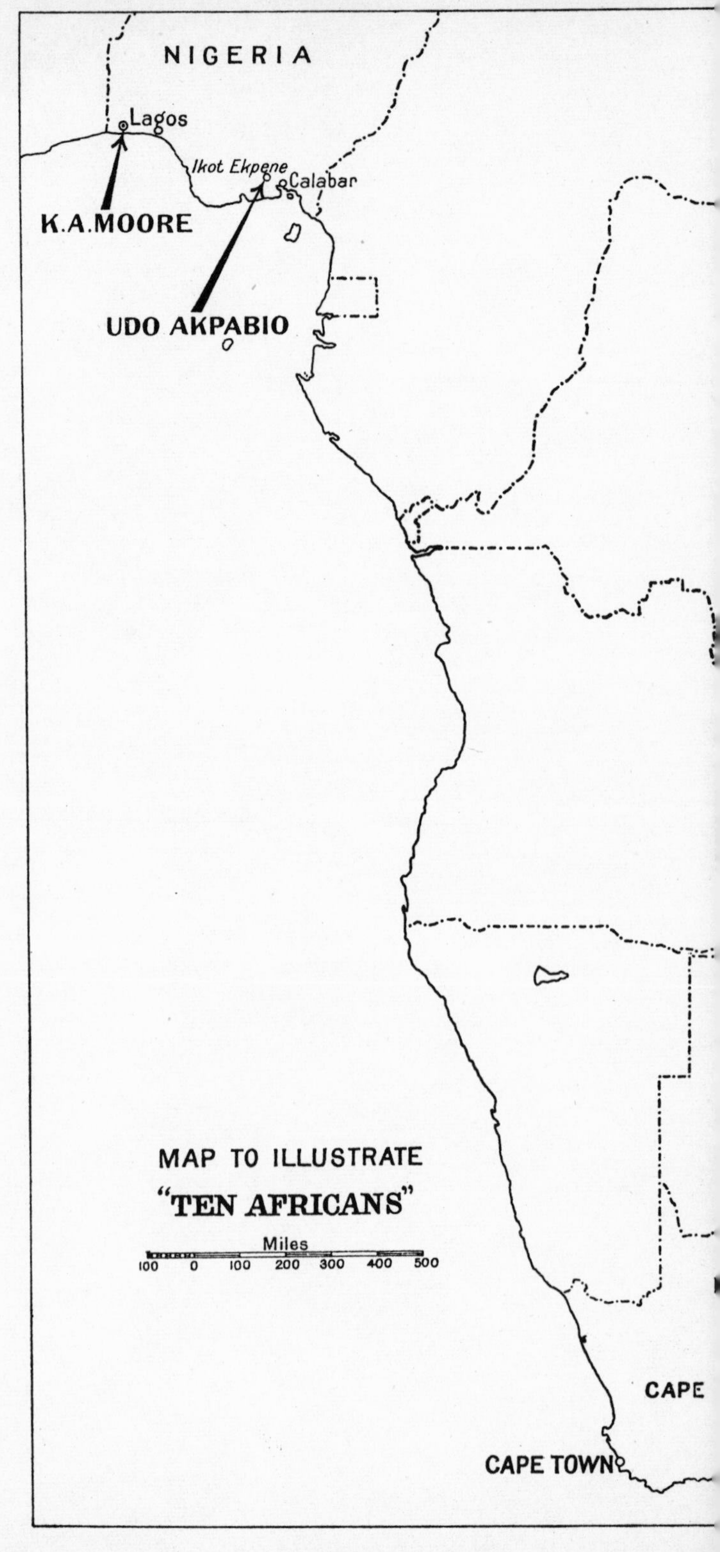
NIGERIA
Lagos
Ikot Ekpene
Calabar
K.A.MOORE
UDO AKPABIO
MAP TO ILLUSTRATE
"TEN AFRICANS"
Miles
100 0 100 200 300 400 500
CAPE
CAPE TOWN

UGANDA
Kampala
Entebbe
LAKE VICTORIA
KENYA
Mumias
L. Baringo
Kisumu
MAU
Nyeri
Ft. Hall
Naivasha
Kikuyu
Nairobi
MASAI
Machakos
Mogadishu
Kismayu
PARMENAS MOCKERIE
MT KILIMANJARO
Moshi
Taveta
Tsavo
Voi
L. Jipe
Arusha
Mtondia
Takaungu
Mombasa
LAKE TANGANYIKA
TANGANYIKA TERRITORY
Tabora
Kondoa Irangi
USAMBARA
Magila
Tanga
PEMBA I.
Muhenza
Pangani
Kilamatinde
Bagamoyo
ZANZIBAR
Mpwapwa
Morogoro
Dar-es-Salaam
MARTIN KAYAMBA
Kiberege
Malangali
Kilwa
Abercorn
Tukuyu
Mahenge
Lindi
Fife
Mwamba
Kasama
Manda
Songea
LAKE BANGWEOLO
Mpika
NORTHERN RHODESIA
NYASALAND
LAKE NYASA
BWEMBYA
Serenje
Ft. Jameson
RASHID BIN HASSANI
Ft. Johnston
Liwanda
Zomba
Blantyre
AMINI BIN SAIDI
EAST AFRICA
R. Zambezi
SOUTHERN RHODESIA
MATABELELAND
Chindi
Shangani
Gwelo
Victoria
Beira
MATOPPO HILLS
Bulawayo
PORTUGUESE
NDANSI KUMALO
TRANSVAAL
Pretoria
ORANGE FREE STATE
Vryheid
ZULULAND
Glencoe
Dundee
Tugela R.
R. Mfolozi
Greytown
Eshowe
NATAL
Pietermaritzburg
GILBERT COKA
Richmond
Durban
TRANSKEI
King William's Town
East London
NOSENTE
STANFORD, LONDON.